The Governance Report 2019

Hertie School

OXFORD

The Governance Report

2019

OXFORD
UNIVERSITY PRESS

OXFORD
UNIVERSITY PRESS

Great Clarendon Street, Oxford, OX2 6DP,
United Kingdom

Oxford University Press is a department of the University of Oxford.
It furthers the University's objective of excellence in research, scholarship,
and education by publishing worldwide. Oxford is a registered trade mark of
Oxford University Press in the UK and in certain other countries

First Edition published in 2019

Impression: 1

Published in the United States of America by Oxford University Press
198 Madison Avenue, New York, NY 10016, United States of America

British Library Cataloguing in Publication Data
Data available

Library of Congress Cataloging in Publication Data
Data available

ISBN 978–0–19–882150–2

Printed and bound in Great Britain by Clays Ltd, Elcograf S.p.A.

Managing Editor: Regina A. List
Book design: Plural | Severin Wucher
Cover illustration: Emilia Birlo
Information graphics: Plural | Kilian Krug
Typeset in Publico and TheSans

The Governance Report 2019 is funded by the Robert Bosch Stiftung GmbH

Table of Contents

Preface   7
Foreword   9
Acknowledgements   11
List of Figures, Tables, and Boxes   12
List of Abbreviations   14

I.   **Health Policy and Health Governance**   17
      KLAUS HURRELMANN, MUJAHEED SHAIKH, *and* CLAUS WENDT

II.   **Health and Well-being Worldwide**   27
      ELODIE BESNIER *and* TERJE ANDREAS EIKEMO

III. **Governing Health Inequalities**   51
      CLARE BAMBRA

IV.   **The Global Governance of Outbreaks**   67
      SUERIE MOON *and* ANNA BEZRUKI

V.   **Global Health Governance**   83
      ILONA KICKBUSCH *and* AUSTIN LIU

VI.   **Politics and Power: The Case of the Global Opioid Epidemic**   103
      ANDRÉ J. VAN RENSBURG *and* PIET BRACKE

VII. **Healthcare as Social Investment**   121
      HANNA SCHWANDER

VIII. **Behavioural Insights for Health Governance**   135
      CHRISTIAN TRAXLER

IX.   **Innovative Governance and Health Reforms in Europe**   149
      ELLEN M. IMMERGUT, ANDRA ROESCU, *and* BJÖRN RÖNNERSTRAND

X.   **Digital Health: Key Challenges**   171
      ROBIN GAULD

XI.   **Health Governance Challenges and Recommendations:**   187
      A Summary
      MUJAHEED SHAIKH, CLAUS WENDT, *and* KLAUS HURRELMANN

References   197
About the Contributors   231

Preface

Health promotion, protection for all people, and healthcare for patients continue to represent some of the most important policy challenges facing countries and the world today. This edition of the Governance Report offers a multidisciplinary look at some of these challenges on multiple levels–from local to global–and at ways to manage them now and into the future within the context of a rapidly changing environment.

The Governance Report 2019 is the seventh in an annual series about the changing conditions of governance, the challenges and opportunities involved, and the implications and recommendations that present themselves to analysts and policy-makers.

The Governance Report is an interdisciplinary effort to examine state-of-the-art governance. In doing so, it enlists experts from the Hertie School in Berlin as well as from other institutions. Special attention is paid to institutional designs and approaches, changes, and innovations that both state and non-state actors have adopted in response to shifts that have been occurring.

The results are available in an annual series that includes a compact report and an edited volume, both published by Oxford University Press, as well as a dedicated website at www.governancereport.org. Together, they are designed to provide both policy-makers and analysts with ideas, knowledge, and tools to consider and implement policies and programmes that lead to better solutions to public problems.

Launched in February 2013 by my predecessor, Helmut K. Anheier, the first edition examines the challenges of financial and fiscal governance and proposes a new paradigm of responsible sovereignty for tackling global issues. In the 2014 edition, the focus turns to the administrative capacity of public administrations, whereas in 2015, the Report considers the governance of the European Union and assesses the status of the European integration project, highlighting the practical and political dilemmas involved. The 2016 edition, a collaborative effort with the OECD, focuses on the governance of infrastructure by emphasising the complexity and trade-offs faced by decision-makers, project managers, businesses, and the population at large in setting priorities, choosing projects, and implementing them. In the 2017 edition of the compact report, we explore what is being done to counteract the democratic malaise experienced in many countries and shed light on how to manage and care for democracy itself. The 2017 edited volume focuses on developments in the field of governance indicators since the first Report was published. Marking the tenth anniversary of the global financial and economic crisis, the 2018 edition of the compact report teases out implications of the crisis for current governance and discerns what lessons have and can be learned such that governments and international actors would be in a better position to stave off a crisis of similar magnitude and complexity.

For this 2019 edition of the compact report, we asked Hertie School Professor of Public Health and Education Klaus Hurrelmann and Claus Wendt, Professor of Health and Health Systems at the University of Siegen, later joined by Mujaheed Shaikh, the Hertie School's new Professor of Health Governance, to assemble renowned health experts to closely examine the key challenges (present and future) healthcare systems are facing, identify best practices in terms of effective governance, and discuss potential solutions to cogently tackle future challenges.

Finally, the Governance Report series seeks to provide evidence to support decision-making processes by developing a new generation of indicators. The dashboards, presenting data on variables either taken from existing sources or collected by our indicators team, provide a wealth of information for policy-makers and researchers that can be extracted and analysed according to the issue or question at hand. The dashboards and analytical tools described in each edition of the Report are available at www.governance report.org.

The preparation of this edition of the Governance Report was funded by the Robert Bosch Stiftung as part of the project 'Restart! A Heath Care Reform Workshop' ('Neustart!'). The project aims to develop reform proposals for sustainable healthcare in Germany. We are delighted about this cooperation, which will continue beyond the publication of this Report.

Henrik Enderlein
President, Hertie School
Berlin, June 2019

Foreword

Together with the Hertie School, we are very pleased to be able to present to you *The Governance Report 2019*. What role does the Robert Bosch Stiftung play in this edition, which focuses on health governance? Health was always one of Robert Bosch's major interests. It was through his initiative that the Robert Bosch Hospital in Stuttgart was established and began operating in 1940. Robert Bosch wanted to have an impact on people, 'not only to alleviate all kinds of hardship, but also to promote their moral, physical, and intellectual development.' For more than fifty years, the Stiftung has been pursuing Robert Bosch's legacy and now continues his social and societal engagement, applying modern means to contemporary challenges.

Not only is the Stiftung financially supporting this Governance Report on health governance, but it is also funding the professorship at the Hertie School devoted to health governance, under the leadership of Professor Dr. Mujaheed Shaikh. Through this professorship, we seek to deepen research on future-ready governance and administrative structures in the health field, bring the research results into teaching, and, ultimately, convey them to the (professional) public.

Health governance is a relatively new field of research in Germany, and, in light of current healthcare challenges, its significance is likely to increase. Changes in the disease spectrum, technological innovation, global health issues, and, not least, the desire to establish a more citizen- and patient-centred healthcare system in Germany all require a comprehensive reorientation of governance principles and thus new and sustainable approaches to health governance.

This edition of the Governance Report on health governance and the health governance professorship are being supported as part of our initiative 'Restart! A Health Care Reform Workshop' ('Neustart! Reformwerkstatt für unser Gesundheitswesen'), which we launched in the fall of 2018. The initiative offers citizens and experts the opportunity to actively shape tomorrow's healthcare provision–taking bold measures to reform the system for everyone and for our future. The initiative's aim is to contribute toward the changes necessary to guarantee the appropriate care required to meet the needs of all people in Germany well into the future. We envision a healthcare system that is people-oriented, patient-centred, multiprofessional, of high quality, and open to innovation; in short, a healthcare system that focuses on keeping people healthy, that takes their quality of life into consideration when in therapy or care, and that people can trust, even when in the most vulnerable of situations.

We are delighted to be working on Restart! with such a strong and expert partner as the Hertie School. We are convinced that in the coming years, with complementary research and in cooperation with the Health Governance professorship, we can generate and set in motion forward-looking ideas for reforming the healthcare system in Germany and beyond.

Bernadette Klapper
Senior Vice President Health, Robert Bosch Stiftung
Stuttgart, June 2019

Acknowledgements

Many people have been involved in developing this edition of *The Governance Report*, in addition to the authors of the various chapters.

We appreciate the ideas and constructive criticism provided by members of the Hertie School community, especially faculty. This Report could not have come together without the work of Regina A. List, the Governance Report's Managing Editor. Hertie School staff members Angelika Behlen, Ashley Lauren Branton-Bamford, Magriet Cruywagen, Chiara Josten, Regine Kreitz, and Ellen Thalman provided support in innumerable ways.

We also wish to thank the Board of the Hertie School for encouraging this Report, and for providing critical feedback and direction. In addition, we would like to mention the members of the Report's original International Advisory Committee: Craig Calhoun (Arizona State University), William Roberts Clark (Texas A&M), John Coatsworth (Columbia University), Ann Florini (University of Maryland), Geoffrey Garrett (University of Pennsylvania), Mary Kaldor (London School of Economics), Edmund J. Malesky (Duke University), Henrietta Moore (University College London), Woody Powell (Stanford University), Bo Rothstein (University of Gothenburg), Shanker Satyanath (New York University), James Vreeland (Princeton University), Kent Weaver (Georgetown University), Arne Westad (Harvard University), and Michael Zürn (Wissenschaftszentrum Berlin and Freie Universität Berlin).

At Oxford University Press, we thank Dominic Byatt for seeing the original promise in this enterprise and to Céline Louasli and the production team for guiding us through. Jessica Leong Cohen's proofreading skills ensured that the manuscript was as error-free as posssible.

For the Report's look we are grateful to the team of Severin Wucher and Kilian Krug at Plural in Berlin, and to artist Emilia Birlo for the cover art.

Finally, we are grateful to the Hertie Foundation for its ongoing support and to Evonik, Stiftelsen Riksbankens Jubileumsfond, and the Berggruen Institute for their support in launching the Report series. For this edition on health governance, we owe special thanks to the Robert Bosch Stiftung for providing funding as part of the project 'Restart! A Heath Care Reform Workshop' ('Neustart!').

List of Figures, Tables, and Boxes

Figure 2.1a: Global life expectancy at birth, 1990-2017
Figure 2.1b: Global healthy life expectancy (HALE) at birth, 1990-2017
Figure 2.2a: Global age-standardised death rates by causes, 1990-2017
Figure 2.2b: Global age-standardised DALYs rates by causes, 1990-2017
Figure 2.3a: Global age-standardised death rates for selected CMNN causes, 1990-2017
Figure 2.3b: Global age-standardised DALYs rates for selected CMNN causes, 1990-2017
Figure 2.4:   Life expectancy at birth by region, 1990-2017
Figure 2.5a: Crude death rates by country income groups and main causes, 2017
Figure 2.5b: Crude DALYs rates by country income groups and main causes, 2017
Figure 2.6a: Crude death rates by WHO regions and main causes, 2017
Figure 2.6b: Crude DALYs rates by WHO regions and main causes, 2017
Figure 2.7:   Percentage of deaths due to selected injury causes by age and sex, 2017
Figure 3.1:   Income inequalities in self-reported health across Europe, 2016
Figure 3.2:   Educational inequalities in non-communicable diseases in Europe
Figure 3.3:   Probability of smoking by educational status in Europe
Figure 5.1:   Flows of development assistance for health from source to channel to health focus area, 1990-2018
Figure 5.2:   Proportion and amount of assessed contributions and voluntary contributions to WHO across biennia from 1998 to 2017
Figure 6.1:   A map of developed forms of power
Figure 6.2:   Global incidence rates of opioid use, by income group, 1990-2017, compared to the US
Figure 6.3:   Global prevalence rates of opioid use, by income group, 1990-2017, compared to the US
Figure 6.4:   Global rates of disability-adjusted life years related to opioid use, by income group, 1990-2017, compared to the US
Figure 6.5:   Global death rates attributable to opioid use, by income group, 1990-2017, compared to the US
Figure 7.1:   Cross-national trends in public spending on healthcare, old-age benefits, and unemployment in the OECD as a share of GDP, 1980-2015
Figure 7.2:   Public support for higher government spending on selected welfare state branches

Figure 7.3:   Public support for additional spending on different welfare state branches according to education levels
Figure 9.1:   Public and private medical expenditure, 2016, with 1989 as reference
Figure 9.2:   Financing sources of healthcare expenditures in selected OECD countries, 2016
Figure 9.3:   Unmet need due to cost, 2016
Figure 9.4:   Unmet need due to cost versus out-of-pocket payments, 2016
Figure 9.5:   Bribery in selected European health systems, 2016
Figure 9.6:   Public satisfaction with the state of health services, 2002-16

Table 5.1:   Examples of innovations in global health governance
Table 5.2:   Health-related high-level discussions at the United Nations General Assembly and Security Council, 2000-18
Table 5.3:   Selected challenges in global health governance and their implications
Table 8.1:   Selected cases of behaviourally informed applications to health problems
Table 9.1:   Patient rights in Europe

Box 6.1:   The death of Cameron Weiss: an illustrative example of the opioid crisis in the US
Box 6.2:   PAIN fake prescription flyer
Box 7.1:   Main 'worlds of welfare capitalism'
Box 10.1:   Digital Health Charter considerations

List of Abbreviations

AI	artificial intelligence
AIDS	Acquired Immune Deficiency Syndrome
AMR	antimicrobial resistance
BIT	Behavioural Insights Team (UK)
BRI	Belt and Road Initiative
BRICS	Brazil, Russia, India, China, and South Africa
CDA	Christian Democratic Appeal (Netherlands)
CDC	Centers for Disease Control and Prevention (US)
CEPI	Coalition for Epidemic Preparedness Innovations
CMNN	communicable, maternal, neonatal, and nutritional
CVD	cardiovascular disease(s)
DALYs	disability-adjusted life years
DEA	Drug Enforcement Administration (US)
DRC	Democratic Republic of Congo
EHR	electronic health record
EU	European Union
FCTC	WHO Framework Convention on Tobacco Control
FIND	Foundation for Innovative Diagnostics
FPÖ	Austrian Freedom Party
FSMB	Federation of State Medical Boards
G7	Group of Seven
G20	Group of Twenty
GDB	Global Burden of Disease (Study)
GDP	gross domestic product
GHSA	Global Health Security Agenda
GP	general practitioner
GPMB	Global Preparedness Monitoring Board
HALE	healthy life expectancy
HiAP	Health in All Policies
HIV	Human Immunodeficiency Virus
HL7	Health Level 7
HTA	health technology assessment
IHME	Institute for Health Metrics and Evaluation
IHR	International Health Regulations
IMF	International Monetary Fund
IMR	infant mortality rate
ISSP	International Social Survey Programme
JEE	Joint External Evaluation
LDS	Liberal Democracy of Slovenia
LMICs	low- and middle-income countries
MDGs	Millennium Development Goals
MERS	Middle East respiratory syndrome

MICs	middle-income countries
MSF	Médecins Sans Frontières
NCD	non-communicable disease
NHS	National Health Service (United Kingdom)
NP	nurse practitioner
NPM	New Public Management
NTD	neglected tropical disease
ODA	official development assistance
OECD	Organisation for Economic Co-operation and Development
PA	physician assistant
PAIN	Prescription Addiction Intervention Now
PDI	person-dependent intervention
PEF	Pandemic Emergency Financing Facility
PHR	personal health record
PII	person-independent intervention
PIP	Pandemic Influenza Preparedness
PP	People's Party (Spain)
PSOE	Spanish Social Workers' Party
PvdA	Labour Party (Netherlands)
R&D	research and development
RCT	randomised controlled trial
RoG V	Role of Government (module)
SARS	Severe Acute Respiratory Syndrome
SDGs	Sustainable Development Goals
SDI	Socio-demographic Index
SMS	Short Message Service
TB	tuberculosis
TCM	traditional Chinese medicine
TRIPS	Trade-Related Aspects of Intellectual Property Rights (Agreement on)
UHC	universal health coverage
UKIP	United Kingdom Independence Party
UN	United Nations
UNAIDS	Joint United Nations Programme on HIV/AIDS
UNDESA	United Nations Department of Economic and Social Affairs
UNGA	United Nations General Assembly
UNICEF	United Nations Children's Fund
VVD	People's Party for Freedom and Democracy (Netherlands)
WHE	WHO Health Emergencies Programme
WHO	World Health Organization
WHO AFRO	WHO African region
WHO EMRO	WHO Eastern Mediterranean region
WHO EURO	WHO European region
WHO PAHO	WHO Region of the Americas

WHO SEARO   WHO South-East Asia region
WHO WPRO   WHO Western Pacific region
WTO   World Trade Organization

I. Health Policy and Health Governance

KLAUS HURRELMANN, MUJAHEED SHAIKH, *and* CLAUS WENDT

Virtually every single area of life in modern societies is influenced by the state of a population's health. Professional productivity, cultural creativity, political and social participation, and citizens' quality of life directly depend on their state of health (Hurrelmann 1989; Hurrelmann and Laaser 1996). Unsurprisingly, the demand for healthcare is ever increasing, and today's healthcare systems are by far the most expensive infrastructural sectors in all highly developed countries, with a continually rising share of health expenditures in GDP (Gerdtham and Jönsson 2000).

After an initial slowdown following the financial and economic crisis that began in 2008, health spending is back on a growth trajectory (OECD 2018a; see also Wegrich and Ziaja 2018). Concurrently, health systems across the world face new economic, political, social, and organisational challenges. Furthermore, present-day healthcare systems are not only highly complex and fragmented but are also primarily geared towards the requirements, constraints, and imperatives of the professional actors in the healthcare system, sometimes in opposition to the demands, needs, preferences, and value orientations of citizens, patients, and users.

> *Health promotion, protection for all, and healthcare for patients continue to represent some of the most important policy challenges.*

Despite vast efforts, it has not yet been possible to reorganise this important sector and implement an effective user-oriented and user-centred structure. Health promotion, protection for all citizens, and healthcare for patients continue to represent some of the most important policy challenges. *The Governance Report 2019* provides an overview of the key challenges (present and future) healthcare systems are facing, identifies best practices in terms of effective governance, and discusses potential solutions to cogently tackle future challenges within the context of a rapidly changing external environment.

This introductory chapter summarises the main themes covered in the Report by describing the concept of 'health governance', underscoring its importance for health policy, introducing key challenges for effective governance, providing examples of governance actions thus far, and introducing the contributions found in the Report.

Challenges to Healthcare

The demand for healthcare is derived from the demand for health (Arrow 1963). Due to an ageing global population and an increase in the prevalence of chronic illnesses, the demand for healthcare services is constantly rising (Strunk et al. 2006). Simultaneous advancements in medical technology that improve healthcare provision and consequently health status have contributed to elevated demand and increased costs (Newhouse 1992).

The promotion and preservation of citizens' health has become one of the most important challenges for leaders in politics, business, science, and civil society. The reasons include:

- The health of the population is one of the most important individual and social resources of modern societies. This resource becomes more vulnerable as the population becomes more diverse in many places due to migration and as family structures change such that there are more and more single parents and more and more people living alone.
- In times of demographic change with an ageing population and increasing chronic illness, maintaining health is becoming increasingly important. Patients, however, are in general socially unorganised and politically incapable of action. The majority of them do not have sufficient competence to understand the complicated health system or even the politics surrounding it.
- Health affects all parts of society and has an influence on many areas of life and work, such as education, employment, leisure behaviour, and consumption, which in turn also affect health. The challenge of maintaining and strengthening health therefore links several social sectors and areas of life.
- The use of health-related products and services is growing exponentially, accounting for an ever-increasing share of gross national product (OECD 2018a). The expanding healthcare market has become one of the most important factors for economic growth.
- Medical progress and the advancing economisation of the healthcare system (e.g. by profit-oriented hospital operators) lead to negotiation conflicts among the professions. For example, doctors see themselves as potential losers, while accountants and insurance merchants are potential winners.
- The digitalisation of all healthcare processes poses new social, political, and economic challenges for healthcare systems.
- In times of far-reaching social, economic, and political upheavals, terrorist threats, large migration movements, low economic growth rates, and high employment uncertainty, large sections of the population live in perceived insecurity.

Overall, the resulting challenges are enormous. These include the tasks of optimising the ratio of resources to outcomes and developing a new approach to health with a strong emphasis on health maintenance, well-being, and quality of life. In addition, testing new ethical standards for health systems and care, new priorities for care, and new forms of funding is becoming increasingly important.

The Concept of Health Governance and Its Relevance

Overcoming the existing and future challenges to healthcare delivery is only possible by addressing the entire management of the system, its control, and its coordination. This is precisely the concept of health governance. Health governance refers to all the actions and means that a society uses to achieve collective solutions for the maintenance and promotion of health as a common good. It addresses both the entire health system (governance of health systems) and individual organisations and institutions of the health system (governance of health institutions) (WHO 2014a).

According to the definition found in the WHO Action Plan on Health Systems Governance (WHO 2014a), the primary aims of health systems governance are to establish goals and guiding strategies for health-related decisions, to initiate the development of laws, regulations, decisions, and strategies, and to provide resources to ensure the achievement of the goals. Health institutions governance involves the monitoring, control, and provision of incentive mechanisms to hold healthcare institutions and organisations accountable and to reconcile the interests and goals of different institutions.

Health governance–the set of processes, mechanisms, and actions of all decision-makers in politics, science, business, and civil society that aim to protect and promote the health of the population–includes strategic leadership, strong intersectoral approaches to health promotion, development of national health capacity, and enforcement of jointly developed policy goals. In a globally networked and interdependent world, health governance combines local, regional, national, and international approaches. It is based on a broad concept of health, considering health 'as an emerging property of many social systems; it therefore require[s] action in many systems, sometimes with and sometimes without the involvement of the health sector' (Kickbusch and Gleicher 2012: x). Ideally innovative governance would promote intelligent systems and organisations that have the capacity to learn, to adapt their processes and rules dynamically to changing contexts, and thus to achieve optimal performance (World Bank 2017e).

The resulting system changes are a challenge for all types of political regimes. Often reforms only succeed in certain areas and are inappropriate, often they follow the particular interests of individual groups of actors, and often they do not take place at all. This leads to misallocation, drives up costs, reduces the acceptance of the system by its clients, and undermines the credibility of important actors, in particular doctors and health policy-makers. One of the tasks of health systems governance is to establish an overall coordination system that prevents each of the individual actors from following their own interests and trying to enforce them with all means available to them. In the corporatively designed German health system, for example, such self-interested action has led to a standstill in structural reforms.

Healthcare systems are under tremendous pressure to reform. Over the coming years, demographic changes that result in an ageing of societies around the world will intensify. Since the 1970s, political actors have pointed to a cost explosion in healthcare. However, in those earlier years, healthcare systems mainly experienced a financing crisis that in social insurance countries was partly related to changes in the wage ratio, i.e. the share of national income accounted for by wages (Wendt 2019). In tax-financed systems, by contrast, healthcare had to compete for resources with other public responsibilities and was therefore always under stricter state control than alternative means of financing. At the time, healthcare spending increased due to medical technological and healthcare innovations, growing numbers of medical doctors and other healthcare providers, and higher expectations of and demands on the healthcare system.

In most countries, economic growth and cost control mechanisms contributed to keeping health expenditure growth rates modest until the 2000s (Shaikh and Gandjour 2019). What has changed since then is that the pace of increase of the number of older people, and among them many multimorbid patients, is accelerating. At the same time, the share of the working-age population and thus the financial basis of the healthcare system and the potential number of qualified healthcare personnel are all declining. Therefore, new healthcare governance models are required to cope with the simultaneous challenges of ageing populations, growing demand, shortage of healthcare personnel, and limited scope for increasing healthcare spending.

Achieving the goal of an efficient health policy of importance to society as a whole requires cooperative and integrated approaches, commitment and leadership competence in all parts of society, and the cooperation of various social actors. Governance literature in the field of healthcare has pointed towards governance activities at the local, regional, national, and international level and the involvement of at least three different types of actors: state, non-governmental, and market (Giaimo and Manow 1999; Moran 2000; Rothgang et al. 2010). To face these unprecedented challenges and implement reforms successfully, concerted effort and participation from all these actors is crucial, thus underpinning the importance of health governance.

Health Systems and Governance Thus Far

At the level of healthcare systems, analytical models of health governance have been developed to better capture and understand health reform processes and how healthcare systems respond to external and internal pressures. From an international comparative perspective, two different governance processes in healthcare systems can be distinguished. The first focuses on actors and institutions in the healthcare arena and primarily asks how various constellations shape the overall development of healthcare systems. The second focuses on the institutional design of healthcare systems and asks how institutional differences are related to access to healthcare services and how institutions are related to health and health inequalities.

Early concepts of healthcare system governance aimed at a better understanding of how doctors' autonomy influenced the overall structure of the healthcare systems. From the mid-1980s onwards, scholars distinguished between different models of governance according to the role of actors in healthcare financing, service provision, and regulation (Frenk and Donabedian 1987; Hurrelmann et al. 2011; Marmor and Okma 1998; Moran 2000). Based on this work, Wendt and colleagues (2009) developed a methodological framework to capture the role of the state, societal actors, and the market in all three dimensions. Using this methodological framework for analysing governance changes in healthcare, it has been shown that major changes have been taking place in financing, service provision, and regulation and in healthcare systems with different actor constellations. Futhermore, changes in one or another of these dimensions imply changes in governance arrangements as well. For instance, when private financing increases, market mechanisms are often strengthened.

Governance changes are taking place in particular in the regulation dimension. Rothgang et al. (2010) have analysed the actors regulating the healthcare system along six relationships between healthcare providers, patients, and funders: who regulates (1) healthcare financing, (2) coverage, (3) providers' access to the healthcare market, (4) patients' access to healthcare providers, (5) payment of providers, and (6) the benefit package? It has been shown that healthcare systems that have been dominated traditionally by different actor constellations have become more similar over time. At one end of the spectrum, those with a high degree of state regulation such as the British National Health Service (NHS) have implemented more market competition mechanisms and are currently debating how to improve patient choice. Healthcare systems such as Germany's with a long tradition of self-regulation by non-profit actors have introduced more competition and stronger state regulation at the same time. And, at the other end of the spectrum, the United States healthcare system that relies on market competition more than other healthcare systems do has increased public funding and state regulation in recent decades.

'Internal markets' in Britain and choice of sickness funds in Germany and the Netherlands are examples that demonstrate that healthcare governance is changing. However, there is no clear trend towards privatisation and market competition, as is demonstrated by state regulation of contribution rates in Germany, and the strong state regulation of private insurers in Germany, the Netherlands, and Switzerland (Wendt 2019). Furthermore, many healthcare systems have implemented more robust regulation as well as incentives such as private co-payments to curtail excessive and unnecessary healthcare utilisation.

Regulating patients' access to healthcare providers and services is a particularly powerful governance tool. It is of importance to guide patients and their families through the healthcare system, and it has been demonstrated to support equality of access (Reibling and Wendt 2012). Since general practitioners (GPs) are often the first point of contact for patients with the healthcare system, they have been assigned the role as a gatekeeper in a number of healthcare systems. Their responsibility, however, is not to keep patients away from the healthcare system but to guide them to necessary healthcare services. In such a system patient choice is restricted. Yet, the trade-off in the best way to guide patients through the healthcare system should not only be between gatekeeping and free-choice systems. Health policy actors are currently searching for solutions that better combine patient choice and patient pathways based on expert knowledge.

While the above governance approaches primarily target system-wide and institutional practices, major governance changes are also taking place in several countries in the field of workforce development, in particular in primary care. Improvement in primary care provision is considered a key strategy for higher patient satisfaction, good access to care, and future sustainability of healthcare systems. One of the main trends is that in the primary sector, healthcare provision takes place to a lesser extent in single-doctor practices and increasingly by multiprofessional teams. In the British NHS, this has been achieved through changes in the reimbursement of GPs.

The advantage of a primary healthcare centre with a multiprofessional team is that patients have a one-stop point of contact for service delivery, which is a huge improvement in particular for multimorbid and chronically ill patients. Strong primary care systems have better health outcomes, reduce inequality of access, and support more effective healthcare utilisation (Kuhlmann et al. 2018). In England, a primary care model has been developed with strong gatekeeping and multiprofessional teams led by GPs. Nurses have received new roles and higher responsibilities within these teams. The Netherlands has different types of primary care provider models that are all informed by the idea of integrated care and people-centredness. As in England, there are new roles for nurses with nurse-specialists having prescribing rights and with patients having direct access to other provider groups such as physiotherapists. In Sweden, multiprofessional teams also provide services, and there is a strong commitment to people-centred care. In Germany, in contrast, team approaches and gatekeeping models are poorly developed, and ambulatory care is organised around office-based GPs and specialists. Integrated community-centred models have been set up as pilots but so far not throughout the country (Kuhlmann et al. 2018).

From a governance perspective, these are highly relevant developments since skill-mix changes can be included in workforce planning frameworks. In England, for instance, it is estimated that GPs can be partly substituted by other professionals: a high percentage of traditional GP tasks might potentially be taken over by non-physicians such as nurse practitioners (NPs). Simulation models for Canada estimated a significant productivity gain if NPs were fully integrated in family physician practice. For the Netherlands, it is calculated that physician assistants (PAs) and nurse specialists could reduce the requirement of GPs, and an expert committee in the US estimates that NPs and PAs could partly compensate for the expected shortage of GP services (Maier et al. 2018). More generally, a number of countries have developed new professional roles and have included the potential substitution of GP and specialist medical services in their workforce planning in order to be able to provide sustainable people-centred care in the future.

> *Governance models and practices must meet existing needs and future demands not only locally, but also globally.*

While policy-makers have made significant reforms in trying to organise the health sector better, involved multiple societal players in the process, and instituted appropriate governance mechanisms, the external environment is continuously evolving. Governance models and regulatory practices must therefore meet existing needs and future demands not only locally, but also globally.

Global Challenges for Health and Well-being

Globalisation processes now challenge existing modes of governance that have so far mainly been institutionalised at the national and subnational levels. While the changes resulting from these processes do not replace systems at the national or subnational level, they introduce new dimensions of transnational and intra-national governance and thereby widen the diversity and complexity of existing modes of governance in the health policy arena (Kuhlmann et al. 2015a).

Global governance has become increasingly important in preventing, monitoring, and responding to the outbreak of infectious diseases, and debates regarding compulsory vaccination demonstrate that national health policy actors respond to global developments (see Moon and Bezruki, Chapter 4 in this Report). The Sustainable Development Goals that are part of the 2030 Agenda for Sustainable Development adopted by the United Nations General Assembly in 2015 mark a new step in the development of global health governance. Goals such as healthy lives and promotion of well-being at all ages call for integrated approaches that are a challenge not only for developing but also for highly developed countries.

Action plans relating to universal health coverage, antimicrobial resistance, health and climate change, and human capital development require and are being addressed by global governance approaches (see Kickbusch and Liu, Chapter 5 in this Report). While there has been significant progress concerning the increase of life expectancy and the improvement of several indicators of mortality, health inequalities within and across countries remain or even increase. Furthermore, non-communicable diseases that have become the leading cause of ill health and death represent a growing burden globally (see Besnier and Eikemo, Chapter 2 in this Report).

Despite the progress made so far, the sustainability of achievements in global health and the governance mechanisms set out in the past is questionable, given the changing paradigms and sets of new and persistent challenges. The need for restructuring global health governance is felt now more than ever, and the reasons lie beyond the usual political and economic dimensions.

Report Overview

*T*he *Governance Report 2019* assembles nine contributions from health and policy experts from the Hertie School and other institutions that identify governance challenges of modern-day health policy and analyse existing and potential responses. The first group of contributions describes national, global, and transnational governance challenges for health policy. Elodie Besnier and Terje Andreas Eikemo (Chapter 2) and Clare Bambra (Chapter 3) map the current state of affairs concerning the level and distribution of various aspects of health both globally and within Europe. Bambra, in particular, presents concrete cases of good and bad health governance. Suerie Moon and Anna Bezruki (Chapter 4) draw attention to global health security challenges and the need for broader stewardship that transcends beyond just the health sector.

The second group of contributions focuses on innovative and comprehensive strategies for health policy by adopting a multilevel lens. These chapters elaborate on selected governance approaches as they are applied and place strong emphasis on the individual, national, and global levels as well as on multilevel and transnational governance. Ilona Kickbusch and Austin Liu (Chapter 5) trace the evolution of global health governance mechanisms and question their sustainability in light of current changes in the world

HURRELMANN, SHAIKH, *and* WENDT

order and growing challenges presented by the global health economy and investments in national health systems. By emphasising the centrality of politics to health governance and using the opioid epidemic as a case study, André Janse van Rensburg and Piet Bracke (Chapter 6) suggest ways to ensure that multiple, often conflicting interests are considered and represented in the policy-making process. Hanna Schwander (Chapter 7) highlights the role of healthcare within the welfare state and, by way of examples implemented in a number of European countries, illustrates how health policies conceived under the social investment approach could contribute to reducing health inequalities. Teasing out the findings of selected behavioural science studies, Christian Traxler (Chapter 8) provides insights not only on what works (and what does not) to address several health policy issues, but also on the potential pitfalls of attempting to simply adopt approaches in other contexts without testing and adapting them. Ellen Immergut, Andra Roescu, and Björn Rönnerstrand (Chapter 9) examine changes in the politics of healthcare governance in Europe since the 1990s, arguing that there has been a paradigm shift that places greater focus on satisfying citizens, good governance, and transparency, i.e. a shift from market management to democratic management in healthcare governance.

Looking even further ahead, Robin Gauld (Chapter 10) illustrates the increasing role of digitalisation and technology in providing current and future healthcare services. In doing so, the chapter outlines not only the promise these developments hold but also the key challenges that healthcare systems should expect, offering a charter for digital health governance.

Conclusion

As noted earlier in this introduction to the Report, health governance refers to all the actions and means that a society uses to achieve collective solutions for the maintenance and promotion of health as a common good. By its nature and as the contributions in this Report lay out, effective governance is a multilayered concept that requires the participation of individual, local, regional, national, and global actors. Given the multitude of actors, potentially conflicting objectives, and global and systemic threats, coordination and cooperation are mammoth tasks that require effective stewardship both nationally and globally. A concrete target perspective must be defined that requires stakeholders and institutions within and outside the health system to work together in order to achieve the goal in the period envisaged.

Nationally and subnationally, principal-agent problems in the delivery of healthcare require strong stewardship to prevent individual actors from acquiring immense control and acting in their own interests as opposed to the common goal of population health and well-being. A larger influence of the state could be strongly encouraged with the aim of diluting the power of such actors.

At the patient level, healthcare closer to home is being increasingly demanded. Multiprofessional care that is in close proximity to people is becoming the ideal model of healthcare provision. Patient-centred health-care must therefore be prioritised.

Changing demography and patient expectations of care provision will naturally change the role of hospitals services. Patient-centred care will require decentralised, multiprofessional outpatient health centres such as those in England and the Netherlands, restructuring of hospitals in terms of both product and process, and enhanced coordination and cooperation among multiple healthcare teams.

This Report's concluding chapter neatly summarises the governance challenges touched on here and in the individual chapters, their implica-tions, and the strategies that governance actors can adopt for instituting effective governance models for successfully delivering future healthcare. Specifically, we provide recommendations keeping in mind the multilevel nature of governance, i.e. global actions and national and regional measures, and the role of the individual in the delivery and receipt of care.

II. Health and Well-being Worldwide

ELODIE BESNIER *and* TERJE ANDREAS EIKEMO

I n September 2015, members of the United Nations General Assembly adopted the 2030 Agenda for Sustainable Development, committing to a shared vision of a world 'where physical, mental and social well-being are assured' and to the goal of 'ensur[ing] healthy lives and promot[ing] well-being for all at all ages' (United Nations 2017). This phrasing directly refers to the World Health Organization (WHO) definition of health as 'a state of complete physical, mental and social well-being and not merely the absence of disease or infirmity' (WHO 1946), thus emphasising the key role of health as both a promoter and a component of sustainable development. This definition also implies that health is well-being, making the two concepts essentially synonymous. Although this conception of health as well-being is not universally accepted, most definitions of these concepts acknowledge the interconnections between them, characterising health as a component (OECD 2017a) or a measure of well-being (Commission on Social Determinants of Health 2008).

> *Most definitions of health and well-being acknowledge the interconnections between the two concepts.*

To achieve the Sustainable Development Goals (SDGs) by 2030, assessing the current state of the global population's health and measuring the progress made are essential to inform global health governance and to develop, implement, and evaluate relevant policies. To this end, this chapter provides an overview of the current health status and burden of disease of the global population, as well as the main changes, variations, and trends since 1990.[1] This is done in three interconnected steps. First, the chapter presents the progress made in life expectancy, mortality, and reducing the burden of key drivers of ill health. Second, this chapter explores these trends further by describing variations and discrepancies in health between and within countries, highlighting the persistent challenge of health inequalities and its implications for health and well-being. The third section then explores the evolution of the main causes of and risks factors for ill health and mortality over time as well as their implications for future trends and challenges that global health governance will have to address.

The epidemiological data presented in this chapter are primarily extracted from the Institute for Health Metrics and Evaluation (IHME)

Global Burden of Disease (GBD) Study 2017 estimates (IHME 2018 and associated papers). This data source allows cohesive international comparisons of the burden of diseases and injuries over time. For disease- or region-specific data, information from the WHO Global Health Observatory data repository (WHO 2018e), the Organisation for Economic Co-operation and Development (OECD) health and well-being indicators, and the United Nations Department of Economic and Social Affairs (UNDESA) have been added. The estimates produced by each organisation may vary slightly for specific indicators due to differences in the sources used and the methods of estimation. However, they show similar trends in the health, burden of diseases, and longevity of the global population.

Progress in Global Health and Longevity

A number of key indicators show positive trends in the health and longevity of the population globally, suggesting that the world is living longer and healthier. However, some of the most recent changes in life expectancy and disease-specific burden point to a slowdown in this progress.

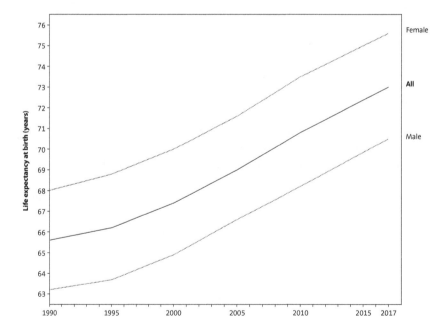

Figure 2.1a **Global life expectancy at birth, 1990–2017**
Source: Adapted from Dicker et al. (2018)

BESNIER *and* EIKEMO

The global population is living longer

Global life expectancy at birth (Figure 2.1a), i.e. the number of years a new-born is expected to live, has continued to improve in the last thirty years, rising from 65.6 years in 1990 to 73 in 2017. During this period, both men and women globally have seen their life expectancy rise at a fairly steady rate. A baby girl born in 2017 can expect to live 75.6 years on average compared to 68 years for those born in 1990. Similarly, baby boys have seen their life expectancy increase from 63.2 years in 1990 to 70.5 years in 2017. The gender gap in life expectancy has remained fairly unchanged over the last thirty-seven years: from 4.8 years in 1990 to 5.1 years in 2017 (Dicker et al. 2018).

At the same time, the number of years a person can expect to live in good health, or their healthy life expectancy (HALE), has risen by 6.3 years in the last twenty-seven years, going from 57 years in 1990 to 63.3 years in 2017 (Figure 2.1b). This increase in HALE benefitted both men and women, although it was slightly higher for women (6.4 years) than for men (6.2 years). However, as life expectancy increased faster than HALE between 1990 and 2017, the number of years in poor health from birth has increased by 1.1 years (Kyu et al. 2018).

While the global population has increased by over 140 per cent between 1990 and 2017 (Murray et al. 2018), the number of deaths has remained fairly

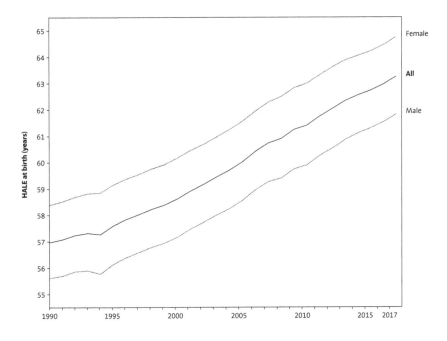

Figure 2.1b **Global healthy life expectancy (HALE) at birth, 1990–2017**
Source: Adapted from Global Burden of Disease Collaborative Network (2018)

stable, with an increase of less than 20 per cent in that period (Dicker et al. 2018; Global Burden of Disease Collaborative Network 2018). This trend is associated with progress in reducing mortality across age groups, with mortality rates in children and young people decreasing the most. Deaths in the first five years of life, known as under-5 mortality, have more than halved since 1990. Under-5 mortality has declined from 85.9 deaths per 1,000 live births in 1990 to 38.9 in 2017 (Dicker et al. 2018; Global Burden of Disease Collaborative Network 2018; Murray et al. 2018).

There has also been a shift in the contribution of different age groups to global mortality. While children under 5 years old made up 25.3 per cent of the total number of deaths in 1990, this contribution dropped to 9.6 per cent in 2017 (Global Burden of Disease Collaborative Network 2018). At the opposite end, older age groups' contribution to the global number of deaths has increased. Since 2008, more than half of the deaths globally occurred in people over 65 years old. In other terms, people today tend to die older than they did a few decades ago. These recent trends are also the continuation of the progress and changes in age at death since the 1950s. At that time, children under 5 years old made up almost half (45 per cent) of the total number of deaths globally (Dicker et al. 2018).

While these trends are encouraging, some nuances within certain groups should be highlighted. The reduction in under-5 mortality was not uniform across the age groups in this category, and progress during the first 28 days (the neonatal period) was comparatively slower (UNDESA 2017). This decrease in mortality has also led to an increase in ill health in certain places. In OECD countries, as infant mortality (deaths during the first years of life) decreased in the last twenty years, the proportion of low birth-weight infants increased, exposing a growing number of infants to a higher risk of poor health and contributing to the current stagnation of reduction in infant mortality in some countries (OECD 2017a).

These objective measures of health contrast with subjective measures such as perceived or self-rated health. For example, while people living in OECD countries gained almost two years of life expectancy at birth between 2005 and 2015, the percentage of adults in these countries rating their health as good or very good has remained stable at just under 70 per cent between 2008 and 2015, after showing an increase of about 2 percentage points between 2005 and 2008 (OECD 2017b). Self-rated health provides a unique perspective on how one's life and capabilities are affected by one's experience of health or ill health (Sen 2009) and has also been linked with healthcare use and mortality in selected populations (Palladino et al. 2016). Together with objective measures of health, they have been used by the OECD well-being index to inform policy decisions (OECD 2017b).

Progress has been made in the fight against major drivers of ill health and death

Since 1990, significant progress has been made in reducing the burden of key global health challenges, especially in the areas of communicable diseases, child health, and maternal health (Figure 2.2a). Both mortality and morbidity due to communicable, maternal, neonatal, and nutritional (CMNN) causes declined between 1990 and 2017 (Kyu et al. 2018; Roth et al. 2018). The global age-standardised death rate[2] due to these causes decreased from 281 deaths per 100,000 population in 1990 to 144 in 2017. Their contribution to the global number of deaths fell from 33.1 per cent of total deaths in 1990 to 18.6 per cent in 2017 (IHME 2018). The reduction of mortality due to these causes was particularly strong in children under 5 years old (Roth et al. 2018).

The burden of ill health due to CMNN causes also declined globally during that period, as the disability-adjusted life years (DALYs) measure shows (Figure 2.2b). DALYs count the years in good health lost due to ill health or premature death in a population. The total number of DALYs and age-standardised DALY rates[3] due to these causes decreased by 41.3 per cent and 49.8 per cent, respectively, between 1990 and 2017 (Kyu et al. 2018). In other words, the loss of good health years due to CMNN causes decreased in the last twenty-seven years.

The reduction of the burden of CMNN causes on health also involves the decrease of major drivers of global mortality and morbidity (Figures 2.3a and 2.3b). Among communicable diseases, these drivers include HIV/AIDS, tuberculosis (TB), diarrhoeal diseases, and malaria. According to the IHME estimates, the number of deaths due to AIDS peaked at 1.95 million in 2006 before falling to 0.954 million in 2017, with a 56.5 per cent decrease in the global age-standardised mortality rate (Roth et al. 2018). These estimates differ slightly from estimates from the Joint United Nations Programme on HIV/AIDS (UNAIDS) and UNDESA, but all these sources concur on the downward trend of AIDS mortality since the mid-2000s (UNDESA 2015a; UNAIDS 2018). In terms of DALYs, the IHME calculates that DALYs due to most HIV/AIDS-related illnesses declined by more than 50 per cent since 1990 in both absolute number and the age-standardised rate, making these causes some of the drivers of the decrease in DALYs due to CMNN causes. However, selected HIV/AIDS-related illnesses, such as multi-drug-resistant TB co-infections, are also among the few DALY causes in that group that have increased in the last twenty-seven years (Kyu et al. 2018).

The reduction of the TB burden has been slower but continuous since the 1990s (UNDESA 2015a; IHME 2018; WHO 2018f). The number of TB deaths decreased from 1.6 million deaths in 1990 to 1.18 million deaths in 2017, while the age-standardised mortality rate per 100,000 population was more than halved, going from 35.4 deaths in 1990 to 14.9 in 2017. Looking

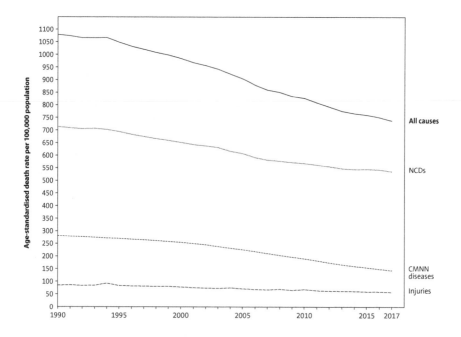

Figure 2.2a **Global age-standardised death rates by causes, 1990–2017**

Source: Adapted from Global Burden of Disease Collaborative Network (2018)

Note: The reference line labelled 'All causes' represents the total death rate and includes CMNN causes, non-communicable diseases, and injuries together.

at health loss due to TB, both the number and the age-standardised rate of DALYs due to TB have been declining, resulting in this disease dropping from the eighth to the fourteenth leading cause of DALYs globally between 1990 and 2017 (IHME 2018).

Since 2007, both the absolute numbers and rates of deaths and DALYs from diarrhoeal diseases have decreased (Kyu et al. 2018; Roth et al. 2018). Yet, these diseases remain one of the top ten leading causes of DALYs globally, higher than HIV/AIDS, malaria, and TB (IHME 2018).

Deaths and DALYs due to malaria have been declining after peaking in 2004 and 2003, respectively (IHME 2018; Roth et al. 2018). However, malaria incidence and mortality trends since 2015 point towards a slowdown in progress (WHO 2018j).

Most communicable diseases have seen a decreasing trend in their mortality and loss of years in good health. Selected neglected tropical diseases[4] such as dengue are the exception as some have seen increased mortality and DALYs (both in absolute numbers and rates) between 1990 and 2017, though Figures 2.3a and 2.3b show little change due to the smaller rate of

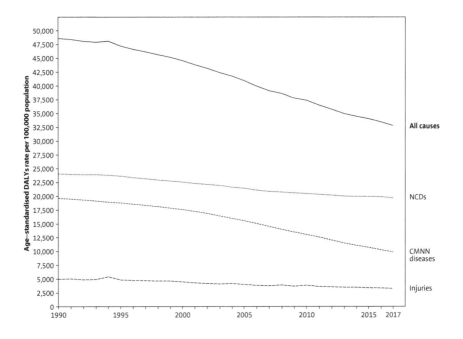

Figure 2.2b **Global age-standardised DALYs rates by causes, 1990–2017**

Source: Adapted from Global Burden of Disease Collaborative Network (2018)

Note: The reference line labelled 'All causes' represents the total death rate and includes CMNN causes, non-communicable diseases, and injuries together.

dengue in comparison to other communicable diseases at the global level (Kyu et al. 2018; Roth et al. 2018).

As for communicable diseases, ill health and deaths associated with pregnancy or occurring in the perinatal period have seen a steady decrease since 1990. According to the WHO Global Health Observatory data, the maternal mortality ratio, or the annual number of female deaths due to causes associated with pregnancy per 100,000 live births, declined from 385 per 100,000 live births in 1990 to 216 in 2015 (WHO 2018e), a 37 per cent reduction (UNDESA 2017). However, this reduction fell short of Millennium Development Goal (MDG) number 5 to reduce the maternal mortality ratio by three-quarters (UNDESA 2015a) and would need to more than double its 2000-15 progress rate to reach the 2030 SDG target (UNDESA 2017). Looking at specific causes of maternal ill health, the age-standardised rate of DALYs due to maternal haemorrhage, i.e. severe bleeding associated with pregnancy or labour, has decreased by more than 76 per cent since 1990 (IHME 2018), one of the most substantial reductions in the age-standardised rate of DALYs due to CMNN causes (Kyu et al. 2018).

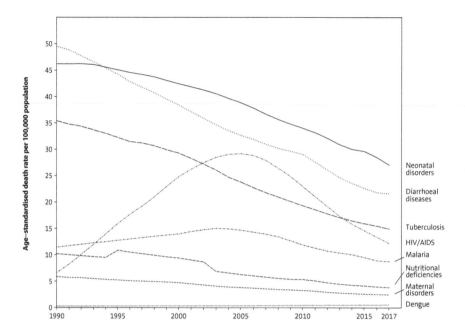

Figure 2.3a **Global age-standardised death rates for selected CMNN causes, 1990–2017**

Source: Adapted from Global Burden of Disease Collaborative Network (2018)

Mortality due to nutritional deficiencies, i.e. ill health caused by inadequate, insufficient nutrition, has followed a similar trend to that associated with pregnancy and the neonatal period, with a 33.6 per cent reduction in the last ten years (Roth et al. 2018).

These global health and well-being trends are undeniably positive. However, the accuracy of these findings and thus their capacity to adequately inform and guide governance decisions depend on the timely availability and quality of data as well as data literacy among policy- and decision-makers. Progress has been made in this field and in the strengthening of reliable data systems (UNDESA 2017). Globally, the share of deaths adequately recorded in relevant registers, an essential statistic to measure the burden of disease, has grown from 18.7 per cent in 1950 to 58.8 per cent in 2015. However, these advances are fragile: in 2016 more than 60 per cent of deaths globally failed to be reported and registered in the death registration system (Dicker et al. 2018). Several gaps remain in the functioning of and details available in vital registration systems. In 2015, only sixty countries had functioning civil registration systems, and only 51 per cent of countries had specific data on maternal causes of death (UNDESA 2015a). Finally, the availability of data disaggregated by sex, socioeconomic status, ethnic group, or other individual and population

BESNIER *and* EIKEMO

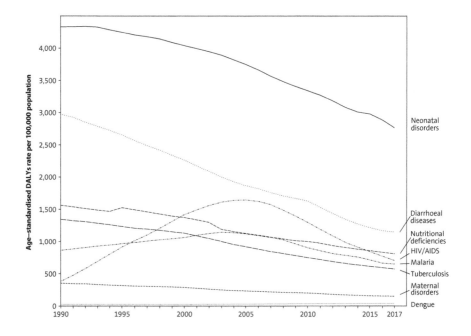

Figure 2.3b **Global age-standardised DALYs rates for selected CMNN causes, 1990–2017**
Source: Adapted from Global Burden of Disease Collaborative Network (2018)

characteristic remains uneven, even among wealthier countries (UNDESA 2015a; Murtin et al. 2017; Lozano et al. 2018). Despite these limitations, available data do show persistent health inequalities between and within countries.

Persistent Inequalities

Despite the progress observed at the global level, wide inequalities persist both within and between countries and world regions.[5] This section describes variations and discrepancies in key health indicators within and between populations, highlighting the cost and implications of such inequalities.

Inequalities between regions and countries

Beyond global averages, we see great heterogeneity between world regions and countries, both in the trends over time and in current health status.

In 2017, life expectancy at birth varied from a low of 51.8 years in the Central African Republic to a high of 84.8 in Singapore (Dicker et al. 2018). Of the 195 countries and territories covered by the IHME GBD project, sixteen countries gained no additional years of life in the last twenty-seven years (Kyu et al. 2018), while certain GBD-defined regions–Sub-Saharan Africa and Central Europe, Eastern Europe, and Central Asia–saw their life expectancy at birth declining in the 1990s (Dicker et al. 2018). As shown in Figure 2.4, a number of high-income countries have seen the pace of increase in life expectancy slow down or stall since the early 2010s, a trend expected to continue in the coming years (Dugarova and Gülasan 2017; OECD 2017a; Dicker et al. 2018). A reversing trend in life expectancy is also observed in countries affected by conflicts (Dicker et al. 2018). By contrast, Sub-Saharan Africa, the region with the lowest levels of life expectancy at birth, has seen progress in life expectancy accelerate, with the largest gain in life expectancy globally since 2000 (Dicker et al. 2018).

Countries with the lowest GBD Socio-demographic Index (SDI)[6] have seen not only the highest increase in life expectancy at birth and HALE between 1990 and 2017 but also the most substantial rise in years spent in poor health: an increase of 1.5 years versus 1.3 years for countries with a high

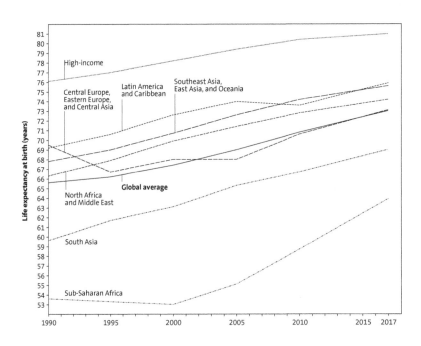

Figure 2.4 **Life expectancy at birth by region, 1990–2017**

Source: Adapted from Global Burden of Disease Collaborative Network (2018)

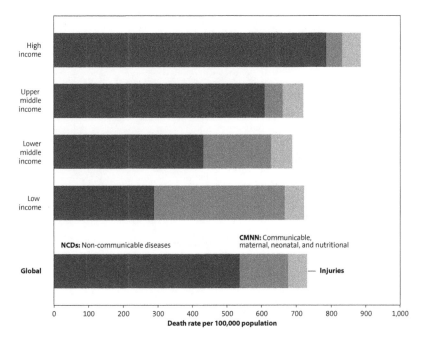

High
income

Upper
middle
income

Lower
middle
income

Low
income

NCDs: Non-communicable diseases   **CMNN:** Communicable,
                                                       maternal, neonatal, and nutritional

Global   — Injuries

0   100   200   300   400   500   600   700   800   900   1,000
Death rate per 100,000 population

Figure 2.5a **Crude death rates by country income groups and main causes,
2017**

Source: Adapted from Global Burden of Disease Collaborative Network
(2018)

SDI. Two countries (Lesotho and Swaziland) and one territory (Guam) have
also seen their HALE decreasing during this period. As with life expectancy
at birth, in 2017 HALE ranged from a low of 44.8 years in the Central African
Republic to a high of 74.2 years in Singapore (Kyu et al. 2018).

The burden of individual causes of death and ill health also varies from
one region or country to another. Low-income countries carry the biggest burden of CMNN causes (Figures 2.5a and 2.5b). For example, in 2013 developing
regions had a maternal mortality ratio fourteen times higher than developed
regions (UNDESA 2015a), and in 2015, 99 per cent of maternal deaths occurred
in low- and middle-income countries (LMICs), including 64 per cent alone in
the WHO African region (WHO 2015c). Child mortality rates also differ significantly across regions. In 2015, for instance, under-5 mortality ranged from 11 per
1,000 live births in Eastern Asia to 86 in Sub-Saharan Africa (UNDESA 2015a).
Encouragingly, Sub-Saharan Africa–the region carrying the highest burden of
under-5 deaths–experienced the largest decline in absolute numbers of child
deaths between 1990 and 2015. The WHO African and South-East Asian regions
alone accounted for three-quarters of children suffering from stunting, a sign
of chronic malnutrition (WHO 2018i). Based on current trends and progress
rates, at least 100 countries and territories are likely to reach the SDG target for

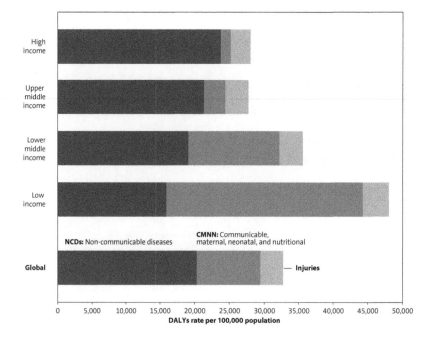

Figure 2.5b **Crude DALYs rates by country income groups and main causes, 2017**

Source: Adapted from Global Burden of Disease Collaborative Network (2018)

reducing under-5 mortality. Much more heterogeneity is found between coun-tries regarding their chances of achieving the SDG targets related to immunisa-tion, HIV/AIDS, or neglected tropical diseases (Lozano et al. 2018).

As presented in Figures 2.5a and 2.5b, high-income countries (as defined by the World Bank) carry the highest crude death and DALYs rates due to non-communicable diseases (NCDs). Yet, the highest absolute numbers of deaths and DALYs due to NCDs are found in middle-income countries (IHME 2018). Since 2000, the risk of dying from one of the four main causes of NCD-related deaths–namely, cardiovascular diseases (CVDs), cancer, chronic res-piratory disease, and diabetes–in adults between 30 and 70 years old glob-ally has decreased from 22 per cent to 18 per cent. Yet, this risk is almost twice as high in LMICs as in high-income countries (WHO 2018i). Low- and lower-middle-income countries have also seen an increase in the contribu-tion of injuries as a percentage of both total deaths and total DALYs between 1990 and 2017 (IHME 2018).

Inequalities between individuals and populations

Health inequalities are also found across population groups and within countries. Variations in health status between men and women globally shows that gender inequalities go beyond biological factors. Women have a longer life expectancy at birth than men in 180 out of 195 countries and territories (Dicker et al. 2018; Kyu et al. 2018). However, the size of the gender gap varies significantly from one region to another (as defined in the IHME GDB project): from 9.1 years in Central Europe, Eastern Europe, and Central Asia to 2.3 years in South Asia (Dicker et al. 2018). The gender gap in healthy life expectancy decreased across all levels of development, with countries with a low SDI having the smallest gender gap in HALE in 2017. Still, while women have seen their life expectancy at birth increase more than men's between 1990 and 2017, they also spend more years in poor health compared to their male counterparts (Kyu et al. 2018). This disparity can be associated with differences in the relative burden of various conditions by gender. Women are more likely to be affected by disabling or debilitating conditions, such as musculoskeletal disorders, depression, or dementia, thus affecting the number of years spent in poor health. By contrast, men are more likely to be affected by lethal conditions such as specific cancers, heart diseases, or injuries, which would affect the number of deaths in that population (Kyu et al. 2018).

Socioeconomic status affects both people's longevity and the burden of diseases. Survey data in LMICs between 2005 and 2013 show that under-5 mortality is 1.7 times higher among rural children than among urban ones, 1.9 higher among children from the poorest households (versus the wealthiest), and 2.8 higher among children whose mothers have no formal education (versus those whose mothers have at least a secondary education) (UNDESA 2015a). These data also show that the prevalence of malnutrition is at least 15 per cent higher in children whose mother had no formal education and, in two-thirds of countries covered, at least twice as high in the poorest quintiles compared to the wealthiest quintiles (WHO 2015e). On the positive side, some of the socioeconomic gaps in child mortality have been narrowing (UNDESA 2015a; WHO 2015e). Inequalities in child mortality and health according to income, education level, and/or living conditions are also found in high-income countries. In the United States, mortality among African American infants is twice as high as for white Americans (OECD 2017a).

Socioeconomic status and being part of specific population groups or minorities affect the distribution of different diseases and health risks. A systematic review of the mental health of the lesbian, gay, and bisexual community in Western countries found a 1.5 times higher risk of depression and a twice higher risk of suicide in this community compared to heterosexual people (King et al. 2008, cited in Langer et al. 2015). In OECD countries, social disparities tend to play a larger role for preventable diseases (OECD 2017a). For example, CVDs are the main contributor to the mortality gap between education levels in the older age group in these countries (Murtin et al. 2017). Poverty and marginalisation are also strongly associated with the incidence of selected communicable diseases. TB is often known as the 'disease of the poor', as poverty is one of the underlying factors driving national epidemics (WHO 2018f). For HIV, so-called key populations–such as sex workers, injected drug users, gay and transgender people, prisoners, and men who have sex with men–and their partners made up 47 per cent of new HIV infections globally in 2017 (UNAIDS 2018).

These health inequalities affect life expectancy. In twenty-five OECD countries, the gap in life expectancy at age 30 between people with the highest and lowest levels of education is six years, reaching more than ten years in certain countries of central and eastern Europe (namely, the Czech Republic, Estonia, Hungary, Latvia, Poland, and Slovakia). This gap by level of education is particularly pronounced among men (OECD 2017a). Relative inequalities in longevity by education level also seem to increase with age (Murtin et al. 2017).

These health inequalities within and between countries, and the premature mortality or preventable cases of ill health associated with them, entail a significant cost to society and governments, with important implications for health and social care systems as well as for the labour market and pension systems (Kyu et al. 2018; see also Bambra, Chapter 3 in this Report, focusing on the European Union (EU)). In the EU, a 2011 modelling study estimates that more than 700,000 avoidable deaths per year and 33 million preventable cases of ill health are due to health inequalities, costing the EU €141 billion in economic losses annually, or 1.4 per cent of GDP (Mackenbach et al. 2011, cited in Murtin et al. 2017). A 2002 modelling study estimated that the economic benefits of reducing Russia's mortality rates due to NCDs and injuries to the levels found in the western members of the EU by 2025 could be between 3.6 and 4.8 per cent of the Russian 2002 GDP (Suhrcke et al. 2007). At the same time, being in poor health also feeds socioeconomic inequalities. Studies carried out across the WHO European region in the 1990s and 2000s found that people suffering from chronic diseases were more likely to be unemployed, retire early, and/or tend to have lower wages (Busse et al. 2010).

Country-specific and Global Challenges

The last twenty-seven years have seen a transformation of the burden of diseases globally. With a shift from communicable diseases being the main contributor to ill health and death to NCDs becoming the leading cause, this epidemiological transition has led to improvement in mortality and longevity but also new challenges for individual countries and the international community. According to IHME (2018), in 2017 the leading causes of death globally were heart diseases, strokes, chronic pulmonary diseases, respiratory infections, and dementias such as Alzheimer's disease. The leading causes of DALYs globally were neonatal disorders, heart diseases, stroke, respiratory infections, and chronic pulmonary diseases. The main cause of injuries was road injuries, ranking eleventh in global causes of death and eighth in global causes of DALYs.

The persistent threat of communicable diseases

As noted earlier, the global burden of communicable diseases has been decreasing over the last few decades, with the age-standardised DALY rate they caused decreasing by 41.3 per cent between 1990 and 2017 (Kyu et al. 2018). Yet, communicable diseases still heavily affect people's health and well-being in several regions and tend particularly to impact children and working-age populations. Communicable diseases accounted for over 40 per cent of deaths and DALYs in low-income countries in 2017. They also remain among the top five leading causes of death and DALYs in children and young people globally (IHME 2018). At the same time, the emergence of new infectious diseases and the risk of outbreaks in a context of globalisation require continuous investment in preparedness, surveillance, and response capacity (WHO 2015c; see also Moon and Bezruki, Chapter 4 in this Report).

As previously mentioned, the mortality and incidence rates of HIV/AIDS, TB, and malaria have been declining globally (IHME 2018; Roth et al. 2018; WHO 2015c, 2018f, 2018i). However, these global trends hide significant variations by age groups and regions. In 2017, the Sub-Saharan African region had the highest number of people living with HIV, malaria cases, and TB deaths but also had the highest rates in reducing the burden of malaria and HIV since 2010 (UNDESA 2015a; UNAIDS 2018; WHO 2018f, 2018j). New HIV infections are higher among women, yet there are more deaths among men, highlighting a gender gap in treatment (UNAIDS 2018). By contrast, men tend to be more affected by TB, although regional variations exist (WHO 2018f). Young people and working-age adults over 15 years old carry the main share of TB and HIV/AIDS burden, while malaria is of particular concern for children under 5 years old, who comprised 63 per cent of malaria deaths in 2017 (IHME 2018; WHO 2018f, 2018i).

These three diseases also highlight the growing global health challenge of antimicrobial resistance (AMR). AMR is the ability of bacteria, viruses, and other microorganisms to develop resistance to the drugs used to treat the diseases they cause, making these medicines less effective or ineffective and hampering our capacity to treat or cure those affected. A number of treatments for infectious diseases, including antibiotics, now face AMR, posing a global threat to health systems' capacity to control and treat infections (WHO 2015b). TB is a strong example of this phenomenon. In 2017, an estimated 558,000 TB cases were resistant to one or more of the main TB drugs. More than half of these cases occurred in three of the world's largest emerging economies, i.e. China, India, and Russia, while the highest rates of drug-resistant TB are found in countries formerly part of the Soviet Union (WHO 2018f).

Since 1990, the burden of vaccine-preventable diseases has been significantly reduced (Kyu et al. 2018). Some diseases like poliomyelitis (polio) are close to being eradicated, with 80 per cent of the world's population living in polio-free regions in 2015 (WHO 2015c). Since 2007, the number of deaths due to measles fell by 57 per cent globally, those due to tetanus by 54.9 per cent, and those due to whooping cough and diphtheria by 23.3 per cent and 23.9 per cent, respectively (Roth et al. 2018). However, the risk of outbreak or re-emergence of these diseases remains. In 2014, seven countries reported imported cases of polio (WHO 2015c). Despite progress in immunisation, global coverage of the measles vaccine is still insufficient to prevent outbreaks (WHO 2018i). Additionally, the persistence of pockets of populations with lower vaccination rates in countries with high national levels of immunisation has led to the resurgence of measles, mumps, pertussis, or polio in areas where these diseases were considered controlled. Alongside the issue of access to immunisation services, vaccine hesitancy, or the refusal or delaying of immunisation despite services being available, is found in all world regions and is impacting immunisation rates globally (WHO 2014b). It is a complex challenge for governments, health systems, health professionals, and communities that requires multicomponent interventions at the individual, community, and population levels.

Finally, recent outbreaks such as Severe Acute Respiratory Syndrome (SARS) in Southeast Asia in 2003, cholera in Haiti and the Dominican Republic in 2010-11, and Ebola in West Africa in 2014-16 illustrate the global effects and disruptions infectious diseases can cause (WHO 2015c), thus calling for a global approach to infectious diseases surveillance, prevention, and control.

The growing burden of NCDs

With 62 per cent of DALYs and 73.4 per cent of deaths globally in 2017, NCDs have become the world's leading cause of ill health in the last twenty-seven years. Since 1990, the absolute numbers of DALYs and deaths caused by NCDs have increased, but their age-standardised mortality and DALY rates have declined (Kyu et al. 2018; Roth et al. 2018). We also see different trends for individual NCDs. Crude DALY rates increased for seven large groups of NCDs, from a 3 per cent rise for cancers to a 34 per cent rise for diabetes and kidney diseases. Crude death rates increased for eight categories of NCDs, with the highest growth found for diabetes and kidney diseases (49 per cent) and neurological disorders (61 per cent). CVDs and cancers remained the leading causes of death and DALYs globally in 2017, with CVDs alone accounting for almost a third of all deaths and almost 15 per cent of all

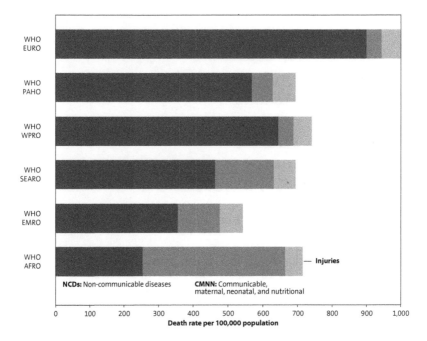

Figure 2.6a **Crude death rates by WHO regions and main causes, 2017**

Source: Adapted from Global Burden of Disease Collaborative Network (2018)

Note: WHO regions are abbreviated as follows: WHO EURO: European region; WHO PAHO: Region of the Americas; WHO WPRO: Western Pacific region; WHO SEARO: South-East Asia region; WHO EMRO: Eastern Mediterranean region; WHO AFRO: African region.

DALYs (IHME 2018). According to both UNDESA and IHME projections, the current rate of progress in reducing the burden of NCDs and associated risk factors would not allow the world or any individual country to reach the related SDG targets (UNDESA 2017; Lozano et al. 2018).

Some regional variations exist behind global trends, with an epidemiological transition occurring as income and development levels rise. As shown previously in Figures 2.5a and 2.5b, in 2017, low-income or low-SDI countries and their health systems were facing a double affliction: a rising burden of NCDs while communicable diseases and perinatal conditions were still among the main causes of death and ill health. At the other end of this epidemiological transition, NCDs make up 89 per cent of the deaths and 85 per cent of the DALYs occurring in high-income countries. Looking at regional groups as defined by WHO (Figures 2.6a and 2.6b), the European region (which includes all the countries formerly part of the Soviet Union) has the highest burden of NCDs both in terms of crude rate and as a percentage of their total burden of diseases, while the WHO African region has the lowest (IHME 2018).

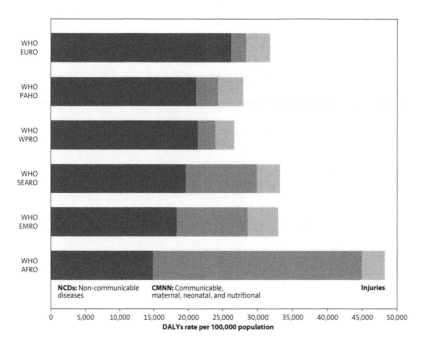

Figure 2.6b **Crude DALYs rates by WHO regions and main causes, 2017**
Source: Adapted from Global Burden of Disease Collaborative Network (2018)

NCDs affect men and women differently. Across all age groups, the mortality rates from CVDs and cancers are higher for men than for women, but those due to dementias and especially Alzheimer's disease are higher among women (OECD 2017a; IHME 2018).

The growing burden of NCDs is driven not only by ageing and population growth but also by the increase of specific risk factors like obesity. For example, the rising prevalence of obesity may explain the stalling of CVD mortality reduction in Western countries (Roth et al. 2018), and is discussed further two sections below. The ageing of the population results from both increased life expectancy and reduced fertility. In 2015, people over the age of 60 made up 12 per cent of the global population. This share is expected to rise to 16.5 per cent globally by 2030, growing from 24 per cent of the European population in 2015 to 30 per cent in 2030, from 21 to 25 per cent in North America, from 17 to 20 per cent in Oceania, and from 11 and 12 per cent in Asia and Latin America, respectively, to 17 per cent. By contrast, with 60 per cent of its population under 24 years of age in 2015, Africa's population over 60 is projected to reach only 6 per cent by 2030 (UNDESA 2015a, 2015b; Dugarova and Gülasan 2017).

The ageing of the population in much of the world and the associated burden of NCDs–most of them requiring long-term care–have direct implications for policy and planning, especially for the health and social care sectors (OECD 2017a; Kyu et al. 2018). According to the OECD, government and compulsory insurance expenditure for long-term care has increased faster than health expenditure, at an OECD average rate of 4.5 per cent a year (OECD 2017a). Globally, the number of workers per person over 60 is expected to drop from 7 in 2015 to 4.9 in 2030 (UNDESA 2015b). This will require measures both to respond to the workforce needs of the labour market and to ensure that people of retirement age are supported and cared for, either through pension systems or informal means.

Injuries disproportionately affect men's and young people's health

The global burden of injuries and violence has remained relatively stable in the last ten years, with small increases in the absolute number of deaths and DALYs they cause but declining mortality and DALY rates (Kyu et al. 2018; Roth et al. 2018). However, certain causes of injuries, particularly interpersonal violence, have seen increasing trends. In 2015, interpersonal violence and homicide were the driving force behind the American region's burden of injuries (OECD countries excluded), the highest as a proportion of total disease burden across all world regions (WHO 2015c). The absolute number of DALYs and the age-standardised DALY rate caused by sexual violence increased by 12.4 per cent and by 0.6 per cent, respectively, in the last twenty years (Kyu et al. 2018). The global number of deaths due to conflicts and terrorism, while small compared to other causes, increased by 118 per cent between 2007 and 2017. Almost a quarter of these deaths occur in children and adolescents under 15 years old (Roth et al. 2018).

The leading injury cause of both mortality and morbidity continues to be road injuries, with an age-standardised DALY rate of 871.1 per 100,000 population and a crude death rate of 16.3 per 100,000 population in 2017 (IHME 2018; Kyu et al. 2018). Despite lower levels of vehicle ownership in low-income countries compared to high-income ones, the crude death rates from road injuries is higher in the former, with sub-Saharan Africa having the highest rate globally according to 2013 data (UNDESA 2017; WHO 2018i). Taking all injury causes together, the WHO Region of the Americas and the Eastern Mediterranean region have the highest burden of injury both in terms of rate and as a percentage of their total burden of disease (IHME 2018).

The impact of injuries on specific population groups is significant (Figure 2.7). For all causes of injuries, men's health is disproportionately affected compared to women's, across all world regions and most age groups (IHME 2018; Kyu et al. 2018; Roth et al. 2018). Men are 75 per cent more likely to commit suicide (UNDESA 2017; WHO 2018i) and account for the majority of deaths by homicide and wars (WHO 2015c). The availability of global data on

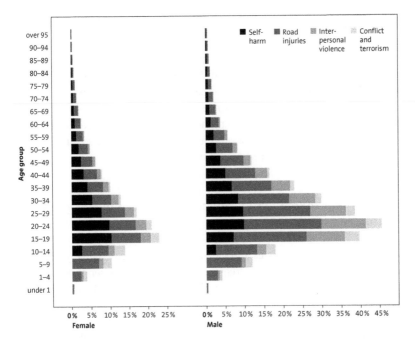

Figure 2.7 **Percentage of deaths due to selected injury causes by age and sex, 2017**

Source: Adapted from Global Burden of Disease Collaborative Network (2018)

violence against women remains limited. However, surveys across 79 countries suggest that one third of women worldwide have experienced physical or sexual violence (WHO 2015c). Finally, injuries are the leading cause of death in adolescents and young adults, with self-harm and interpersonal violence being the leading causes of death in 15 to 29 year olds globally (IHME 2018). The burden falling disproportionately on young people raises challenges for the health and well-being of the future workforce and of the next generation.

Understanding risk factors: towards a multisectoral approach to health

The contribution of behavioural, environmental, and metabolic risk factors to ill health and death varies according to causes, age groups, and countries' levels of income and development. Between 1990 and 2017, exposure to risks of high body mass index, ambient particulate matter pollution (air pollution), and high fasting plasma glucose (a marker for diabetes)–three risk factors associated with NCDs–has increased most among individual

BESNIER *and* EIKEMO

risks globally. At the same time, exposure to risks of unsafe sanitation services, unhealthy diet rich in trans fats, and indoor air pollution has declined the most, all three risk factors being associated with NCDs and two–unsafe sanitation services and indoor air pollution–with communicable diseases (Stanaway et al. 2018).

In adults, the prevalence of obesity almost doubled between 1980 and 2014 (WHO 2015c), with it being higher in women than in men (WHO 2015c; OECD 2017a). The rise of child obesity is of particular concern because of the long-term health and quality of life impacts of this risk factor. Between 1975 and 2016, the number of obese children and adolescents has multiplied by more than ten. In 2016, WHO estimated that one in five children globally was either overweight or obese (WHO 2018i). While child obesity prevalence is highest in high-income countries, it is growing faster in LMICs, leading some regions to face a double burden of malnutrition (Kyu et al. 2018; WHO 2018i). For example, the WHO Eastern Mediterranean region has similar prevalences of overweight (high weight for height) and undernutrition called 'wasting' (low weight for height, a sign of acute insufficient food intake or illness) in children under 5 years old (WHO 2018i). Both forms of malnutrition have been linked to lower educational attainment and poorer health, leading to poorer economic prospects as adults (OECD 2017a; WHO 2018i). Addressing obesity involves preventive and structural action from the local to the global level, going beyond the health sector to include international trade, food production systems, education, and urban planning (WHO 2018i).

Moving to environmental risks, 92 per cent of the world's population in 2016 was estimated to be breathing air with pollution levels above WHO recommended limits (Dugarova and Gülasan 2017). Outdoor air pollution is decreasing in most OECD countries (OECD 2017a) but has been increasing in other regions, particularly in the WHO South-East Asia region and the WHO Western Pacific region (WHO 2015c). Almost 90 per cent of the mortality due to outdoor air pollution occurs in LMICs (WHO 2015c). Although increasing at the global level, persistently limited access to clean cooking fuels and technologies (a key contributor to indoor air quality) in Sub-Saharan Africa and parts of Asia drives their comparatively higher rates of mortality due to indoor pollution (UNDESA 2017; WHO 2018i). Women and children are particularly exposed to this type of pollution (UNDESA 2017). Finally, while decreasing globally, the burden associated with unsafe drinking water and sanitation systems remains significant in Sub-Saharan Africa, as reflected in a mortality rate due to these risks that was four times the global average in 2016 (WHO 2018i).

Both alcohol and tobacco remain among the top ten leading health risks (IHME 2018). Both of these risk factors are drivers of the NCD epidemic and in the case of alcohol, of the injury burden (WHO 2015c). Such behavioural risks tend to increase with countries' income and development levels (Stanaway et al. 2018). Smoking has decreased globally, reaching an age-standardised prevalence of 19.9 per cent of people aged 15 and older in 2016 (WHO 2015c, 2018e). Global alcohol consumption per year remained stable between 2010 and 2016 at 6.4 litres of pure alcohol per person aged 15 and older, although consumption has increased in certain countries and particularly in Southeast Asia (OECD 2017a; WHO 2018i). Although declining since 2010, the highest smoking prevalence and alcohol consumption in 2016 are still found in the European region (OECD 2017a; Lozano et al. 2018; WHO 2015c, 2018e). Both of these risks disproportionately affect men (OECD 2017a; Stanaway et al. 2018; WHO 2018e, 2018i). Alcohol abuse excluded, abuse of other substances has risen since 2007. The age-standardised mortality and DALY rates caused by drug use have risen by 34.1 per cent and 12.1 per cent, respectively (Kyu et al. 2018; Roth et al. 2018).

Many of these risk factors are linked to health inequalities. An OECD study covering thirty-five of its members between 1995 and 2015 found that people with lower levels of education are more likely to pursue unhealthy lifestyles such as smoking, unhealthy diets, and lack of physical exercise (OECD 2017a). Studies in both developed and developing countries show that smoking prevalence is higher among the poorest households (Townsend 2015; WHO 2015c). In European countries, low-income groups also have higher mortality due to alcohol and smoking (Anderson 2015; Murtin et al. 2017). A 2010 review in European countries found that poor and less educated people tend to be more exposed to air pollution (Deguen and Zmirou-Navier 2010, cited in OECD 2017a).

A better understanding of these risks and their role in the disease burden as well as of the role of living conditions and socioeconomic factors in health has led to a broader approach to health promotion involving the wider determinants of health, empowerment, and participation (Commission on Social Determinants of Health 2008; McDaid et al. 2015; OECD 2017a; WHO 2017c). The link between income and health, both at country and individual levels, is well established (Wilkinson and Pickett 2009; OECD 2017a). However, research tends to show that the distribution of wealth, power, and resources across the population, inequalities, and cohesion also play a role in making society live healthier and longer (Commission on Social Determinants of Health 2008; Wilkinson and Pickett 2009). Education, health spending, employment, and working conditions have also been linked with health and life expectancy (OECD 2017a; see also Bambra, Chapter 5 in this Report). As most policies and actors influencing these factors sit outside the health system, addressing these determinants requires coordinated action across sectors as well as policy coherence across branches of governments. Health in All Policies, an approach that aims at assessing the health impact of public policies across sectors, has been emphasised and promoted as a way to ensure such coherence for health at different levels of government (Commission on Social Determinants of Health 2008; WHO 2013, cited in

OECD 2017a). At the same time, the contribution of health to other sectors and the multiple benefits of investing in health provides further arguments for a holistic approach to health (McDaid et al. 2015; Dyakova et al. 2017; Nurse et al. 2014; see also Schwander, Chapter 7 in this Report).

Health and Well-being Worldwide: Implications for Global Governance

Undeniable progress has been made in improving people's health over recent decades. Life expectancy has increased, and several global indicators of mortality and ill health show encouraging trends. However, we also see a transformation–rather than a reduction–of the health challenges decision-makers and health actors have to face. The decline of mortality has been uneven across regions and population groups. A persisting burden of communicable diseases requires continuous effort both from the countries and regions carrying the biggest share of this burden and from the international community in addressing outbreaks as well as keeping individual members' own burden of communicable diseases under control. The rise of NCDs as the leading cause of death and ill health has strong implications for policy and governance across sectors as well as for the sustainability of health systems. This growing burden of NCDs is further fuelled by increasing exposure to risk factors that are key drivers of the NCD epidemic. Some Western countries are already seeing the effect of these trends on their population's health, with progress toward extending life expectancy slowing down or stagnating. While proportionately smaller, the burden of injury, violence, and conflict, especially on young people, calls for long-term, concerted plans both to reduce their burden and mitigate their impact on the health of the generations currently affected.

Global health governance and leadership have achieved some clear success in lessening the burden of selected causes of death and in reducing ill health globally (see also Kickbusch and Liu, Chapter 5 in this Report). For example, the era of the MDGs between 2000 and 2015 has been associated with the reduction of child and maternal mortality as well as the reversal of the AIDS-related mortality trend (UNDESA 2015a; WHO 2015c). The new SDGs include a commitment to continue building on the progress made with the MDGs while providing a more multisectoral, global approach to health (United Nations 2017). As such, they offer the opportunity to better address the determinants of health and reduce disparities between and within countries in the global burden of diseases and injuries.

Endnotes

1   The year 1990 is the baseline throughout this chapter because reliable, comparable global health data are not consistently available for the various indicators used before this date. In addition, 1990 was the baseline used for the Millennium Development Goals' targets.

2   The *crude rate* reflects the actual, observed rate of a health issue in a population. It is calculated by dividing the actual *number* of the health issue of interest by the number of people in the population of interest. To be able to compare areas of different sizes, rates are expressed according to a standard population size (e.g. 100,000 population). Crude rates differ from *age-standardised rates*, which represent information—not empirical data—that has been statistically adapted to allow accurate comparison of populations over time. As the age structure of a population influences several health measures (e.g. the prevalence of certain diseases, mortality, and so on), these rates are standardised on a reference population's age structure in order to compare them accurately without the distortions that can be caused by the over- or underrepresentation of specific age groups in a population.

3   DALYs are a *summary* measure that captures the burden of a health condition or health issue in a population. It expresses the loss of an equivalent year of complete health, further to ill health and premature deaths. As with other epidemiological measures and depending on what it is used for, DALYs can be expressed as actual numbers, crude rates, or age-standardised rates.

4   Neglected tropical diseases (or NTDs) are a group of 19 infectious diseases found mainly in the tropical and subtropical areas of the world. As they particularly affect poor or hard-to-reach populations living in developing countries, NTDs have historically been rather low on the global health agenda, a low priority status that resulted in a lack of data, resources, and control or treatment options for these diseases (hence, the term 'neglected'). In 2012, WHO adopted an NTD Roadmap with targets for the detection, prevention, control, and treatment of these diseases (WHO 2012, 2018g).

5   Regions can be defined geographically (as the IHME GBD regions do), according to countries' ranking for specific indicators (i.e. the World Bank's income categories or the IHME GBD Socio-demographic Index), or according to countries' membership in specific organisations (e.g. WHO, OECD, or the EU). In this chapter, the name of the indicator or the organisation is mentioned when referring to such regional groupings. Further details on the difference between regional groupings can be found on the WHO website (WHO 2018b).

6   The IHME GBD Socio-demographic Index (SDI) is a summary measure of a country's or territory's development status, expressed on a scale from 0 to 1. It is built on the average of 3 indicators strongly associated with health outcomes: income per capita, average years of schooling, and total fertility rate (Dicker et al. 2018).

III. Governing Health Inequalities

CLARE BAMBRA

Since the global financial crisis of 2007-9, Europe has experienced considerable economic, social, and political upheaval (Wolf 2015). Across Europe, the economic recovery has been weak and inequitable: unemployment has remained high, particularly amongst young adults and those with low skills, wages have stagnated, and living standards have declined. Relatedly, health inequalities–defined in this chapter as systematic, avoidable, and important differences in health (Whitehead 1992)–have also increased. Whilst average life expectancy at birth in the European Union (EU) increased from 79.4 in 2008 to 81.0 in 2016, these increases were smaller amongst men and women with a lower level of education (Forster et al. 2018). For example, in Denmark, the difference in life expectancy at age 30 between men with a low education and men with a tertiary education rose from 4.8 years to 6.4 years. The respective gap for women increased from 3.7 years to 4.7 years. Similarly, in England, health inequalities have also increased (Forster et al. 2018). So, whilst the health of everyone in Europe has improved over the last decade, more privileged groups have benefited the most, leading to increased health inequalities in some countries (Mackenbach et al. 2016). The governance reverberations of the heightened social, economic, political, cultural, and health inequalities across Europe continue to be felt, most notably with the rise of populism (Funke et al. 2016; Castells et al. 2018).

This chapter examines how health inequalities have been governed in Europe since the early 2000s.[1] The chapter starts by providing an overview of the state of health inequalities in Europe. It then outlines the causes of health inequalities, emphasising the importance of governance in shaping the wider social and economic context which in turn influences the magnitude of health inequalities. It uses an overview of the English health inequalities strategy–which ran from 2000-10 and was the most extensive ever attempted in Europe–as a case study of how governance can reduce health inequalities. Austerity in England from 2010-18 is then discussed as an example of how governance can increase health inequalities. The chapter concludes by reflecting on the current and emerging challenges for governing health inequalities in Europe given the threats posed by migration, populism, and continued economic uncertainty.

Health Inequalities in Europe

In this chapter, health inequalities are defined as systematic, avoidable, and significant differences in health by socioeconomic status (Whitehead 1992). Socioeconomic status is a term that refers to occupational class, income, or educational level (Bambra 2011b). Across Europe, people with higher occupational status (e.g. professionals such as teachers or lawyers) have better health outcomes than those with lower occupational status (e.g. manual workers). Similarly, people with a higher income or tertiary-level education have better health outcomes than those with a low income or no educational qualifications (Bambra 2016).

Current levels of health inequalities in Europe are depicted in Figures 3.1-3.3.[2] Figure 3.1 shows inequalities in general health by income group. Good health increases with income in all countries (Eurostat 2018). At the EU level, 60 per cent of people with a low income report to be in good health compared to 78 per cent of people with a high income: a difference

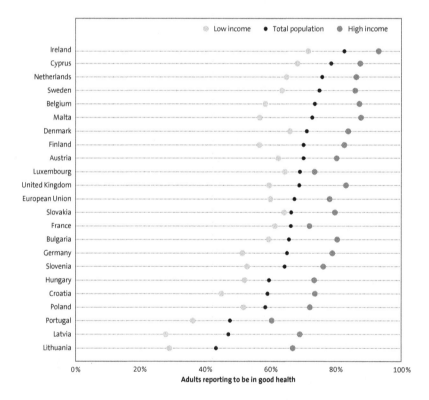

Figure 3.1 **Income inequalities in self-reported health across Europe, 2016**
Source: Forster et al. (2018), based on data by Eurostat (2018) (indicator code: hlth_silc_10), reproduced with permission.

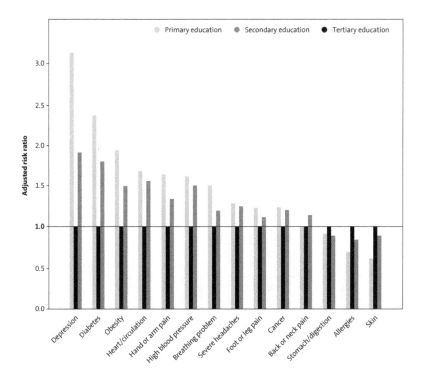

Figure 3.2 **Educational inequalities in non-communicable diseases in Europe**

Source: Forster et al. (2018), based on data by McNamara et al. (2017b) from the European Social Survey 2014, reproduced with permission.

Notes: Adjusted risk ratios estimate the probability of self-reporting a particular NCD for individuals with primary and secondary education vis-à-vis highly educated people, net of the effect of age. Regressions for a pooled European sample also control for country-fixed effects.

of 18 percentage points. Figure 3.1 also shows how inequalities in general health vary across Europe. For example, the health gap is 20 percentage points in Ireland and Portugal but almost 40 in Lithuania.

Figure 3.2 shows educational inequalities in long-term, chronic diseases (called non-communicable diseases, or NCDs) (McNamara et al. 2017b). Again, there are clear inequalities across Europe. For instance, someone with a low education is over three times more likely than someone with a tertiary education to report depression. As Figure 3.2 also indicates, educational inequalities in Europe are highest for depression, diabetes, and obesity.

There are also socioeconomic inequalities in health behaviours: rates of smoking and alcohol consumption are higher in lower socioeconomic groups, whilst rates of physical activity and consumption of fruit and vegetables are lower (Huijts et al. 2017). For example, as Figure 3.3 shows, smoking follows a clear social gradient: in all European countries except Portugal,

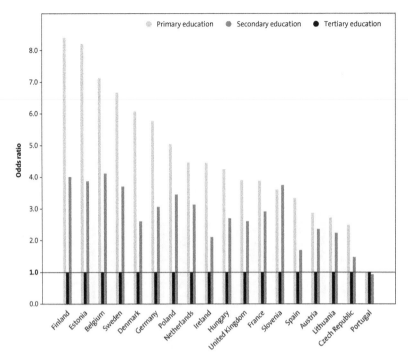

Figure 3.3 **Probability of smoking by educational status in Europe**

Source: Forster et al (2018), based on data by Huijts et al. (2017) from the European Social Survey 2014, reproduced with permission.

Notes: Odds ratios represent the probability of being a daily smoker given primary or secondary education, respectively, relative to individuals with tertiary education. All results are adjusted for gender, age, and age-squared.

the likelihood of smoking daily is higher for individuals with a primary or secondary education than for their more highly educated peers (Huijts et al. 2017).

Governing Health Inequalities

Health inequalities have important social and economic consequences for individuals, families, and communities. They also have social and economic implications for the governance of societies. For example, health inequalities result in unnecessary premature deaths, entailing large economic costs in terms of lower productivity and higher healthcare and welfare costs (Mackenbach et al. 2011). Better health and lower health inequalities improve productivity, reflected in higher labour market participation rates, working hours, rates of consumption, and efficiency (Bambra et al. 2018). The costs of inequalities in health across the EU amount to 9.4 per cent of GDP. It is estimated that 700,000 deaths per year in the EU are attributable to social inequality and that health inequality accounts for 20 per cent of the total costs of healthcare and 15 per cent of the total costs of social security benefits. Increasing the health of some 50 per cent of the European population with lower secondary education or less to the average health of the 50 per cent with at least higher secondary education would improve labour productivity by 1.4 per cent of GDP each year–meaning that within five years of these health improvements, the EU's GDP would be more than 7 per cent higher (Mackenbach et al. 2011).

Further, health inequalities are not genetic or biological in origin: the World Health Organization (WHO) Commission on the Social Determinants of Health (2008) established that health inequalities are socially determined and caused by differences in exposure across the life course to key social, economic, and cultural factors. The social determinants of health are the conditions in which people work and live. They can be seen as the 'causes of the causes' of health inequalities: there are clinical causes of disease, there are proximal causes (e.g. health behaviours), and then underpinning them are the social causes. For example, one of the underpinning clinical causes of stroke is hypertension (high blood pressure), the proximal cause of the high blood pressure could be poor diet, whilst the social cause could be low income and the inability to afford a healthy diet (Bambra 2016). Following the WHO Commission on the Social Determinants of Health (2008), the main social determinants of health are considered to be: access to health services, housing and living conditions, personal and community capabilities, working conditions, unemployment, and social protection. These are all policy areas that are at the centre of governance debates.

Access to health services

Universal, free access to healthcare is vital to reducing health inequalities across the life course (Gelormino et al. 2011; Asaria et al. 2016). However, across Europe, there are high inequalities in mortality amenable to healthcare, and people from lower socioeconomic backgrounds are less likely to access and use healthcare services than those in higher socioeconomic groups with the same health need (Forster et al. 2018). Inequalities in access to healthcare arise from accessibility (e.g. due to geographic proximity of services, attitude of healthcare professionals, or health literacy levels) and affordability (due to service costs including out-of-pocket payments) (Bambra et al. 2014).

Housing and living conditions

People living in poorer quality or insecure accommodation have worse health than others (Gibson et al. 2011). High housing costs can have a negative effect on health as expenditure in other areas (such as diet) is reduced, and costs may also lead to anxiety and worry (Stafford and McCarthy 2006). Low housing quality (such as damp homes, poor safety or sanitation, or overcrowding) also negatively impact on health (e.g. increased rates of respiratory disease) (Gibson et al. 2011). People with a low income are particularly likely to be exposed to poor housing as they are more likely to be renting, are less able to afford better quality housing, and have less security of tenure (McNamara et al. 2017a).

Personal and community capabilities

Lower rates of social capital, control, resilience, and trust are associated with worse health outcomes (Phelan et al. 2004). Social isolation and loneliness are linked with poorer health outcomes, including lower life expectancy (Shiovitz-Ezra and Ayalon 2010). Access to good quality education and lifelong learning go hand in hand with better health outcomes, as does volunteering (Jenkinson et al. 2013). Literacy and health literacy are also important for health (e.g. in terms of accessing services, the labour market, etc.) (Aaby et al. 2017). There are lower levels of personal and community capabilities in lower socioeconomic groups and communities, thereby impacting on health inequalities (Milton et al. 2012).

Working conditions

The health problems associated with the physical work environment such as noise, heavy loads, and exposure to chemicals are more prevalent amongst manual than non-manual workers: manual workers have a 50 per cent higher exposure to the majority of physical hazards than professional occupational groups do (Bambra 2011b). People in lower-status jobs also experience higher exposure to adverse psychosocial working conditions such as low job control, high work demands, high job insecurity, and low workplace social support (Marmot et al. 2006). These result in an increased risk of stress-related morbidity, including coronary heart disease, adverse health behaviours, obesity, musculoskeletal conditions, and mental health problems (Marmot et al. 2006; Bambra 2011b).

Unemployment and social protection

Unemployment increases the chances of poor health, including an increased likelihood of mortality, poor mental health and suicide, self-reported ill health, limiting long-term illness, and risky health behaviours (Bambra 2011b). Further, people from lower socioeconomic groups are disproportionately at risk of unemployment and its ill health effects (Bambra 2011b). Social protection policies can mitigate the effects of unemployment on health (Bambra and Eikemo 2009; O'Campo et al. 2015). In general, there is evidence that providing income protection for people who are unemployed or experiencing sickness, old age, or other situations of need (e.g. single parenthood, inactivity, or underemployment) is associated with better population health outcomes such as lower infant mortality rates (IMR), better child health and well-being, and lower mortality rates for all age groups and across all socioeconomic groups (Bambra 2013).

Governance matters

These social determinants of health, including healthcare, housing, education, and employment, are many of the issues that dominate governance and policy agendas across Europe. Key contemporary political discussions (How can we fund better healthcare? How can we provide affordable housing? How can we have a more highly skilled workforce? How can we reduce youth unemployment?) all relate to the distribution across society of the social determinants of health. So, as health inequalities are substantially shaped by the social determinants of health, and the social determinants of health are themselves the subject of considerable governance debates, policy development, and implementation, it stands that in turn governance systems, politics, and policies matter for health inequalities in Europe (Bambra 2016).

Governance can thereby be seen as the 'causes of the causes of the causes' of health inequalities (Bambra 2016). To return to the earlier example of the causes of stroke or heart disease: the immediate clinical cause could be hypertension (high blood pressure); the proximal cause of the hypertension could be poor diet, of which the social cause is having a low income, the causes of which are political and governmental, i.e. people have low incomes because the political and economic system allows them to have low incomes. Wages could be regulated so that they are higher, laws could make it easier to organise collectively in trade unions to bargain for better wages, or food prices could be controlled or subsidised (Bambra 2016). These macroeconomic and political factors are largely under the control or influence of national governments and international and global levels of governance such as those of the EU or the International Monetary Fund (IMF) (Schrecker and Bambra 2015). In this sense, inequalities in health and disease are produced by the structures, values, and priorities of political and economic systems of governance (Krieger 2011). Health inequalities are determined–at least in part–by the wider political, social, and economic system and the actions of the state and international-level actors: politics can make us sick or healthy (Schrecker and Bambra 2015). So, again, governance systems, politics, and policies really do matter for health inequalities. The next sections will demonstrate this further through case studies of contrasting governance approaches that have reduced or increased health inequalities in England.

How Governance Can Reduce Health Inequalities: The English Health Inequalities Strategy

In 1997, a Labour government was elected in England on a manifesto that included a commitment to reducing health inequalities. This led to the implementation between 2000 and 2010 of a wide-ranging and multifaceted health inequalities reduction strategy for England (Mackenbach 2010) in which policy-makers systematically and explicitly attempted to reduce inequalities in health. The strategy focused specifically on supporting families, engaging communities in tackling deprivation, improving prevention, increasing access to healthcare, and tackling the underlying social determinants of health (Mackenbach 2010). For example, the strategy included large increases in levels of public spending on a range of social programmes, the introduction of the national minimum wage, area-based interventions such as Health Action Zones, and a substantial increase in expenditure on the healthcare system. The latter was targeted at more deprived neighbourhoods when, after 2001, a 'health inequalities weighting' was added to the way in which National Health Service (NHS) funds were geographically distributed, so that areas of higher deprivation received more funds per head to reflect higher health need (Bambra 2016). Furthermore, the then-government made tackling health, social, and educational inequalities a public service priority by setting public service agreement targets. The key targets of the Labour government's health inequalities strategy were to: (1) reduce the gap in life expectancy at birth between the most deprived local authorities and the English average by 10 per cent by 2010; and (2) cut inequalities in IMR by 10 per cent by 2010.

There has been some debate about the effects of the English health inequalities strategy. Prominent early studies (Mackenbach 2010, 2011a, 2011b) concluded that although the strategy can be considered a partial success, it failed to reach its ambitious targets. However, these studies were published very shortly after the end of the strategy period, by which time it is unlikely that the impact had been fully realised. The studies also could not take into account the trend in inequality after the strategy period had ended. Although the studies mentioned above and others (Department of Health 2008, 2009;

Marmot et al. 2010; Hu et al. 2016) found no effect on or increases in inequalities during the strategy period, later studies found that inequalities in the key social determinants of health–including unemployment, child poverty, housing quality, access to healthcare, and educational attainment–did decrease during the strategy period (Buck and Dixon 2013; Asaria et al. 2016; Taylor-Robinson et al. forthcoming). Now, analyses using longer follow-up data have shown that these changes in the social determinants went hand in hand with changes in health inequalities (Bambra 2012; Barr et al. 2014; Barr et al. 2017; Robinson et al. 2019).

Barr et al. (2017) found that inequalities in life expectancy declined during the English health inequalities strategy period, reversing a previously increasing trend. Before the strategy, the gap in life expectancy between the most deprived local authorities in England and the rest of the country increased at a rate of 0.57 months each year for men and 0.30 months each year for women. During the strategy period this trend reversed, and the gap in life expectancy for men declined by 0.91 months each year and for women by 0.50 months each year. Barr et al. (2017) also found that since the end of the strategy period the inequality gap has increased again at a rate of 0.68 months each year for men and 0.31 months each year for women. At the end of the English health inequalities strategy period, the gap in male life expectancy was 1.2 years smaller and the gap in female life expectancy was 0.6 years smaller than it would have been if the trends in inequalities before the strategy had continued.

Further, Robinson et al. (2019) investigated whether the English health inequalities strategy was associated with a decrease in inequalities in IMR. They found that prior to New Labour's health inequalities strategy (1983-98), the gap in infant mortality between the most deprived local authorities and the rest of England increased at a rate of three infant deaths per 100,000 births per year. During the strategy period (1999-2010), the gap narrowed by 12 infant deaths per 100,000 births per year, and after the strategy period ended (2011-17) began increasing again at a rate of four deaths per 100,000 births per year.

Another area of strategy success was around reducing inequalities in mortality amenable to healthcare, i.e. mortality from causes for which there is evidence that they can be prevented given timely, appropriate access to high-quality care (Nolte and McKee 2011). NHS funding was increased from 2001 when the aforementioned health inequalities weighting was added to the way in which NHS funds were geographically distributed to target funding to areas of higher deprivation. Analysis has shown that this policy of increasing the proportion of resources allocated to deprived areas was associated with a reduction in absolute health inequalities from causes amenable to healthcare (Barr et al. 2014). Increases in NHS resources to deprived areas accounted for a reduction in the gap between deprived and affluent areas in male mortality amenable to healthcare of 35 deaths per 100,000 and female mortality of 16 deaths per 100,000. Each additional £10 million of resources allocated to deprived areas was associated with a reduction in four male deaths per 100,000 and two female deaths per 100,000 (Barr et al. 2014).

So, the most recent data shows that the English strategy did reduce health inequalities in terms of life expectancy, infant mortality, and mortality amenable to healthcare. However, it has to be acknowledged that the decreases were on the modest side. Arguably, the English health inequalities strategy may have been even more effective in reducing health inequalities if there had not been a gradual 'lifestyle drift' in governance whereby policy went from thinking about the social determinants of health alongside behaviour change to focusing almost exclusively on individual behaviour change (Whitehead and Popay 2010). Only so much can be achieved in terms of reducing health inequalities by focusing only on individual-level behaviour change or the provision of treatment services such as smoking cessation programmes or by increasing access to healthcare services. There is a need to also address the more fundamental social and economic causes. Whilst some policies enacted under the 1997-2010 Labour governments focused on the more fundamental determinants such as the implementation of a national minimum wage, the minimum pension, tax credits for working parents, and a reduction in child poverty, as well as significant investment in the healthcare system, there was, however, little substantial redistribution of income between rich and poor. Nor was there much by way of an economic rebalancing of the country (e.g. between north and south). Further, in wider policy areas, the Labour governments continued the neoliberal approach of Thatcherism, including, for example, further marketisation and privatisation of the healthcare system (Scott-Samuel et al. 2014). The strategy might also have been even more effective if it had been sustained over a longer time period. But the global financial crisis of 2007-9 led to the premature end of the English health inequalities strategy, a change of governing political party, and the increase again in health inequalities.

How Governance Can Increase Health Inequalities: Austerity in the United Kingdom

The global financial crisis of 2007-9 led to a long period of recession across Europe. Banks increasingly required state bailouts, and stock markets posted massive falls which continued as the effects in the 'real' economy began to be felt with high unemployment rates of around 8.5 per cent in the UK and the United States, 10 to 12 per cent in France and Italy, and more than 20 per cent in Spain and Greece. The IMF announced that the global economy was experiencing its worst period since the 1930s: the Great Recession (Gamble 2009).

European governance responses to the Great Recession varied. Whilst some countries such as Iceland responded with stimulus, others such as Spain, Greece, and the UK implemented austerity (Reeves et al. 2013). In 2010, a Conservative-led coalition government was elected in the UK on a platform of austerity (Kitson et al. 2011). Austerity in the UK–the third most extensive austerity regime in Europe (Reeves et al. 2013)–was characterised by a drive to reduce public deficits via large-scale cuts to central and local government budgets, reduced funding for the healthcare system, and large reductions in welfare services and working-age social security benefits.

Beatty and Fothergill (2016) have estimated that the UK welfare reforms implemented as a result of austerity between 2010 and 2015 have taken over £20 billion a year out of the economy. This is equivalent to around £470 a year for every working-age adult in the country. Local government spending has also fallen by well over 30 per cent since 2010. Research shows that these welfare and local budget cuts have hit the poorest parts of the country the hardest (Beatty and Fothergill 2016), with austerity disproportionately impacting the availability of key services in these areas, widening social inequalities within them and spatial inequalities between them and other areas (Pearce 2013; Bambra and Garthwaite 2015). The poorest areas of the country have been worst affected, with the 'old industrial areas'–places like Liverpool, Middlesbrough, Hartlepool, Burnley, and Stockton-on-Tees–losing up to £900 per person (Beatty and Fothergill 2014). These 'reforms' have also disproportionately impacted low-income, working-age households (Browne and Levell 2010). Low-income families with children, for example, have been subjected to numerous welfare cuts since 2010, including the abolition of child benefit and child tax credit for the third child or more; reductions in the value of tax credits; below-inflation up-rating of most working-age benefits; housing benefit reforms, including the underoccupancy charge (most commonly referred to as 'bedroom tax'); introduction of universal credit; and household caps on total benefit receipt (regardless of how many children are in the household) (Beatty and Fothergill 2016).

The politically driven austerity programme started to impact on health inequalities quickly by unequally changing the underpinning social determinants of health, most notably in terms of poverty (Pearce 2013). Whilst relative child poverty declined between 2007 and 2013, there have been sharp increases since: child poverty (defined as living in a household with income below 60 per cent of the median household income after housing costs) rose by 2 percentage points between 2014 and 2017, and it is projected to increase further through to 2022 (Hood and Waters 2017)). By 2017 there were 4.1 million children in England living in relative poverty, amounting to 30 per cent of all English children. This compares to 2015 estimates of less than 10 per cent of children living in poverty in countries such as Austria, Denmark, Finland, Iceland, Norway, Slovenia, Sweden, and Switzerland (OECD Social Policy Division 2015). Food poverty has also emerged in the

UK as a consequence of austerity governance with over one million people a year now accessing emergency food banks. The majority of food bank visits are as a result of delayed, stopped, or reduced welfare payments (Garthwaite et al. 2015). Alongside food poverty, many more are now also experiencing fuel poverty as energy costs rise whilst incomes fall (Bambra 2019).

In terms of the health effects of austerity governance, studies have found that there are important variations in the effects of recessions and economic downturns on population health depending on policy responses. In a wide-ranging and well publicised analysis of the health effects of austerity, Stuckler and Basu (2013) concluded that the overall effects of recessions on the health of different nations vary significantly by political and policy context: those countries (such as Iceland or the US) that responded to the financial crisis of 2007-9 with an economic stimulus fared much better–particularly in terms of mental health and suicides–than those countries (e.g. Spain, Greece, or the UK) that chose to pursue a policy of austerity. Similarly, Karanikolos et al. (2013) found that across Europe, weak social protection systems exacerbated the health and social crisis in Europe. Previously, in the context of the Asian recession of the late 1990s, Hopkins (2006) found that, while in Thailand and Indonesia where social welfare spending was reduced, mortality rates increased, in Malaysia where no cutbacks occurred, mortality rates were unchanged. On the basis of several decades of data prior to the Great Recession, Stuckler et al.'s (2009) study of twenty-six European countries concluded that greater spending on social welfare could considerably reduce suicide rates during periods of economic downturn. In the UK, there is evidence that the pressures that austerity has placed on key social and healthcare services resulted in up to 10,000 additional deaths in the first seven weeks of 2018 compared to the same period in previous years (Hiam and Dorling 2018).

In terms of health inequalities, studies suggest that austerity has increased health inequalities in England. For example, Barr et al. (2015) found that inequalities in mental health and well-being increased at a higher rate between 2009 and 2013. Further, people living in more deprived areas experienced the largest increases in poor mental health (Barr et al. 2016) and self-harm (Barnes et al. 2016). It has also been shown that austerity is having a disproportionate impact on the health of vulnerable groups, especially those individuals and families, including children, on the lowest incomes, with mental health problems, or in receipt of welfare benefits (MacLeavy 2011; Mattheys et al. 2018). For example, Taylor-Robinson et al. (forthcoming) found that increases in child poverty since the implementation of austerity governance were associated with increased inequalities in IMR in England, with every 1 per cent increase in child poverty associated with an extra 5.8 infant deaths per 100,000. Inequalities in IMR, life expectancy, and mortality amenable to healthcare also increased from 2010 onwards (Barr et al. 2015; Barr et al. 2016; Robinson et al. 2019). Internationally, Niedzwiedz et al. (2016) found that reductions in spending levels or increased conditionality may have adversely impacted on the mental health of disadvantaged social groups.

These findings about the effects of austerity on health inequalities are in keeping with previous studies of the effects of public sector and welfare state contractions on increases in health inequalities in the UK, the US, and New Zealand in the 1980s and 1990s. Such prior research into austerity-style governance suggests that cuts to the social safety net will only serve to increase health inequalities. Indeed, these older studies are almost certain to understate the scale and multitude of the health consequences (Pearce 2013) given the larger scale of the subsequent spending cuts this time around. Nonetheless, they provide the best available evidence at this stage of the effects on health inequalities of the 'austerity epidemic' (Schrecker and Bambra 2015).

A US study found that whilst premature mortality (deaths under age 75) and IMR declined overall in all income quintiles from 1960 to 2002, inequalities by income and ethnicity decreased only between 1966 and 1980, and then increased between 1980 and 2002 (Krieger et al. 2008). The reductions in inequalities (1966-80) occurred during a period of welfare expansion in the US (the War on Poverty) and the enactment of civil rights legislation, which increased access to welfare state services. The increases in health inequalities occurred during a period when public welfare services (including healthcare insurance coverage) were cut, funding of social assistance was reduced, the minimum wage was frozen, and the tax base was shifted from the rich to the poor, leading to increased income polarisation.

Research into the health effects of Thatcherism (1979-90) has also concluded that the large-scale dismantling of the UK's social democratic institutions and the early pursuit of austerity-style policies increased socioeconomic health inequalities. Thatcherism deregulated the labour and financial markets, privatised utilities and state enterprises, restricted social housing, curtailed trade union rights, marketised the public sector, significantly cut the social wage via welfare state retrenchment, accepted mass unemployment, and implemented large tax cuts for the business sector and the most affluent (Scott-Samuel et al. 2014). In this period, whilst life expectancy increased and mortality rates decreased for all social groups, the increases were greater and more rapid amongst the highest socioeconomic groups, so that inequalities increased.

These findings are mirrored in studies of welfare state reductions in New Zealand (Shaw et al. 2005; Pearce et al. 2006; Pearce and Dorling 2006; Blakely et al. 2008) which found that whilst general mortality rates declined, socioeconomic inequalities amongst men, women, and children in all-cause mortality increased in the 1980s and the 1990s then stabilised in the early 2000s. Likewise, spatial inequalities in health between local areas and regions increased. The increases in health inequality occurred during a period in which New Zealand underwent major structural reform, including a less redistributive tax system, more targeted social benefits, introduction of a regressive tax on consumption, privatisation of major utilities and public housing, user charges for welfare services, and a more deregulated labour market. The stabilisation of inequalities in mortality in the late 1990s and early 2000s was during a period in which the economy improved and there were some improvements in services (e.g. better access to social housing, more generous social assistance, and a decrease in healthcare costs).

These historical increases in health inequalities were not inevitable–they were the result of a clear political choice to implement a particular form of governance. Similarly, austerity in response to the global financial crisis of 2007-9 was a clear governance choice. It has led to increased health inequalities in England and reversed the gains made under the previous health inequalities strategy.

Health Inequalities in a Changing Europe

This chapter has examined how health inequalities have been governed in Europe since the early 2000s. It has outlined the extent of current health inequalities across Europe and explored their causes, emphasising the importance of governance in shaping the social determinants of health. It presented two contrasting case studies, the English health inequalities strategy and austerity in the UK, both of which show that governance matters for health inequalities. Governance–through the implementation of positive social and health policies–can decrease health inequalities, saving lives. In contrast, governance–as we have experienced with post-financial crisis austerity in Europe–can also result in increased health inequalities by reducing the social safety net.

There are clear lessons for policy-makers in Europe from the English experience. Austerity and reducing the social safety net may increase health inequalities, but there is also evidence from England that policies that address the social determinants of health by supporting families, engaging communities in tackling deprivation, improving prevention, increasing access to healthcare, and reducing poverty through expanding the welfare state and increasing wages can reduce health inequalities: governance matters.

Health inequalities may be ubiquitous, but the English case studies suggest that they are not inevitable or insurmountable: they can be reduced. Across Europe, there is increasing evidence demonstrating how public policies can reduce health inequalities–through public regulation mechanisms (e.g. taxation of tobacco, sugar taxation, minimum pricing for alcohol), via social policy tools (e.g. reducing poverty through more generous social protection policies), or by increasing healthcare access (Bambra et al. 2014; Thomson et al. 2018; Hillier-Brown et al. forthcoming). Health inequalities can be reduced, but there needs to be a real desire to do so, and ultimately a governance choice must be made to do so (Bambra 2016). There needs to be the political will and the accompanying action to change the social determinants of health.

However, policy-makers in Europe are today faced with the effects of major new challenges to reducing health inequalities, including migration, the rise of populism, and continued economic volatility. These interlinked, contemporary challenges are each examined briefly below.

Across Europe, migration rates have increased over the last decade. For example, in 2011 in Greece around 6.6 per cent of the population were non-EU migrants with a further 1.8 per cent of the population coming from within the EU (Eikemo et al. 2018). Partly as a result, populist radical right parties have been gaining votes and prominence. These parties–including Rassemblement National (French National Front), Austrian Freedom Party (FPÖ), Italian Northern League, Alternative for Germany, Law and Justice (Poland), Dutch Party for Freedom, UK Independence Party (UKIP), True Finns Party, and Sweden Democrats–are nationalist, authoritarian, and populist (privileging the 'common sense' of 'the people' over elite knowledge) (Falkenbach and Greer 2018). As such, they pose a threat to traditional political parties and democracy, and–by marginalising issues of health and welfare in favour of focusing on migration, crime, and security–they pose a challenge to the future governance of health inequalities.

They pursue exclusionary policies, trying to restrict access to social welfare benefits, including healthcare, by non-citizens (mostly migrants): welfare chauvinism (Falkenbach and Greer 2018). This means that these parties focus political debate on issues other than health and social justice and also try to exclude some of the most vulnerable groups (e.g. migrants who have some of the highest health needs) from the health and welfare system. This can lead to more general cuts to welfare. For example, from 2017 to 2019, Austria was governed by a coalition of the FPÖ and conservative parties. The coalition made considerable spending cuts to the welfare system, specifically in relation to migrants, such as a 25 per cent reduction in the budget of the unemployment service (Falkenbach and Greer 2018). Other notable areas of public health policy under threat from populist radical right parties include tobacco control (e.g. the Austrian coalition cancelled the planned public smoking ban) and reproductive health rights (e.g. in the US, Trump champions restricting access to abortions and birth control, including trying to remove Planned Parenthood service from Medicaid, the health insurance for the poorest (Rosenbaum 2019)).

Another way in which populist radical right parties pose a challenge to the governance of health inequalities is through contributing to the broader economic volatility within the global financial system. Europe has had a very sluggish recovery from the 2007-9 crisis, with wages in countries like the UK still below their pre-crash levels and unemployment rates particularly high amongst youth in countries like Spain and Greece with long-term rates of over 20 per cent. There are growing concerns that Europe is on the brink of another widespread recession with Brexit (brought about in part by the mainstream influence of the populist radical right UKIP) (OECD 2016) and the protectionist trade and tariff wars initiated by US President Trump seen as major contributory factors. Indeed, Brexit itself is considered to have huge impacts on health policy, including employment within the NHS, access to and regulation of medicines, and food prices to name but a few (for a full overview see Fahy et al. 2019).

Recessions have mixed impacts on health: they have detrimental health effects for those losing jobs or in fear of losing their jobs, but all-cause mortality, deaths from cardiovascular disease, motor vehicle accidents, and hazardous health behaviours decrease during economic downturns, whilst deaths from suicides, rates of mental ill health, and chronic illnesses increase in some–but not all–countries (Bambra et al. 2016). However, as noted earlier in this chapter, the policy responses chosen by governments matter: it is not recession in and of itself that matters, but how governments respond to it. After the 2007-9 crisis, countries that chose to invest in the economy and protect public spending did not have significant changes in population health, whilst those countries that pursued austerity had significant increases in mental ill health and suicide. In terms of inequalities (e.g. the UK as described earlier in this chapter), the negative health impacts of recessions–filtered through austerity–disproportionately impact those on the lowest incomes who are in most need of social welfare protection. How European governments respond to another recession will be vital in terms of future patterns of health inequalities, and the pressure towards welfare chauvinism from populist radical right parties may lead to a further round of austerity (Falkenbach and Greer 2018).

So, whilst there is a growing evidence base to suggest that multifaceted governance approaches such as the English health inequalities strategy can reduce health inequalities–through action on the social determinants of health–the threats of populism and further economic volatility and austerity pose significant challenges to the future of health equity.

Endnotes

1   This chapter draws on research conducted by the author as a Leverhulme Research Leadership Award holder (Leverhulme grant reference RL-2012-006) and as senior investigator in CHAIN: Centre for Global Health Inequalities (Norwegian Research Council grant reference 288638).

2   With thanks to Timon Forster for redrawing Figures 3.1–3.3.

IV. The Global Governance of Outbreaks

SUERIE MOON *and* ANNA BEZRUKI

O utbreaks of infectious disease are increasingly understood as economic, political, and security threats, in addition to the clear risk they pose to human health (Heymann et al. 2015). The term 'global health security' has been usefully defined as 'action to reduce the vulnerability of people around the world to new, acute, or rapidly spreading risks to health, particularly those threatening to cross international borders' (Kickbusch et al. 2015: 1069). While a number of threats could fall under this umbrella, such as nuclear accidents or natural disasters, this chapter focuses specifically on acute outbreaks of infectious disease given their frequency and disruptive nature.

Many aspects of global health security are inherently transnational and thus require effective global governance.

While national capacities to prevent, detect, and respond to outbreaks are a critical first line of defence, many aspects of global health security are inherently transnational and thus require effective global governance. For example, mitigating international panic and developing scientific understanding of emerging pathogens both require international cooperation, even among the most well-resourced states. Oftentimes, disease threats emerge in resource-limited settings and can quickly cross borders, making international assistance and cooperation even more critical. Since the turn of the millennium, there have been significant changes in the global governance of outbreaks of infectious disease, some of which were undertaken in direct response to large-scale outbreaks, including the 2014 West African Ebola crisis.

This chapter examines the global governance challenges in preparing for, and responding to, outbreaks of infectious diseases to determine how prepared the world is for major outbreaks. It begins by providing a brief history of global governance arrangements, followed by an identification of gaps across four issue areas: country commitments under the International Health Regulations (IHR); science, technology, and knowledge-sharing; the international health and humanitarian system; and the cross-cutting issues of financing, leadership, monitoring, and accountability. The chapter concludes that the global health system has exhibited an important ability to evolve, but particular attention needs to be paid to persistent weaknesses in the cross-cutting issues if we are to adequately govern the global risk of outbreaks.

Foundations of the Current System

The way in which the world governs the threat of outbreaks has evolved considerably since the nineteenth century. Understanding current arrangements for the global governance of outbreaks may benefit from a brief review of its history.

History of efforts to improve global governance of outbreaks

The risk of outbreaks prompted the first formal intergovernmental arrangements for health cooperation, which can be traced back to 1851 when the first International Sanitary Conference was held in Paris. European governments convened to establish arrangements to minimise the spread of certain infectious diseases. Thirteen governments[1] signed the first International Sanitary Convention in 1892 to notify each other when cholera was detected in their territories and to refrain from restricting travel or trade unless scientifically justified. Notably, the main objective was to protect economic interests and prevent the spread of infectious disease, not to protect public health in outbreak-affected countries.

The 1948 creation of the World Health Organization (WHO), together with the United Nations (UN) system more broadly, established a far more ambitious vision for what international cooperation could and should achieve for health. The WHO Constitution (WHO 1946), which recognised 'communicable disease' as 'a common danger' to all countries, mandated the organisation to provide aid to governments during emergencies (upon request) and to 'stimulate and advance work to eradicate epidemic, endemic and other diseases'. In the ensuing decades, WHO would launch major programmes, including but not limited to the control of infectious diseases. WHO wore many hats: running operations in countries, issuing technical normative guidelines that carried significant weight particularly in developing countries, conducting political advocacy on health issues, and providing an international arena for political and policy debates through its biannual meetings of member states (the Executive Board and World Health Assembly).

However, by the 1990s WHO was in decline. It suffered from weak leadership and was caught between competing blocks in the Cold War. In addition to a barrage of critiques from the public health community regarding its lack of efficacy and bureaucratic lumbering, it also fell victim to the anti-UN sentiment rising in the United States (Chorev 2012; Clift 2013; Godlee 1997; Smith 1995; Walt 1993). After the World Health Assembly voted to freeze WHO's core budget in 1982 and its single largest funder, the US government, withheld its contributions to WHO's regular budget in 1985 as part of the country's broader policy shift relating to the UN (Brown et al.

2006; Mackey and Novotny 2012), the search for alternatives to WHO–and the state-centred, multilateral model of global governance it represented– began in earnest.

In parallel with these developments at WHO, in the 1990s the broader development community increasingly began to recognise the importance of health as a critical input for both human security and economic growth. Several important features of this era merit mention (additional detail is provided in Kickbusch and Liu, Chapter 5 in this Report). First, the growing recognition of the importance of health attracted new funds and new funders, such as the Bill and Melinda Gates Foundation, who preferred not to channel their resources through what they viewed as an ailing WHO. One result was the rapid increase in the numbers and types of actors working in health. Second, WHO found itself frequently competing with the newer global health actors for funding and influence. The dismantling of WHO's capacity to address outbreaks in the new millennium can be seen as a reflection of disagreement among its funders and member states regarding what its role and core functions should be. Third, much of the new funding and initiatives focused on vertical interventions for a few health challenges (e.g. childhood immunisation, maternal health, HIV, tuberculosis, and malaria), which yielded important achievements but did not emphasise building health systems that could handle unexpected challenges such as outbreaks of infectious disease. These underlying features shaped the ways in which the global community sought to govern the threat of outbreaks.

Impetus for reforms: the 2002-3 SARS and 2014-5 West African Ebola crises

Outbreaks of infectious disease occur regularly, most contained before they cross borders or reach headlines. It is only major crises that have prompted a review of global governance arrangements and subsequent reforms. The two most influential have been the Severe Acute Respiratory Syndrome (SARS) in 2002-3 and Ebola in West Africa in 2014-15.

The deadly SARS virus was first identified in humans in southeast China in 2002. It quickly spread to nearly thirty countries, stopping economies, travel, and tourism in its tracks. China initially withheld information on the outbreak from WHO and the global community, increasing levels of panic and allowing continuing spread of the virus. WHO Director-General Gro Harlem Brundtland took a major political risk and publicly called on China for greater transparency. She also issued a travel advisory for Toronto after cases were identified there, despite strong disagreement from Canadian authorities. Eight thousand cases later, the outbreak was brought to a halt, but economic losses were estimated to have reached at least US$11.8 billion in East Asia and Canada (Keogh-Brown and Smith 2008).

SARS prompted a major revision of the International Health Regulations (IHR), which had not been significantly revised since 1969. Recognising the value of Brundtland's muscular response, governments delegated greater authority and responsibility to WHO, such as allowing it to consider outbreak information from non-state actors in its decision-making (Fidler 2005). The revised IHR underscored WHO's role as not only a technical organisation but also a political actor whose decisions could have global consequences. WHO had played a critical role in collecting, interpreting, and sharing with governments highly-sensitive information, a function that would not have been possible for a non-state actor or public-private partnership.

However, SARS may also have inadvertently laid the groundwork for WHO's future failures during the West African Ebola crisis. It is possible that the Chinese government sought to avoid a repeat of having its national policies publicly rebuked and criticised by the head of WHO, and that it therefore chose to invest significant diplomatic capital in backing one of its own–Margaret Chan, who led Hong Kong's response to SARS–to become WHO's Director-General in 2006 (Moon 2018).

Chan's governing approach gave much greater deference than Brundtland to member states–as highlighted during the West African Ebola crisis a decade later. The government of Guinea had resisted WHO calling greater international attention to the Ebola outbreak in its territory in 2014, given the significant economic repercussions this could cause. Despite clear and mounting evidence that the outbreak had crossed borders, broken records, and was out of control in urban areas of Liberia and Sierra Leone where human Ebola cases had never previously been identified, WHO waited five months after the first confirmed case to declare an international emergency. Ebola created panic worldwide, especially after a handful of cases spread beyond the three worst-affected countries and to Europe and the US. It took over two years and several billion US dollars to extinguish the outbreak, which resulted in 11,000 deaths, disproportionately among health workers who had already been in scarce supply in these countries. WHO faced a crisis of confidence in its ability to carry out one of its core functions. Yet Ebola also reminded leaders that no country could afford a dysfunctional WHO.

Reform efforts focused on WHO, rather than on creating new or alternate organisations. After a decade of rapid growth of actors in global health, governments and other major funders had little appetite to create yet another. Two priorities emerged: to rebuild the operational capacity to deal with outbreaks that had been dismantled at WHO and to create a peer review system for national preparedness, recognising that weak country health systems could pose threats far beyond their borders (Gostin et al. 2016). Managing outbreaks also became one of the top three priorities (alongside universal health coverage and health promotion) in WHO's 2019-23 five-year workplan (WHO 2018c).

Disease Outbreak Issues Requiring Improved Global Governance

Despite the high political attention paid to outbreaks following the 2014-5 West African crisis (which we refer to as the 'post-2014' period), the reforms that were implemented in the short window of political opportunity that followed have been partial. A recurring theme in analyses of outbreak preparedness is a cycle of 'panic and neglect'–and this cycle has yet to be broken (World Bank 2017b). Below four issue areas are identified where many new initiatives were launched, but where important gaps remain (Leigh et al. 2018; Moon et al. 2017).

Country commitments under the IHR (2005)

All 194 WHO member states have made a set of commitments under the IHR (WHO 2005), in recognition of the interdependence among countries in effectively preventing, detecting, and responding to outbreaks. Compliance with these commitments has been problematic, however, as clearly illustrated by more recent crises.

National health system capacities

National capacity to manage outbreaks is widely recognised as a top priority. The post-2014 era witnessed a significant push to add external peer review to capacity assessments that had traditionally been conducted domestically. The voluntary Joint External Evaluation (JEE) process was initially developed under the aegis of the Global Health Security Agenda (GHSA), a group of over sixty countries and intergovernmental organisations collaborating to improve global preparedness for health-related emergencies. WHO later took over coordination of the JEEs. As a universal membership multilateral organisation, WHO arguably created more widespread political acceptance for the JEEs, since GHSA was widely perceived as a US creation. As of early 2019, 114 countries had completed JEEs, with an additional twenty-two planned, covering over two-thirds of all member states (WHO n.d.b)–a remarkable change in norms and practices in a short time period.

Post-2014, the roles of both WHO and the World Bank in country preparedness significantly expanded. In 2017, WHO's new Health Emergencies Programme (WHE) supported health emergency responses in forty-four countries and worked with thirty-nine countries to improve preparedness (WHO 2017b). The World Bank is providing financing for preparedness and response through several initiatives, including the creation of the Pandemic

Emergency Financing Facility (PEF), which is to provide insurance to countries in case of outbreaks; an expansion of the Crisis Response Window, which provides grants for emergency response efforts; and Catastrophe Deferred Drawdown, which provides immediate liquidity to countries experiencing unexpected financial shocks, including health emergencies (Ayotte et al. 2019; Glassman et al. 2018). In addition, the World Bank committed in July 2017 to provide support to at least twenty-five countries to develop pandemic preparedness plans (World Bank 2017c; Glassman et al. 2018).

A number of new initiatives to strengthen national capacities were also launched post-2014 (see a more detailed listing of these in Leigh et al. 2018). Among these was the creation of the African Centres for Disease Control by the African Union, officially launched in January 2017 with support from the US Centers for Disease Control and Prevention (CDC) (CDC 2015; Manlan 2017). The mission of the African Centres is to strengthen surveillance, information systems, laboratory systems, and emergency preparedness.

Finally, one of the clearest lessons to emerge from the West African Ebola outbreak was the importance of community engagement, in light of the recognition that community-led behaviour change was key to breaking transmission chains. Research suggests that effective community engagement in an outbreak is reliant on ongoing, two-way conversations between responders and community members and that responders should work to be transparent, contextually responsive, and accountable to communities (Ryan et al. 2019). Post-2014, several initiatives were launched to facilitate international actors partnering closely with communities in outbreak response. For example, the United Nations Children's Fund (UNICEF) created an initiative to address the need for a more systematic approach to communications and community engagement with affected peoples (UN OCHA 2017). UNICEF and academic partners also established a global partnership to carry out research on effective community engagement and risk communication needs (Global Health Crises Task Force 2017). In addition, the WHO Research and Development (R&D) Blueprint included guidance on engaging communities while conducting clinical research in emergencies (Hankins 2016).

However, persistent challenges in community engagement remain, including how to assess whether new community engagement strategies have been adopted or are successful. Some challenges can be seen clearly in the Ebola outbreak in the Democratic Republic of the Congo (DRC), first declared on 1 August 2018. Control of the epidemic is hindered by mistrust and tension between local communities, on the one hand, and the government and Ebola responders, on the other, with locals delaying seeking care, not disclosing all their contacts, and in some cases, committing violent attacks against healthcare facilities and workers (Green 2019; Matfess 2018; Nguyen 2019). Some of these attacks have been carried out by organised rebel militia groups with unclear motivations (Aizenmann 2019; de Freytas-Tamura 2018; Matfess 2018; Nguyen 2019). In response to the militia-led violence, some organisations, including Médecins Sans Frontières (MSF), have ceased operations in some locations, while others are now being protected by the military and the police (Aizenmann 2019). However, attempts to reduce militia-led violence by bringing in the military or police to protect Ebola responders may further sow mistrust, and potentially violent reactions, among the general population (Nguyen 2019; Burke 2018; Aizenmann 2019). Even if strategies are effective at increasing trust among the general population, disease-control activities may still be hindered in certain areas due to the risk of militia violence.

In general, much attention has rightly been paid to increasing national core capacities, but significant challenges remain. Particularly in developing countries where health spending can fall far short of meeting basic needs, a persistent tension exists between calls to invest in preparedness for outbreaks which may happen in the future and the many competing demands for health services today. This tension is visible in the different voices pushing for achieving universal health coverage, a target of the Sustainable Development Goals and clear priority for the current WHO leadership, and those advocating for greater investment in outbreak preparedness. The risk that these two goals compete for attention and funds is real, despite the theoretical possibility that these goals can be mutually reinforcing. More research is needed to better understand how each agenda is being implemented, and whether or how any complementarities can be realised.

As JEEs progress, it is becoming clear that both major funding and sustained political attention will be needed to address the identified weaknesses in national systems, yet neither is likely to materialise in most countries. International assistance can play a role in the poorest or most fragile countries, which are often highlighted as high-risk countries for outbreaks, but such assistance has been slow to materialise, with a few important exceptions. Nor are high-income countries necessarily ready for outbreaks, as highlighted in 2015 when the Middle East respiratory syndrome (MERS) spread rapidly through South Korea's sophisticated but unprepared hospital system. Monitoring changes in capacity in all countries over time will be critical.

Trade and travel restrictions

The need to prevent travel and trade restrictions unwarranted on scientific or public health grounds is widely recognised and formed the original nineteenth-century raison d'être for international health cooperation. Such restrictions exacerbate the economic impact of outbreaks, make it harder for international organisations to support affected countries, and disincentivise outbreak reporting. This issue has received relatively little attention post-2014, though a few initiatives have sought to improve the flow of information between governments, WHO, and the travel industry (Morhard 2019; World Travel and Tourism Council 2018; WHO 2015a).

Overall progress in this area is insufficient. A wide range of relevant public and private stakeholders is involved in trade and travel restrictions including airlines, shipping, tourism, individual travellers, and multiple government ministries beyond health. Norms and expectations for reasonable responses by private firms during outbreaks remain undefined. Because they do not fall under the clear responsibility of any single intergovernmental body such as WHO, monitoring and accountability are a major challenge. In order to develop a comprehensive, systematic monitoring framework, new sources of data on private stakeholder reactions would need to be developed, and the method for collecting data on government reactions would need to be strengthened (Herten-Crabb et al. 2017). Understanding of the causes and impacts of trade and travel restrictions is limited, as is political engagement to strengthen accountability for unwarranted measures.

Science, technology, and knowledge-sharing

One of the most logical and important areas for international cooperation in outbreaks is generating rapid, accurate scientific understanding of the characteristics of relevant pathogens, as well as developing and deploying technologies to control them. However, arrangements to facilitate such cooperation are thin and largely inadequate.

Knowledge generation and sharing

Despite widespread recognition that knowledge on outbreak-prone pathogens should be shared quickly and widely, governance arrangements to ensure this takes place are weak. There is a lack of incentives and inadequate infrastructure, in addition to complex regulatory, ethical, and legal questions that governments, scientists, health workers, and others must navigate during and outside of emergencies.

Data-sharing platforms. There are no overarching frameworks for data-sharing on pathogens of pandemic potential. However, many different platforms have been developed by various public and private actors to facilitate rapid flows of epidemiological and research data (Argimón et al. 2016; CDC n.d.; Nuffield Department of Women's and Reproductive Health n.d.; WHO n.d.a). It is difficult to assess, however, whether these platforms meet all data-sharing needs, or how widely they are or are not being used.

Sample-sharing. Similarly, there is widespread awareness that rapid sharing of pathogen samples and related benefits (e.g. data, vaccines, diagnostics) between laboratories is critical for understanding and tracking pathogens and developing and deploying countermeasures to control them. However, ensuring that this occurs remains difficult, with very little information publicly available regarding the extent to which reliable sharing of either samples or benefits takes place. The four-year intergovernmental negotiation to address this issue for pandemic influenza produced the ground-breaking 2011 WHO Pandemic Influenza Preparedness (PIP) framework, which established norms and arrangements for sharing both influenza samples and related benefits such as vaccines across countries. However, there has been no political push to extend PIP beyond influenza, meaning that other pathogens are not subject to these international rules. PIP was workable, in part, due to the specific economic incentives that exist for influenza, namely, the existence of a regular annual seasonal influenza vaccine market. Extending PIP to other pathogens where no such market exists may not be feasible. That said, some of the principles of sample-sharing and benefit-sharing are broadly applicable beyond influenza, but no government has prioritised tackling this issue. Another crisis may be required before any major actor decides to invest the significant political capital required to negotiate new rules to address sample- and benefit-sharing.

While no overarching international framework exists for sample-sharing beyond influenza, WHO has developed a Material Transfer Agreement to facilitate pathogen- and benefit-sharing between research entities and countries (WHO 2017a). Anecdotal evidence points to regular sharing of pathogens between laboratories and countries, but there is limited transparency on the extent, speed, or terms on which such sharing occurs.

Clinical trials. Clinical trials were organised in record time during the West African Ebola crisis to test potential vaccines and drugs for efficacy against the virus. These trials were developed and conducted by a diverse group of actors, including the WHO, the US National Institutes of Health, research universities, national public health organisations, aid organisations, and pharmaceutical companies (National Academies of Sciences, Engineering, and Medicine 2017), and were funded by various public and private actors, including governments, the European Commission, the Wellcome Trust, and the Bill and Melinda Gates Foundation (European Commission 2015; Fitchett et al. 2016). However, questions subsequently arose regarding the lack of timely sharing of trial results and how to address challenging ethical and operational issues such as informed consent and randomisation in an emergency. The US National Academies of Sciences, Engineering, and Medicine (2017) conducted a post-crisis review, concluding that the randomised controlled trial was an ethical and appropriate design to use even during epidemics, and that in most circumstances it should indeed be used. It recommended that clinical research be embedded in the local healthcare system and that during an epidemic an independent rapid research response workgroup should convene to prioritise products for trial, assess trial designs, and monitor and evaluate them (Leigh et al. 2018). The WHO R&D Blueprint includes guidance on clinical trial study designs to be used during emergencies, assists researchers in exploring design methodology options, and provides a modelling platform to simulate different trial designs under disease outbreak scenarios (WHO 2017a).

There are ongoing challenges with conducting clinical trials, including strengthening research capacity in resource-poor settings. An international group of experts convened by the World Bank highlighted the need to mobilise political and financial investment in appropriate physical research infrastructure, a trained health research workforce, functional ethics committees, regulatory capacity, and expertise in the social sciences (World Bank 2018a).

Surveillance. A number of both well-established and newer initiatives exist in the area of surveillance, focusing on specific diseases, zoonoses, countries/ regions, or new technologies (DiSARM n.d.; Epihack n.d.; Global Virome Project n.d.; Metabiota n.d.; Susumpow et al. 2014; UC Davis Veterinary Medicine n.d.; WHO Global Observatory for eHealth 2016). It remains unclear, however, whether these add up to a coherent and functional global surveillance system able to combine data from multiple sources and to pick up signals through the noise. It is also an open question whether all countries have the adequate baseline surveillance capacity needed to feed into global systems.

Health technology research, development, and deployment

Health technologies such as diagnostics, drugs, and vaccines can play a key role in controlling disease transmission, reducing suffering, and saving lives. A major challenge, however, is that such technologies are unlikely to be developed without concerted public action because markets for the products are too small, risky, and/or unpredictable for commercial investment. In addition, ensuring that such technologies are available and affordable in countries directly affected by outbreaks is a major unresolved challenge. The R&D Blueprint developed by WHO for pathogens of pandemic potential in response to the West African Ebola crisis provides important guidance for global coordination of R&D efforts, before and during outbreaks. The Blueprint includes a list of ten priority pathogens for which additional R&D is needed,[2] with related roadmaps and target product profiles.

Vaccines. Post-2014, significant attention was dedicated to developing vaccines for pathogens with outbreak potential. Prior to this, no single actor had been mandated with the responsibility for ensuring that technologies are developed for outbreaks globally. In the absence of an adequate market incentive, the majority of such activities were funded for biodefence purposes by governments of the advanced industrialised countries. A candidate vaccine against Ebola was developed and tested in record time during the West African crisis, building off of defence investments made earlier by the Canadian and US governments. It was a significant and rare achievement that multiple clinical trials of Ebola candidate vaccines were launched within months during the emergency, which highlighted both the feasibility of such research and the need to plan such trials far in advance (Henao-Restrepo et al. 2017; Kennedy et al. 2017; Pavot 2016).

The Coalition for Epidemic Preparedness Innovations (CEPI) was launched in 2017 by the governments of Norway and India, the Gates Foundation, the Wellcome Trust, and the World Economic Forum to address at least some of these problems. It channels funding to labs developing platform technologies or vaccines against target pathogens. CEPI is one of the largest and most visible of the post-2014 'reforms' of the global system. While CEPI was developed and launched quickly, critics have raised a number of concerns, including that the Board's priority pathogens were not the most appropriate, that the organisation has not fulfilled its transparency commitments, and that it will be unable to ensure that the resulting vaccines will be available and affordable in the hardest-hit countries during an actual emergency (Liu and Torreele 2019; Leigh et al. 2018).

Diagnostics and therapeutics. Some advances in diagnostics and therapeutics have been made in response to recent outbreaks. For example, more than a dozen diagnostics that can detect Ebola virus in a matter of hours now exist (WHO 2017a). New initiatives continue to be formed. For example, the Foundation for Innovative Diagnostics (FIND) announced in January 2019 that CEPI will support the expansion of its programme to build diagnostic capacity for Lassa fever (FIND 2019). Investments in therapeutics are also being made by public health research funds, academic research centres, and private pharmaceutical firms–and, importantly, tracked by WHO (WHO 2017a).

However, diagnostics and therapeutics for outbreaks have received less attention and funding than vaccines, perhaps because of the personalities involved or because vaccines can protect everyone while drugs and diagnostics are more relevant for directly-affected countries. A recent study found that six out of the ten R&D Blueprint priority pathogens identified by WHO lack adequate diagnostic tests, whether because of a lack of established reference tests, lack of point-of-care diagnostics, or limited commercial availability (Kelly-Cirino et al. 2019). Challenges include a limited market for diagnostics in the absence of an outbreak, limited access to samples, and the need for special laboratory equipment and/or skilled personnel to use existing diagnostics (Kelly-Cirino et al. 2019). Similar challenges exist for the development and uptake of new therapeutics. FIND has called for the development of a forum to tackle barriers to diagnostic development and uptake for outbreaks (Kelly-Cirino et al. 2019; FIND 2018).

Overall, there is significant investment in R&D for new outbreak-related technologies and a relatively clear WHO-centred system to set priorities for and monitor the R&D system. However, difficult questions remain unresolved regarding who will get priority access to scarce technologies in the event of an outbreak, how to fill R&D gaps, and whether investments can be sustained in the time that elapses between sporadic disease events.

International health and humanitarian system

A major subject of analysis post-2014 was how well the international health and humanitarian aid systems functioned during the crisis, with a particular emphasis on WHO and the UN coordination machinery.

The World Health Organization

WHO was the single most scrutinised organisation before and after the West African Ebola crisis, and it is where many of the reform efforts have focused. As noted earlier, protecting people from health emergencies is now one of the three strategic priorities articulated in WHO's thirteenth general programme of work (2019-23) (WHO 2018c). Much of WHO's efforts have been focused on strengthening its operational capacity through the creation of the previously mentioned WHE. One criticism of WHO during the West African Ebola outbreak was that it did not have the staff, organisational capacities, or culture to respond quickly and nimbly to a fast-moving outbreak (Kamradt-Scott 2016; WHO 2015d). WHE was established in 2016 'to help Member States build their capacity to manage health emergency risks and, when national capacities are overwhelmed, to lead and coordinate the international health response to contain outbreaks and to provide effective relief and recovery to affected populations' (Executive Board, 138 2016).

However, at least as important as WHO's operational role is its political function. WHO retains a central role gathering and interpreting information daily on potentially risky disease events, assessing when an outbreak should be declared a 'public health emergency of international concern', and providing governments with policy guidance on trade and travel restrictions. Many actors besides WHO have capacity to operate on the ground, such as the US CDC or MSF. But no other actor has the authority to monitor countries to ensure an adequate level of preparedness or to issue global travel warnings that can bring economies to a halt, for example. Thus, WHO senior staff are particularly crucial for managing political pressure from member states in the broader interests of global public health.

Finally, the sustainability of all these efforts remains at risk due to unstable and inadequate funding for both outbreaks and WHO more broadly.

Between 2000 and 2017, the proportion of WHO's budget guaranteed by its member states fell from 47 percent to 20 percent, leaving it increasingly reliant on voluntary contributions to meet expanding demands (its total budget also doubled during this time) (WHO 2016b, 2018d). Governments proved unwilling to support a Germany-backed proposal to increase significantly their obligatory contributions to WHO, though they did approve a small increase of 3 per cent–an important symbolic victory but of limited practical consequence (Ravelo 2016, 2017). Member states seem to prefer an organisation they can more easily control.

The broader humanitarian aid system

When outbreaks overwhelm the health sector, the broader humanitarian aid system becomes critical. Post-2014 reviews highlighted the importance of strengthening the humanitarian sector's outbreak response capacity and coordination (Moon et al. 2017). In April 2017, WHO issued an updated framework to try to improve coordination on health threats (WHO 2017b). UN agencies also sought to improve information-sharing on health threats within the UN system and to improve coordination of external communications on health crises. In addition, the UN's main coordination body for humanitarian aid developed a new protocol that links its emergency capacities with WHO (Inter-Agency Standing Committee 2016; Leigh et al. 2018).

Responding to outbreaks in conflict settings remains a major challenge for both health and humanitarian organisations, as the Ebola outbreak that began in 2018 in the DRC clearly illustrates. Because of their intergovernmental nature, UN agencies face significant challenges operating in civil conflicts because one party to the conflict is a member state while the other is not. There are a limited number of other actors with the capacity to respond in such settings (Leigh et al. 2018). Ensuring the thinly-stretched humanitarian system can help when outbreaks grow into humanitarian crises remains difficult.

Cross-cutting issues

Each of the three specific areas discussed above is critical for managing outbreaks, and all share four cross-cutting challenges: financing, leadership, monitoring, and accountability.

Financing

The Commission on a Global Health Risk Framework for the Future estimated that US$4.5 billion in additional annual spending was needed to reach sufficient levels of national preparedness for health emergencies, and an additional $1 billion per year for R&D (GHRF Commission 2016). Post-2014 there was a significant mobilisation of international funds. For example, the US government made major investments to launch the multi-country partnership GHSA in 2014, followed by a US$1 billion commitment to GHSA for the West African Ebola crisis (Michaud et al. 2017). Australia, South Korea, Japan, and Canada have also been multi-million-dollar funders of GHSA-related activities. Private foundations, such as the Gates Foundation and Wellcome Trust, provided significant funds for outbreak-related R&D in particular, through support of CEPI and other initiatives.

The World Bank Group, in concert with WHO, developed the previously mentioned PEF with the stated goal of providing a quick disbursal of funds to countries experiencing an outbreak of a specific set of covered infectious diseases, including influenza, coronaviruses, and filoviruses (World Bank 2017c). The project has a US$61 million cash component and a US$425 million insurance component. Its first grant was approved in May 2018 from the cash component to help finance the response to the Ebola outbreak in the DRC (World Bank 2017d, 2018b). However, questions have been raised about the PEF, including the programme's financial sustainability; its eligibility criteria; the benefit of new mechanisms for financing outbreak response, rather than preparedness and more direct investment in strengthening national health systems; and the risk that governments or investors might gain financially from larger outbreaks (Glassman et al. 2018; Katz and Seifman 2016; Stein and Sridhar 2017; Allen 2019; Abe et al. 2019).

However, despite significant activity to mobilise financing and estimate funding needs, timely data on investments and financing flows remain elusive. The costs of controlling major outbreaks have been documented, but the global cost to prevent them is less well understood. Given the poor state of many national health systems, wide funding gaps seem likely. A major governance question is therefore selecting priorities for investments in preparedness. However, debate remains on what those priorities should be, who should set them, and on what basis. Investments should build capacities to both respond to emergencies and deliver day-to-day benefits for populations, but research is urgently needed on whether, which, and how investments in preparedness can do so (Moon and Vaidya 2018).

In addition, tracking of financing remains a major challenge, and political commitments do not necessarily translate into funding. For example, in 2015, Group of Seven (G7) members committed to assisting at least sixty countries to implement the IHR, and in 2016, they committed to assisting seventy-six countries and regions to develop national preparedness plans (G7 2015, 2016). However, specific funding was not committed, making it difficult to track progress. Although prior commitments were referenced, no further commitments were made by the G7 in 2017 or 2018 (G7 2017, 2018; Leigh et al. 2018).

Significant funding gaps remain, even simply for WHO. WHO created a Contingency Fund for Emergencies in 2015, which has yet to reach its target of US$100 million and has been depleted faster than it has been replenished (Ravelo 2018). WHO funding is chronically unstable, with high dependency on voluntary funding, as noted previously.

Overall, monitoring and accountability for financing are extremely weak. No aggregate estimates of global investments in outbreak preparedness or response were identified, and data on national investments have been especially difficult to find. Without such estimates, it is impossible to track whether global financing totals or gaps are increasing or decreasing over time (Leigh et al. 2018).

Leadership, monitoring, and accountability

The steady stream of outbreaks over the past decade has helped to keep this issue on the political agenda, with the West African Ebola crisis a watershed moment. As discussed above, many new initiatives have been launched over the past decade. However, there is no governing framework to ensure that this proliferation of efforts sum up to a functional whole.

WHO has played an essential stewardship role in many areas, including country capacity assessment, R&D, and emergency response. However, many aspects of outbreak management require engagement outside the health sector, such as travel and trade, or provision of aid in large-scale humanitarian crises. The 2016 final report of an expert panel convened by then UN Secretary-General Ban Ki-Moon called on the UN to take a systematic role in overseeing global readiness for outbreaks (High-Level Panel on the Global Response to Health Crises 2016), but current UN Secretary-General Antonio Guterres has to date not claimed it.

Monitoring and accountability also cut across all the disease outbreak issues. A number of initiatives have been launched, including a bolstered role for WHO in monitoring countries' preparedness (WHO 2016a). Johns Hopkins University has also developed an independent assessment of country preparedness (Nuzzo 2017). Beyond country level, it is critical to assess overall global capacity, but this requires in-depth investigation and specialised expertise. In its final report, the UN Secretary-General's Global Health Crises Task Force recommended that the Secretary-General implement a new independent mechanism for reporting on the status of the world's preparedness for disease outbreak (Global Health Crises Task Force 2017). The Global Preparedness Monitoring Board (GPMB), created by WHO and the World Bank Group, was announced during the 2018 World Health Assembly after several years of discussions (WHO 2018h). Ideally, the GPMB will function as a much-needed accountability mechanism. Key questions remain about its modus operandi and how it will safeguard its independence.

Conclusions

Anumber of broad global trends, such as urbanisation, climate change, deforestation, meat consumption, and intensified travel and trade, raise the risk of outbreaks of emerging and re-emerging infectious diseases. The global community has recognised outbreaks as an important issue that requires effective governance. Recent years have witnessed significant change and progress, such as new and reinvigorated initiatives to strengthen national health system capacities, limit the imposition of trade and travel restrictions, increase knowledge-sharing, and spur R&D.

Still, many systemic weaknesses persist. Maintaining political commitment–and the funding that often follows–is nearly impossible in the absence of outspoken leadership from the highest levels of government. Multiple important needs compete for attention and funds, both within and beyond the health sector. Because political attention is unlikely between crises, it is even more critical to institutionalise monitoring and accountability. Making data on investments for outbreak preparedness readily and publicly available would be a meaningful first step toward improving monitoring and accountability. Enhancing our understanding of the results of those investments for both outbreak preparedness and health systems more broadly is also critical. The GPMB may prove to be an important player in global accountability efforts by providing essential information and analysis; its work over the first few years will be decisive for establishing its credibility as the independent monitoring body the world so clearly needs.

Furthermore, a clear governing framework is needed to ensure that efforts are coherent and that they sum up to a functional, adequate global system. In the absence of overarching stewardship by the UN Secretary-General, piecemeal efforts–while potentially of great benefit–do not necessarily add up to a system that will protect the world from major outbreak-driven emergencies.

Significant reform has always followed major crises. It is unfortunately likely that addressing the unmet needs identified here will require another. When that next window of opportunity arises, it will be critical to institutionalise long-term financing for national and international capacities and to build a clear framework for monitoring and accountability of all actors. At least as important, leadership will be essential to ensure that the global system adds up to more than the sum of its parts.

Endnotes

1   Austria–Hungary, Belgium, Denmark, France, Germany, Great Britain, Italy, Netherlands, Portugal, Russia, Spain, Sweden–Norway, and Turkey.

2   Priorities include Crimean-Congo haemorrhagic fever, Ebola virus disease and Marburg virus disease, Lassa fever, MERS-CoV and SARS, Nipah and henipaviral diseases, Rift Valley fever, Zika, and Disease X, which acknowledges that an epidemic could be caused by a pathogen currently unknown to cause human disease.

V. Global Health Governance

ILONA KICKBUSCH *and* AUSTIN LIU

Health was one of the first areas for which an international governance structure was developed in the context of a new world order that began to emerge in the mid-nineteenth century. In 1851, negotiations started on a first international health agreement to increase protection of the large trading nations from a group of highly infectious diseases such as cholera, plague, and yellow fever. This link to trade was complemented by the emerging field of colonial health and tropical medicine, accompanying conquest and empire. Indeed, the legacy of these two approaches shape global health to this day.

On the one hand, trade and security combined with fear of contagion across continents motivated transborder health cooperation and agreements and have over the last 150 years been major drivers of international health governance innovation. On the other hand, for the last fifty years or so development agencies–many based in countries of the former colonial powers–have provided much of the global health funding and shaped approaches and priorities, often linked as much to foreign policy interests as to development goals. There is also much continuity in the role of philanthropic and humanitarian organisations: the Rockefeller Foundation set out to eradicate yellow fever, as the Bill and Melinda Gates Foundation today focuses on the eradication of polio; the International Committee of the Red Cross's extraordinary commitment to impartiality is echoed by Médicins sans Frontières.

The biggest global health governance innovations after World War II have been (a) the creation of the World Health Organization (WHO) in 1948; (b) the successful eradication of small pox in 1980; (c) new global partnership-based organisations such as the Joint United Nations Programme on HIV/AIDS (UNAIDS), the Global Alliance for Vaccines and Immunisation (now known as Gavi, the Vaccine Alliance) and the Global Fund to Fight AIDS, Tuberculosis and Malaria (the Global Fund) established at the end of the twentieth century; (d) the adoption of ground-breaking normative treaties by WHO and health-related rulings by the World Trade Organization (WTO) early in the twenty-first century; and (e) most recently some of the mechanisms to strengthen global health security such as the Pandemic Emergency Financing Facility (see Table 5.1 for examples). As a new world order is being shaped, it is to be expected that new approaches to global health governance will emerge.

Table 5.1 **Examples of innovations in global health governance**

Innovation	Example (year launched)
New humanitarianism	○ International Committee of the Red Cross (1863)
	○ Médicins sans Frontières (1971)
New philanthropic models	○ Rockefeller Foundation (1910)
	○ Bill and Melinda Gates Foundation (2000)
New intergovernmental organisations	○ Health Organisation of the League of Nations (1923)
	○ World Health Organization (1948)
New international agreements and instruments	○ The first International Sanitary Convention (1892)
	○ International Health Regulations (1969, 2005)
	○ Framework Convention on Tobacco Control (2003)
New global public–private partnerships	○ Global Alliance for Vaccines and Immunisation (2000)
	○ Global Fund to Fight AIDS, Tuberculosis and Malaria (2002)
New mechanisms to strengthen global health security	○ Contingency Fund for Emergencies (2015)
	○ Pandemic Emergency Financing Facility (2017)

Which Paradigms Drive Global Health Governance?

There is no single paradigm that drives global health governance. Global health priorities are usually defined by a biomedical paradigm and frequently echo military language: diseases are the enemy, and a strategy to fight them is developed. Increasingly the biomedical paradigm is data-driven, technocratic, and expressed in popular statements like 'what gets measured gets done'. But throughout the history of public health (and subsequently international and global health), health agendas that prioritise social justice have challenged this view. They highlight that most diseases are inseparable from poverty, inequities, stigma, and social disadvantage. These two paradigms–the biomedical and the social-political–have remained constant drivers of the governance agenda. They continuously raise the questions of which strategies are the most sustainable and which health investments provide the highest returns. In 1978 WHO had provided an answer: it pioneered the Primary Health Care approach, calling on governments to build integrated health systems that empower people and communities, engage in multisectoral policy, and prioritise primary care and essential public health functions.

KICKBUSCH *and* LIU

In the 1990s, a macroeconomic global health paradigm began to quantify both the substantial negative economic consequences of disease and the impact of investment in better health and its determinants. The 1999 *World Health Report* argued that countries need to invest in health to achieve economic growth and social development and estimated that half of the health improvements between 1960 and 1990 in low-income and middle-income countries were from changes in two social determinants: income and education (WHO 1999). The 2001 report of the Commission on Macroeconomics and Health (2001) emphasised the importance of investment not only in the health sector but also in education, water, sanitation, and agriculture to reduce poverty. Macroeconomic arguments, data, and language such as 'best buys' are since used across the spectrum by all global health advocates.

Until the 1980s, the primary responsibility for international health progress was assigned to governments by both the biomedical and the social-political paradigms. Following the end of the Cold War, market-driven, neo-liberal approaches gained the upper hand, and this consensus on the role of governments was weakened. Countries are explicitly divided into donors and recipients, and, while the principles of development assistance were transformed in the 2005 Paris Declaration on Aid Effectiveness and the subsequent high-level forums 'from being purely donor and ideologically driven to a more negotiated practice guided by pacts' (Omaswa 2018), the power remained with the donors. Multistakeholder, win-win partnership strategies beyond government emerged as preferred global health governance approaches in the context of the Millennium Development Goals (MDGs)– the first common United Nations (UN) framework for promoting global development–and have since been enshrined in the Sustainable Development Goals (SDGs).

This focus on development through multistakeholder partnerships led to tensions between political and financial support to a member state-governed international health organisation, such as WHO, and the new health organisations and initiatives governed by partnerships and frequently based on addressing individual diseases. From the perspective of the social-political paradigm, these focused global health efforts presented challenges for global health as they often overlooked emerging and systemic health issues and promoted a 'simplistic linear input-process-outcome model for health' (Marten 2018).

Development assistance for health tripled from about US$12 billion in 2000 to more than US$36 billion in 2015 (IHME 2016), while WHO's programme budget of roughly US$2 billion per annum remained low (comparable to the size of a major university hospital). WHO has had to defend its normative role to produce global public goods in an environment in which development agencies and large foundations prefer organisations whose outputs and outcomes can be measured in the shorter term–lives saved and deaths averted–and which provide them with high visibility. Yet, WHO's normative work provides the basis for much of the work of other organisations and of health systems at country level. For example, a statistical model estimates that, from 2007 to 2014, more than 53 million people in eighty-eight countries participating in the WHO Framework Convention on Tobacco Control (FCTC) stopped smoking, which translates into more than 20 million averted smoking-related deaths (Levy, D. T., et al. 2018).

Engineering a New Governance Order (1998-2008)

The end of the Cold War led to a shift from international health to global health (Frenk et al. 2014), during which a new governance order in global health emerged owing in part to the new multistakeholder governance models and to WHO's enhanced position as a norm-setter.

The new partnerships

During this period that Lidén (2013) calls *The Grand Decade for Global Health 1998-2008*, we witness a strong political commitment to global health through the adoption of the MDGs, in which three of the eight goals (Goal 4: Reduce child mortality; Goal 5: Improve maternal health; and Goal 6: Combat HIV/AIDS, malaria, and other diseases) were dedicated to health. The priority assigned to health was very much influenced by the moral and political force of health activists and protesters in the development arena–initially from AIDS activists–pushing for higher financial contributions and supported by celebrities from the entertainment world. It also profited from the fact that health gains were more easily measurable, a critical factor for the legitimacy of the MDGs. While a group of Western governments were stepping up their official development assistance (ODA) contributions, a major new funder dedicated to saving lives entered the global health arena: the Bill and Melinda Gates Foundation. Given the large resources available to the Gates Foundation, the power balance in global health governance clearly shifted. The funding it has disbursed is greater than that of most of the sovereign states except the United States and the United Kingdom, and it has significantly influenced both global health priorities and their governance (see Figure 5.1) (IHME 2019).

Giridharadas (2018: 30) calls the multistakeholder sphere of action 'market world' and defines it as an 'ascendant power elite that is defined by the concurrent drives to do well and do good, to change the world while also benefitting from the status quo'; it is a world that brings together the wide range of stakeholders from business, philanthropy, academia, media, think tanks, civil society, and governments. This describes well the new global health gov-

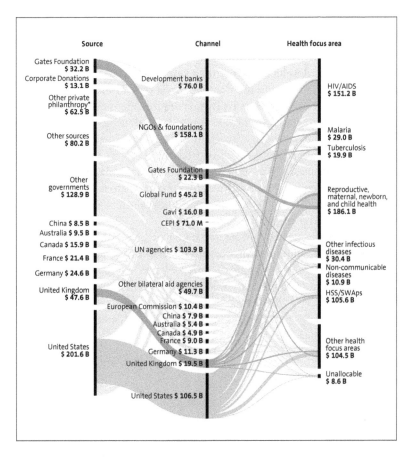

Figure 5.1 **Flows of development assistance for health from source to channel to health focus area, 1990–2018**

Source: IHME (2019), used and modified with IHME's permission.
Notes: *Excluding the Gates Foundation and corporate donations.
2018 estimates are preliminary.

ernance world that wanted to save lives but was not necessarily interested in counteracting the negative impacts of globalisation and trade liberalisation on health. The new global health players wanted a determined change in the modes of governance and more say in priority-setting for global health, but most of them wanted to fight infectious diseases and were not interested in challenging the powers of large industries such as tobacco or alcohol.

In 1996, UNAIDS was launched by six UN organisations and introduced as an inclusive governance model. This multistakeholder composition influenced other multilateral mechanisms and, in the early 2000s, the new institutions that were created exhibited these new governance features. The largest were the Global Alliance for Vaccines and Immunisation, stimulated by a US$750 million grant from the Gates Foundation, and the Global Fund to Fight AIDS, Tuberculosis and Malaria. Many other such partnerships were created for drug development (e.g. the Medicines for Malaria Venture), for funding (e.g. UNITAID, the international drug purchase facility), and for fighting diseases (e.g. the Stop TB Partnership). While these new organisations achieved significant success in fighting infectious diseases–for example, child mortality has been reduced by half–about 100 million people are pushed into extreme poverty each year because of debts accrued through healthcare expenses, and a tsunami of non-communicable diseases (NCDs) is building up around the world, driven by global industries (see Besnier and Eikemo, Chapter 2 in this Report). Bollyky (2018) calls this phenomenon the paradox of progress in global health.

As the money started flowing to the new organisations, the funding of WHO began to be affected. A process got underway by which, while WHO's total budget continued to increase, an ever-larger component of it came from voluntary contributions at the same time as its assessed contributions remained steady. Over this grand decade, member states' assessed contribution share of WHO's budget decreased by half from 47 per cent in 1998 to

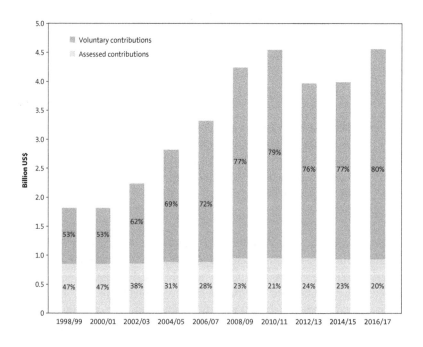

Figure 5.2 **Proportion and amount of assessed contributions and voluntary contributions to WHO across biennia from 1998 to 2017**

Source: WHO (2016b), used with permission of WHO.

KICKBUSCH *and* LIU

23 per cent in 2008, as shown in Figure 5.2 (WHO 2016b). Indeed this rapid increase in earmarked funding to WHO has been described by Sridhar and Woods (2013) as 'Trojan multilateralism', as it reinforces the asymmetry of decision-making between WHO and member states and tightens bilateral monitoring of multilateral action. It comes as no surprise that very few multilateral donors have an appetite to support WHO's action on NCDs, which has a strong evidence-based focus on regulation and taxation of products harmful to health.

Strengthening WHO as a norm-setter

While much of the global health debate and analysis was focused on the new partnerships and the increase of donor funding, it was in this decade under the leadership of Gro Harlem Brundtland as Director-General of WHO from 1998 to 2003 that WHO's role in producing global public goods came back into focus. Two of the most important global agreements in global health that strengthened the political authority of WHO were adopted during her term of office.

Following the outbreak of Severe Acute Respiratory Syndrome (SARS) in 2002-3, the political impetus was finally found to totally revise the International Health Regulations (IHR), a central opt-out treaty framework to ensure global health security that had not been significantly modified since 1969. The purpose and scope of the IHR (2005) is now no longer limited to the notification of specific diseases; instead states are required to notify WHO of all events that may constitute public health emergencies of international concern, and the Director-General has the power to declare such an emergency (Moon 2018).

In this period WHO also for the first time made use of the treaty-making power inherent in its constitution and adopted the above-mentioned FCTC relating to tobacco control in 2003. The FCTC is a landmark treaty as it is the first and only international instrument that regulates the consumption and commercialisation of a legal consumer product, and ideologically it expresses the rejection and isolation of an entire commercial sector (Burci 2018). It represents a new approach to counteract the negative impacts of globalisation and trade liberalisation on health. Moreover, it raises the need for extensive multisectoral diplomacy, in the complex environment of multiple legal frameworks and often competing government agendas (Nikogosian and Kickbusch 2018). In fact two major global health funders, Michael Bloomberg and Bill Gates, launched the Anti-Tobacco Trade Litigation Fund in 2015 to combat the use of international trade agreements to threaten and prevent countries from passing strong tobacco-control laws. This arguably also would not have been possible without the FCTC.

It was also in this decade that the Doha Declaration on the Trade-

Related Aspects of Intellectual Property Rights (TRIPS) and Public Health was adopted at the WTO. The Doha Declaration clarified the rights of WTO members to use TRIPS safeguards. It did not resolve all the problems, but it did give primacy to public health over commercial interest and private intellectual property ('t Hoen 2002). It also shows the power of developing countries, supported by public health advocates and AIDS activists, to drive through an agenda that is at odds with industrialised economies and the multinational pharmaceutical industry. This too arguably 'helped reassert the World Health Organization's authority as the main global health institution through dialogue with the WTO and its members' (Friel 2018).

Despite these important normative breakthroughs in support of global public goods through WHO's work, the shift in balance of power within the multilateral system which defined this decade was reinforced in the period that followed. In the 'grand decade' governments rescinded responsibilities and the leadership of social change (in our case, global health) to self-appointed new players, only some of which were also ready to address the structural power imbalances. In the neoliberal economic environment, states had no appetite for normative global health governance, and WHO was not able to maintain its forceful normative impact and skilled political leadership after Brundtland left office in 2003.

Limits of the Win-win Model (2008-18)

The partnership-based win-win model continues its successful trajectory–this is where the money flows–but in this decade we have started to see its limits especially after major crises. The social-political paradigm regained momentum with the new political space governments created to address health challenges as well as the adoption of the 2030 Agenda for Sustainable Development.

In crisis governments come back into focus

The two defining crises in this decade clearly show the model's limits. The immediate effects of the global financial crisis of 2007-9, the worst since the Great Depression in 1929, were rising unemployment, increasing homelessness, and worsening poverty–all with negative impacts on the health and well-being of people. Continuous development was no longer guaranteed in the high-income economies, and the development trajectory of many low- and middle-income countries (LMICs) was affected. In consequence, the social-political paradigm of global health gained new momentum, and WHO published an influential report on the social determinants of health in 2008

KICKBUSCH *and* LIU

(Commission on Social Determinants of Health 2008). An increase in suicides and outbreaks of infectious diseases were commonly found in countries that adopted strict fiscal austerity due to budget cuts that restricted access to healthcare. In Greece, the human costs of austerity were made dramatically clear: medicines and other supply shortages due to 40 per cent cuts to hospital budgets, job losses of 26,000 health workers, a 52 per cent rise in HIV infections, doubling in homicides, and a 17 per cent increase in suicides (Stuckler and Basu 2013). The increase of health inequalities within countries–despite economic progress–has since become a key concern in global health and resonates with political concerns about the general rise of inequalities worldwide and its political consequences. (In Chapter 3 of this Report, Bambra focuses on health inequalities in Europe.)

The second defining event for global health was the 2014 Ebola outbreak in West Africa. The highly inadequate and late global response (Farrar and Piot 2014) led to severe criticism of WHO and opened a debate on whether there should be a separate agency for health security. It manifested the complexity of dealing with health crises that are the result of the combination of 'dysfunctional health systems, international indifference, high population mobility, local customs, densely populated capitals, and lack of trust in authorities after years of armed conflict' (Farrar and Piot 2014: 1545). In hindsight, the significant budget and job cuts at WHO after the financial crisis, including a two-thirds cut to emergency response staff, might also have set the stage for this health crisis (Fink 2014).

One outcome was a major shift in the governance of health security. While the legal instrument, the IHR, was not reopened for discussion, a number of new governance mechanisms have been created by way of post-Ebola institutional and financial reforms, including: the establishment of the WHO Health Emergencies Programme and the Contingency Fund for Emergencies to help respond to public health crises, the World Bank's support in the financing of pandemic preparedness and the launch of the Pandemic Emergency Financing Facility to transfer pandemic risks to the private capital market, as well as the Global Preparedness Monitoring Board set up by the two agencies. New networks like the Global Health Security Agenda have gained political support and momentum, and a new tool, the Joint External Evaluation, was introduced by WHO to help countries assess the level of their compliance with the IHR. Nevertheless, most of the new mechanisms are designed to support response rather than preparedness (Glassman et al. 2018). The Ebola outbreak in the Democratic Republic of Congo declared in August 2018 is a test case for how well the governance reforms of health security function. (For more detailed analysis on global governance of disease outbreaks, see Moon and Bezruki, Chapter 4 in this Report.)

Governments create new political spaces

Starting with HIV/AIDS an increasing number of health issues have found their way to the United Nations General Assembly (UNGA) or Security Council in New York (see Table 5.2 for examples). That is in large part because they cannot be resolved by the health sector alone and need the political clout of 'high politics' which can serve as a tipping point for collective action (Held et al. 2019). The Global Health and Foreign Policy Initiative was launched in 2007 to make the case for health as a foreign policy issue and ensure a regular debate of global health at the UNGA. While the debate of a health issue at the UNGA is seen as a signal of the importance of global health, there is always the risk that health is made subordinate to the predominant political concerns. The 2018 UNGA negotiations left some health advocates frustrated by the outcome because of the diplomatic trade-offs that member states made between the high-level political declarations on tuberculosis (TB) and NCDs, which significantly weakened the latter (Byatnal 2018).

Partly because of the health security crisis, political attention to health increased significantly in political bodies outside of the UN. Under the leadership of German Chancellor Angela Merkel, health was launched as a priority at the 2015 Group of Seven (G7) Summit of Germany in Schloss Elmau, and then introduced at the 2017 Group of Twenty (G20) Summit in Hamburg. Under the German Presidency, for the first time there was a meeting of G20 health ministers, which continued under subsequent Argentinian and Japanese presidencies. Inviting the Director-General of WHO to a G20 Summit was also unprecedented. This approach reaffirmed that addressing global health risks, especially pandemic preparedness, resilient health systems, and antimicrobial resistance (AMR), is critical to the global economy.

The sustainable development agenda

A critical governance breakthrough was the adoption of the 2030 Agenda for Sustainable Development and its seventeen SDGs in 2015. They are the outcome of a transparent, inclusive process of negotiation and set a very different universal development agenda from the MDGs (Kamau et al. 2018). This shift was further reflected in the decision by the World Bank to drop the term 'developing countries' in the 2016 edition of its World Development Indicators and to no longer distinguish between 'developed' and 'developing' countries in the presentation of its data. As former UN Secretary-General Ban Ki-moon said: 'The 17 Sustainable Development Goals are our shared vision of humanity and a social contract between the world's leaders and the people' (United Nations 2015). SDG 3–ensure healthy lives and promote well-being for all at all ages–moves from a disease-focused to an integrated approach, with the goal to overcome the biomedical, disease-based paradigm. Now the SDGs help

Table 5.2 **Health-related high-level discussions at the United Nations General Assembly and Security Council, 2000–18**

UN Organ	Date	Topic	Outcome
UN General Assembly	6/2001	Special Session on HIV/AIDS	A/RES/S-26/2: Declaration of Commitment on HIV/AIDS
	6/2006	High-Level Meeting on AIDS	A/RES/60/262: Political Declaration on HIV/AIDS
	6/2011	High-level Meeting on AIDS	A/RES/65/277: Political Declaration on HIV and AIDS: Intensifying Our Efforts to Eliminate HIV and AIDS
	9/2011	High-level Meeting on NCDs	A/RES/66/2: Political Declaration of the High-level Meeting of the General Assembly on the Prevention and Control of Non-communicable Diseases
	7/2014	Second High-level Meeting on NCDs	A/RES/68/300: Outcome Document of the High-level Meeting of the General Assembly on the Comprehensive Review and Assessment of the Progress Achieved in the Prevention and Control of Non-communicable Diseases
	4/2016	Special Session on Drugs	A/RES/S-30/1: Our Joint Commitment to Effectively Addressing and Countering the World Drug Problem
	6/2016	High-Level Meeting on Ending AIDS	A/RES/70/266: Political Declaration on HIV and AIDS: On the Fast Track to Accelerating the Fight against HIV and to Ending the AIDS Epidemic by 2030
	9/2016	High-level Meeting on AMR	A/RES/71/3: Political Declaration of the High-level Meeting of the General Assembly on Antimicrobial Resistance
	9/2018	High-level Meeting on TB	A/RES/73/3: Political Declaration of the High-level Meeting of the General Assembly on the Fight Against Tuberculosis
	9/2018	Third High-level Meeting on NCDs	A/RES/73/2: Political Declaration of the Third High-level Meeting of the General Assembly on the Prevention and Control of Non-communicable Diseases
UN Security Council	7/2000	HIV/AIDS	S/RES/1308 (2000) [on the responsibility of the Security Council in the maintenance of international peace and security: HIV/AIDS and international peacekeeping operations]
	6/2011	HIV/AIDS	S/RES/1983 (2011) [on impacts of HIV/AIDS epidemic in conflict and post-conflict situations]
	9/2014	Ebola outbreak in West Africa	S/RES/2177 (2014) [on the outbreak of the Ebola virus in, and its impact on, West Africa]
	5/2016	Protection of health workers	S/RES/2286 (2016) [on protection of the wounded and sick, medical personnel and humanitarian personnel in armed conflict]
	10/2018	Ebola outbreak in the Democratic Republic of the Congo (DRC)	S/RES/2439 (2018) [on condemning attacks by armed groups in the Democratic Republic of the Congo and their role in exacerbating the Ebola virus outbreak]

bring broad global health agendas like universal health coverage (UHC), AMR, health effects of climate change, and human capital to the fore. In 2017, recognising the enormous need for cooperation, Germany's Chancellor Angela Merkel, Ghana's President Nana Akufo-Addo, and Norway's Prime Minister Erna Solberg wrote a joint letter to WHO's Director-General asking WHO to coordinate a Global Action Plan on Healthy Lives and Well-being for All to accelerate SDG implementation. This could potentially be a significant new contribution to global health governance.

After two decades of increased funding for global health, in the present political climate it is uncertain not only whether the level of financing of global health initiatives and organisations can be upheld (Morrison 2018) but also whether the mechanisms established in the 'grand decade' are best suited to support countries to make health progress, ensure health security, and build the health systems they require. The SDGs aim to address the misconception that 'the world is divided into two', i.e. developed/developing, rich/poor, high-income/low-income, North/South, West/Rest, and Us/Them (Rosling et al. 2018), but the development industry is not yet geared towards this major transformation. The priority global health challenges require both the willingness to invest in 'others' and in global public goods for all.

Governance and Power Under Reconstruction

Global health governance is under reconstruction, and some argue that we are at the onset of a 'new world health era' (Pablos-Méndez and Raviglione 2018). In the face of a changing political environment, in the coming decade we will need new approaches to manage the global health economy, spur national investment in health systems, and support global public goods for health.

An uncertain trajectory

Already significant concern has been voiced that the world is not on track to reach the vast majority of targets under SDG 3 on health (Lozano et al. 2018). The reasons lie in the political and economic domains and in the complex nature of a new set of health challenges and risks that need to be addressed, most of them human-made. The last two decades in global health showed a shift of ideology from government action towards multistakeholder solutions and a power shift in the relations between philanthropy and the state, described as disruptive philanthropy (Horvath and Powell 2016). But the last ten years have also shown the limits of this model and the need for strong government action in the field of global health. The next decade will see ideological shifts fuelled by high inequalities, geopolitical change driven by non-Western powers (Seifmann and Pannenborg 2018), as well as new asymmetries of power and knowledge in the wake of the digital transformation (Zuboff 2019).

In the political sphere the disintegration of the post-war global order, the opt-out of the US from many multilateral commitments, the weakening of Europe, and the rise of the rest, especially China, will significantly impact the present system of global health governance. Politically, there have been calls for ODA to be pulled back into the foreign policy sphere (where it had also resided during the Cold War) to primarily support foreign policy and national interests (Payne 2019).

In a research study, Held et al. (2019: 5) find strong agreement that 'shifting geopolitical rivalries and domestic political forces have always influenced consensus building within multilateral institutions.' The biomedical and the social-political paradigm are both gaining strength. The data-, efficiency-, and technology-driven approach to fixing health problems that has been dominant for nearly two decades in many development agencies and philanthropic organisations is reinforced by medical breakthroughs and great digital potential (see Gauld, Chapter 10 in this Report, for more on digital health). At the same time the dominant global health approaches are challenged on many fronts by academics, civil society advocates, and voices from the global South as neglecting health inequalities and health determinants and placing the individual and free market at the centre. The social-political paradigm is gaining strength as the SDGs call to 'leave no one behind'.

Non-Western governments assume new roles in global health governance

Stuenkel (2016: 2) points out the fallacy that 'history is seen as a Western-led process, which creates little awareness of non-western contributions to ideas on global order.' This applies to the roles G20 countries and Brazil, Russia, India, China, and South Africa (the BRICS) play in the governing bodies of global organisations, in the context of South-South relations, at the regional level, and by providing global goods. This is a significant gap in global health analysis and research which has been dazzled by the 'grand decade'.

Much more attention must be given to the contribution of emerging economies in the trajectory of global health. For example, the complexity of roles of India between being a rising power, a key economic actor in the global health industry, an aid recipient, a donor, and a partner can be seen in the case of its engagement with the Global Fund. First and foremost, India plays a major role as the 'pharmacy of the world', as a supplier of affordable low-price drugs. This defines many of its negotiation positions in global fora, especially in relation to discussions on intellectual property.

Treating millions of AIDS patients every year through the programmes of global health organisations like the Global Fund is dependent on the generic products from India. 'If we didn't have India, no way could we have accessed those 15 million people at those costs of $2 billion,' UNAIDS executive director Michel Sidibé said at a BRICS meeting. The cost would have been closer to US$150 billion (Guha 2016). This, for instance, is not reflected in major aid indices that focus on Development Assistance Committee donors of the Organisation for Economic Co-operation and Development.

At the same time, between 2003 and 2019, India as a grant recipient of the Global Fund received US$1.1 billion to fight HIV/AIDS, and since 2010 it has reduced new infections by 46 per cent and AIDS-related deaths by 22 per cent. 'In a demonstration of solidarity and shared responsibility', India donated US$20 million to the Global Fund in the 2016 replenishment conference (The Global Fund to Fight AIDS, Tuberculosis and Malaria 2018). In further positioning itself as a responsible global health actor, India hosted the Global Fund's Preparatory Meeting of the Sixth Replenishment in February 2019.

On the other hand, China has stepped up its development activities considerably, including creating a new International Development Cooperation Agency in 2018. Chen and Yang (2018) argue that China's initial focus on avoiding epidemics is related to the fact that outbreaks could constrain trade and the economy, especially along the corridors of the Belt and Road Initiative (BRI). By August 2018, about ninety countries and organisations, which together account for more than one-third of global GDP and about 65 per cent of the world's population, had joined the BRI–potentially a parallel global governance approach. From 2013 to 2018, China signed over 100 deals with countries participating in the BRI worth more than US$5 trillion in trade volume in a wide range of areas under the initiative (Calado 2018). The global health work is to be promoted through four BRI networks: public health, policy research, hospital alliance, and health industry, all of which will receive significant Chinese government funding.

Despite the magnitude of China's health assistance, especially to Africa, many questions remain regarding the scope of this aid, its effectiveness, and the governance mechanisms that guide the conceptualisation and implementation of such efforts. Also, little information is available to assess the reorientation of Chinese health support to Africa, away from its traditional focus on curative medicine and 'bricks-and-mortar' infrastructure (Lin et al. 2016). One strategic intent is to strengthen traditional Chinese medicine (TCM), with fifty-seven TCM international cooperation projects for the year 2018 as part of the TCM Belt and Road Development Plan (2016-2020) (Song 2018). Criticism of China's BRI is mounting, especially in parts of Europe and the US but also in some countries along the route.

The expanding global health economy requires governance

The SDG drive for solutions at the country level and economic growth in the developing world requires global health organisations to engage in transition strategies to domestic funding in middle-income countries (MICs). Today, more than 400 million people still lack access to essential health services (WHO and World Bank 2015), and 40 per cent of the world's population lacks social protection (ILO 2014). A significant dynamic is underway driven by many of the countries themselves. WHO (Xu et al. 2018) puts a spotlight on the funding of health services: total health spending is growing faster than GDP at 6 per cent on average in LMICs; health system resources are coming more through pooled funds, in particular from government sources; and external funding (aid) represents less than 1 per cent of global health expenditure, of less relevance in MICs but increasing in low-income countries. The emphasis is now on how global health governance can support determined domestic political leadership to invest in health, building strong public health institutions and creating enabling regulatory and legal environments for health.

Moreover, the coming decade will be defined by a significant rise in the health economy and its increasing integration with the growth of technology industries, as health becomes a major application for digital development and artificial intelligence systems. Global healthcare expenditures are expected to continue to rise as spending is projected to increase at an annual rate of 5.4 per cent between 2017 and 2022, from US$7.724 trillion to US$10.059 trillion. The health technology market alone is expected to reach US$280 billion by 2021 (Deloitte 2019). There is clearly a need to better understand the relationship between health and global finance (Kickbusch 2013). There have been proposals to factor a health component into responsible investment initiatives, as well as support divestment strategies from health-harming industries (Krech et al. 2018). At the same time, and as van Rensburg and Bracke describe in Chapter 6 of this Report with regard to the opioid epidemic, aggressive lobbying efforts at both the national and global levels have sought to counteract regulation, such as plain packaging, sugar tax, or minimum drinking age, and strong attacks on the normative role of WHO in relation to the NCDs agenda continue.

National investment in health systems is a governance priority

While Sachs et al. (2019) have proposed that the world's billionaires could easily pledge US$5 billion per year to support global health, the answer lies in better governance and significant investment in health systems. This links global health to national political agendas, and both China and India have, as part of their high-profile national development plans, launched large-scale domestic health programmes. In October 2016, President Xi Jinping announced the Healthy China 2030 blueprint, which makes public health a precondition for all future economic and social development (Tan et al. 2017). In a similar vein, in 2018, India's Prime Minister Narendra Modi called for India to end TB by 2025, five years ahead of the global target–a significant feat as India accounts for one quarter of the global TB burden. He also launched the Ayushman Bharat initiative with the goal to create 150,000 health and wellness centres across the country to deliver UHC as well as a health insurance aimed at providing coverage for poor families.

For Western analysts, these developments carry great ambiguity, as in the developing world the movement for UHC began with the rise of populist politicians: in 2000, Thaksin and his Thai Rak Thai Party proposed the 30-Baht Scheme as a major policy of their rural platform. Thailand today is a champion for UHC and is playing a significant role in the UN High-level Meeting on UHC called for September 2019. Plenty of other politicians have since run on populist platforms that promise to deliver UHC to their people. In his 2014 presidential campaign, President Jokowi, the then-Governor of Jakarta, promised to extend his UHC programme nationwide by issuing Healthy Indonesia Cards (*Kartu Indonesia Sehat*). Ahead of 2019 elections, the Philippines' President Duterte also signed a Universal Healthcare Act that automatically enrols all Filipinos in the National Health Insurance Program.

The willingness to support global public goods must be enhanced

Apart from national investment, the next decade will require action on some of the toughest challenges in global health governance, some of which are highlighted in Table 5.3. It is the combined impacts of rapid demographic, environmental, economic, social, and technological changes that make health-related problems harder to address (Held et al. 2019). This includes the immense concentration of wealth, the need to act decisively on the commercial determinants of health, and the necessity to regulate the rapidly growing global health industry, especially in relation to its synergies with the digital information and communications companies. There is also a clear need to improve pandemic preparedness to be ready for 'disease X'. And more than before societal responses are critical: in its 2019 list of ten major threats to global health, WHO listed vaccine hesitancy, which threatens to reverse progress made in tackling vaccine-preventable diseases (WHO 2019b).

Table 5.3 **Selected challenges in global health governance and their implications**

Challenge	Implication
Antimicrobial resistance (AMR)	AMR could cause an estimated 10 million deaths per year by 2050 and a cumulative cost of up to US$100 trillion in global economic output if the current trajectory is not reversed (Review on Antimicrobial Resistance 2014).
	Its impact on the global economy from 2017 through 2050 would reduce annual global GDP by between 1.1% and 3.8%—as large as the losses in the 2007–9 global financial crisis (World Bank 2017a).
	We still do not know the extent to which AMR will undermine medical and human progress.
Non-communicable diseases (NCDs)	NCDs are collectively responsible for 73% of all deaths worldwide.
	Every year, tobacco kills 8.1 million people, 2.8 million deaths are attributed to alcohol use, and 1.4 million deaths are attributed to diet high in sugar-sweetened beverages. Many more years of productivity are lost due to ill health, disability, or early death (Stanaway et al. 2018).
Disease X	Pandemics can cost an estimated US$60 billion economic losses, or up to US$570 billion all-inclusive losses, per year (Fan et al. 2016; GHRF Commission 2016).
	We are not sure what will be the cause of the next pandemic, which might well be a pathogen that is currently unknown to cause human disease—an 'unknown unknown' (Honigsbaum 2019).
Digital transformation	There have been advances in systems biology and genetic engineering, increases in computing power and informatics, the development of materials science and nanotechnology, and breakthroughs in artificial intelligence and robotics, but we are not yet sure whether they will yield all the benefits that they promise.
	Access to new technologies is already providing new avenues to attack sovereign states for political or financial gain, for example through cyber-attacks on health systems (Cyber Security Policy 2018) or the use of algorithms to manipulate anti-vaccination messages to undermine trust (Broniatowski et al. 2018).
Air pollution and climate change	Nine out of 10 people worldwide breathe polluted air, which causes approximately 7 million premature deaths per year (WHO 2018a).
	Climate change impacts many social and environmental determinants of health, such as air, water, food, and shelter, and speeds up the spread of climate-sensitive diseases and occurrence of natural disasters. The UN Intergovernmental Panel on Climate Change (IPCC 2018) warned that we are close to reaching the point of no return on climate change.
Fragility and urbanisation	Almost a quarter of the world's population—1.8 billion people—were living in fragile contexts (through a combination of challenges such as drought, famine, conflict, and population displacement) in 2016. This could reach 2.3 billion by 2030 (OECD 2018c).
	Urban population globally is projected to grow by 2.5 billion by 2050, with nearly 90% in lower-income nations in Africa and Asia. The increased speed and volume of trade and travel as well as the accelerating rate of urbanisation put poor, overcrowded cities with weak public health infrastructure at risk of outbreaks (Bollyky 2019).

The Grand Disruption

Present global health scholarship is coming under increasing critique. Too much of the global health analytical work has been unidirectional and focused on Western donors, their perspectives, and their solutions–published in the English-language major journals–rather than on the needs and contributions of countries and actors in the rest of the world. Some academics and civil society advocates highlight the lack of voices from the global South (Sheikh et al. 2017) and of women in global health leadership (Dhatt et al. 2017). Some consider global health a neocolonial or postcolonial imperial project which shores up a capitalist neoliberal world order (Biehl 2016). For instance, Dahn et al. (2015) argue that the 'rubber plantation model of international health' has shaped and maintained massive inequity in access to knowledge and resources. Birn (2014) warns that as public multilateral health agencies favour the private sector and philanthropic efforts, they may in fact reinforce the inequities they seek to overcome.

This critique relates to the real world of power relationships. The combined fortunes of the world's twenty-six richest individuals reached US$1.4 trillion last year–the same amount as the total wealth of the 3.8 billion people of the poorest half of the world (Luhby 2019). At the same time, illness still costs Africa US$2.4 trillion in lost productivity every year, especially because of the high burden of NCDs (WHO 2019a). Inequality is endangering political stability across borders. The International Monetary Fund (Lagarde 2019) recognises that this 'winner-takes-most' dynamic at play is unsustainable, and there have also been calls for a Global Green New Deal to tackle climate change and inequality together (Kozul-Wright and Gallagher 2019). In global health, a growing number of authors as well as civil society organisations call for a new political economy moving beyond the belief that the big problems can be remedied through harmony of interest rather than through determined action by governments who are also willing to address corporate power (Labonté and Ruckert 2019).

Many analysts consider the world to be at the cusp of a new world order, under which the global health agenda will be driven by new geopolitical dynamics and national interests. 'Support to international organisations and agreements can no longer be taken for granted, their value base is increasingly being questioned, financing mechanisms are no longer ensured, and political ideology increasingly trumps technical evidence' (Kickbusch and Cassels 2018). Western countries, especially through the G7 process, are still leading the calls for the replenishment of the 'grand decade' mechanisms–the Global Fund and Gavi. But over the next decade Western agency will no longer take centre stage in global health. Non-Western powers have already created a parallel multilateralism in the domain of the global financial institutions (Stuenkel 2016). China's massive global project of connectivity, the BRI, will possibly take on a major role in redefining global health governance.

KICKBUSCH *and* LIU

Nevertheless, it is not yet clear to what extent the emerging powers are ready to engage in global health and where their priorities will lie.

Global health today is perhaps one of the most crowded and diverse fields of global activity: a wide array of institutions, mechanisms, and actors have emerged which build on models that reach far back to historical precedents. The question is whether they are still fit for purpose. All the challenges mapped out in Table 5.3 are interrelated, but the global governance structures are not. A 2018 special issue of *The BMJ* drew attention to nine global health disruptors, each of which has the potential to be a disruptive force for global health governance (The BMJ 2018), but we are not well prepared to deal with any of them. This weakness will have to be addressed through political leadership, particularly at the domestic level, but the current political environment, in which short-term political interests often trump long-term public policy goals, does not give much ground for optimism.

VI. Politics and Power: The Case of the Global Opioid Epidemic

ANDRÉ J. VAN RENSBURG *and* PIET BRACKE

The governance of health and well-being is intrinsically political. Rudolf Virchow's famous maxim that '[m]edicine is a social science, and politics nothing else but medicine on a large scale' highlights the centrality of politics and power in health governance (quoted in Mackenbach 2009). Bambra and colleagues (2005: 187) note that 'health is political because power is exercised over it as part of a wider economic, social and political system', arguing that the political nature of health is underlined by several considerations. For example, within the context of the global neoliberal market economy, some groups have more access to health as a commodity than others do. Furthermore, the social determinants of health are deeply correlated with political action and inaction (Kickbusch 2007), and health is an inexorable feature of citizenship and human rights (Bambra et al. 2005). If health is political, its governance is even more contentious, insofar as health governance relates to dynamic processes of strategic interaction and deliberate rules that frame the duties, roles, and relations between stakeholders (Brinkerhoff and Bossert 2014; Fox and Ward 2008; van Rensburg et al. 2016; Touati et al. 2007). Consumers have become increasingly demanding as well as more knowledgeable about health and disease causation (Kickbusch 2007), further elevating the importance of politics and power in governing health and well-being globally.

> *If health is political, its governance is even more contentious.*

This means that the positions of and relations between three key groups of stakeholders are highlighted for scrutiny, namely (1) states, politicians, and policy-makers; (2) service providers (including pharmaceutical manufacturers, researchers, and healthcare workers); and (3) citizens and consumers (including their families) (Brinkerhoff and Bossert 2014). Politics emerges within these interactions due to the mechanisms of inclusion and exclusion inherent to health governance (Kickbusch 2007). Simply put, health and wellness are the result of politics in terms of both structure (e.g. markets, health systems, culture) and agency (e.g. actions by politicians, service providers, citizens). Health is a strategic public good and the subject of intense political contestation: the governance of health and well-being legitimises or de-legitimises the nature and competence of the state as an entity of power (Mackintosh 2013; see also Immergut, Roescu, and Rönnerstrand, Chapter 9 in this Report).

Despite routine consensus that politics is central to health governance and that health and its promotion 'are profoundly political', there continues to be relative silence in mainstream debates on the influences of politics, power, and ideology on health (Bambra et al. 2005: 187). This silence has become more deafening in the context of global health narratives that increasingly underline risk and risk management in response to public health emergencies, especially in terms of the spread of and response to communicable diseases such as HIV, avian influenza, Zika virus, and Ebola in recent times (Harper and Parker 2014; see also Moon and Bezruki, Chapter 4 in this Report).

This chapter aims to provide a snapshot of the role of politics and power in the governance of health and well-being. It is important to note that the notion of politics does not necessarily refer to partisan politics; in this chapter, politics is used to refer to broader sets of policies and systems that influence and drive power relations in terms of health and well-being (Koplan and McPheeters 2004).

Politics in health governance takes on many forms. It can be conceptualised as unfolding in a cascading manner, in terms of macro-, meso-, and micropolitics (van Rensburg et al. 2016). Macropolitics includes global governance of illness and disease, exemplified by the politicisation of HIV across different regions, countries, and contexts (Piot et al. 2007), and more recently, the role of diplomacy and global political economy in the governmental and non-governmental response to Ebola in West Africa (Benton and Dionne 2015; Hofman and Au 2017; see also Moon and Bezruki, Chapter 4 in this Report). On a meso level, politics and power relations emerge during processes of integration and collaboration across healthcare organisations and service providers, with–among myriad others–examples from Australia (Ehrlich and Kendall 2015), Belgium (Willem and Gemmel 2013), England and the Netherlands (Mur-Veeman et al. 2003), and South Africa (van Rensburg et al. 2018). In terms of micropolitics, the challenges resulting from inter-professional and interdisciplinary collaboration (Jansen 2008) and shifting relationships between patients and providers that resulted in the evolution of traditional patient-provider relationships to patient-centred care and on to person-centred care (de Maeseneer et al. 2012) bear mention.

Cutting across this normative cascade of politics in health governance, and the focus of this chapter, is politics as a form of power, whereby politics involves processes of production and distribution of resources and different sectors of society hold distinct forms of capital (Bambra et al. 2005; Bourdieu et al. 1994; Raphael 2015). Rather than using a single definition of power, we draw from two traditions of power, namely, mainstream and second-stream (Clegg 1989; Scott 2001). Mainstream focuses on the sources of power and

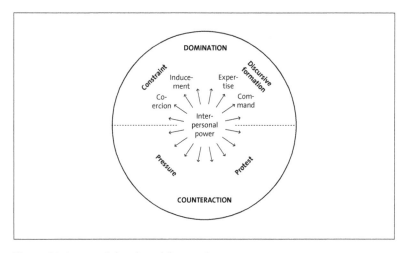

Figure 6.1 **A map of developed forms of power**
Source: Adapted from Scott (2001)

the power of one agent over another, while second-stream emphasises the subtle processes, techniques, and strategies of power employed in politics (Scott 2001).

While this broad conception helps us better understand power as a nuanced social force, we need to go further to find a more appropriate toolkit with which to better understand politics in health governance. Here, it is useful to draw from what Scott (2001: 15) calls 'developed forms of power', an analytic frame that better allows us to interrogate power in terms of its relational dynamics in health governance. The developed forms of power are depicted in Figure 6.1, adapted from Scott's (2001) map of power relations. Two broad forms are distinguished, namely domination and counteraction. Forms of domination include constraint, which unfolds in terms of coercion (the threat of force) and inducement (the promise of rewards), and discursive formation, which encompasses expertise (trust in perceived superior knowledge and skills) and command (the right to give orders and the obligation to obey). 'Power always involves resistance' (Scott 2001: 25), and forms of domination are opposed by forms of counteraction. Institutionalised counteraction, legitimised by those in power, resists in the form of pressure politics through official and legitimate channels. Protest, on the other hand, generally involves organised social movements that seek to challenge and restructure patterns of domination through more radical means (Scott 2001). Domination and counteraction refer to more large-scale power structures, but power also unfolds in face-to-face contexts, on an interpersonal level. While this form of power is dispersed throughout society, and certainly holds a prominent position in the spectrum of power, in this chapter we place the focus on structures of domination and counteraction.

By applying this lens to health governance, the chapter highlights how politics and power shaped the unfolding of analgesic opioid use in the United States and globally, aiming to illustrate how politics manifests and why it matters. As will be shown, globalisation and neoliberal forces augment the ways in which states, politicians, and policy-makers; service providers; and citizens and consumers relate to each other. Finally, the chapter offers reflections on possibilities for improved governance within the contexts of politics and power.

Opioid Use as a Public Health Crisis in the United States

O pioids encompass a range of drugs that activate opioid receptors on nerve cells. Their use in the field of medicine has had profound effects on pain management and is a staple in pain management, especially in providing relief and improving quality of life for people suffering from chronic discomfort. Nonetheless, they have habit-forming qualities that may lead to physical dependence and withdrawal symptoms. Such opioids include illegal substances such as heroin, drugs used for anaesthesia such as fentanyl, and prescription pain-relieving analgesics such as oxycodone, hydrocodone, codeine, and morphine. The use of long-acting opioids for non-cancer pain has been significantly associated with out-of-hospital mortality risk (Chung et al. 2019; Ray et al. 2016). Frequent users of drugs such as hydrocodone and oxycodone often turn to illegally obtained, much stronger opioids such as heroin and fentanyl in order to cut costs and in pursuit of stronger pain relief, leading to built-up opioid tolerance that raises the risk of accidental overdose, even due to a slight dose imprecision (Cicero et al. 2017). By 2011 abuse of opioid analgesics in the US had increased to the point that deaths due to their overdose exceeded those due to overdose of cocaine and heroin combined (CDC 2011). The focus here will be on the politics that drives the growing prescription opioid epidemic.

Much attention has been paid to the rising opioid crisis in the US, where both mainstream media and academic research have scrutinised the increasing number of people dying from opioid addiction. In the US, preventable deaths due to opioid overdose increased 14 per cent in 2017 over the previous year and 633 per cent since 1999 (National Safety Council n.d.a). At an estimated 1 in 96 chance, dying from an opioid overdose is–in 2017, for the first time on record–more likely in the US than dying in a motor vehicle collision (1 in 103), from a fall (1 in 114), or from gun assault (1 in 285) (National Safety Council n.d.b). From 2000 to 2009, the number of newborn babies diagnosed with drug withdrawal increased three-fold, while the number of mothers who used opioids at the time of delivery increased five-fold (Patrick

VAN RENSBURG *and* BRACKE

Box 6.1 The death of Cameron Weiss: an illustrative example of the opioid crisis in the US

Cameron Weiss was a young victim of the opioid crisis in the US state of New Mexico. Following a sports-related injury, Cameron was prescribed Percocet at the age of 16 and was prescribed more opioid-based analgesics following more injuries. The teenager started adding to his dosage by taking opioids from his grandparents' medications, ultimately turning to heroin at a much lower cost than illegally obtained prescription medications. In August 2011, Cameron was found dead at home due to a heroin overdose, mirroring a similar path taken by thousands of Americans who turn to increasingly stronger and more dangerous methods of pain relief.

Following his death, his mother, Jennifer Weiss-Burke, lobbied the state government to pass a bill that would limit the prescribing of pain relief opioid medication for acute pain to seven days in order to reduce the chances for addiction and the number of leftover pills. The bill was designed to exclude cases of chronic pain management. However, pharmaceutical industry lobbyists mobilised to suppress the planned measure. Despite amendments that allowed physicians and prescribers to set their own limits, the bill was defeated in the state House Judiciary Committee before it even came to a full vote. According to Bernadette Sanchez, the state senator who sponsored the measure, 'The lobbyists behind the scenes were killing it.' Crucially, in 2012, most of the members of the judiciary committee had received drug industry contributions, and opioid makers had spent more than double the amount of the previous year on lobbying in New Mexico. Following calls from the US Centers for Disease Control and Prevention for better regulation, by 2016 measures like the one championed by Jennifer Weiss-Burke were adopted in Connecticut, Maine, Massachusetts, New York, and Rhode Island, all exempting prescriptions for chronic pain.
Source: Whyte et al. (2016)

et al. 2012). Various other studies (Gomes et al. 2018; Kiang et al. 2019; CDC 2011) have traced the grim statistics relating to the rapid emergence of the opioid crisis in the US. Further, one analysis suggested that, in the period 1999-2008, the rates of opioid-related death, opioid analgesic sales, and substance abuse admission rates increased strongly and in parallel (CDC 2011).

Results from the Global Burden of Disease study (IHME 2018) paint a bleak picture of the effects of opioid consumption on health and well-being in the US between 1990 and 2017. Since 1990, the rate of new cases (incidence) of opioid use disorder increased from 52.81 cases per 100,000 population to 80.14 (Figure 6.2). Despite a decline since the mid-2000s, the incidence rate has begun rising again. The prevalence rate of opioid use disorder, i.e. how many suffer from it at a given time point, changed from 736.63 per 100,000 population to 1,357.16 (Figure 6.3). Though the rate plateaued somewhat in the mid-2000s, it too is again on the rise. Particularly ominous in relation to the burden on society and individuals in the US is the increase in the rate of disability-adjusted life years (DALYs) due to opioid use: that rate trebled from 365.72 per 100,000 population in 1990 to 1,220.23 in 2017 (Figure 6.4), with little relief on the immediate horizon. Finally, the rate of deaths due to opioid use increased substantially during the period from 1.23 per 100,000 population to 14.57 (Figure 6.5).

This substantial burden of disease associated with prescription opioid use in the US can be ascribed to a multitude of factors, although there do seem to be some drivers that are more central to this discussion. As illustrated by the story of Cameron Weiss, an adolescent whose opioid addiction led to death by overdose, and subsequent efforts to pass legislation to curb opioid prescribing (see Box 6.1), specific kinds of politics and power depicted in Figure 6.1 are involved in driving opioid addiction in the US. For example, the power of expertise was exhibited in the development of extended-release opioids such as Percocet, the pain relief drug first prescribed to Weiss. Hailed at the time as a breakthrough in the management of non-cancer pain, oxycodone–the active ingredient in Percocet and Oxy-Contin–was strongly promoted among the medical community, despite concerns regarding its addictive properties. By no means the only culprit, Purdue Pharma's OxyContin, launched in 1995, has been a marker for the power of new pharmaceutical technologies in changing clinical approaches to pain (Kolodny et al. 2015). Drugs such as OxyContin signified a combination of inducement and expertise, i.e. marketing practices supported by the approval of the medical community (Scott 2001). Purdue Pharma alone spent an unprecedented six to twelve times more on the promotion of Oxy-Contin than was spent promoting competing drugs (US General Accounting Office 2003; van Zee 2009). Pharmaceutical lobbyists' reaction to a pro-regulation bill is a form of counteraction, using pressure to change the outcomes of the legislative process. A key mechanism here is the promotion of a discourse favourable to continued opioid use, packaged in the form of aggressive marketing tactics, guidelines aimed to 'edify' the medical community on the value of prescribing opioids, and fighting accountability and transparency measures aimed to address overprescription and misbranding (US General Accounting Office 2003; McCaskill 2018; van Zee 2009).

A Global Perspective on Problematic Opioid Use

The rise in opioid-related addiction and death in the US has spurred global concern that similar pathways could unfold in other countries and regions, especially given the increasingly globalised nature of pharmaceutical markets. However, concerns about similar opioid-related burdens in other corners of the world are unlikely to hold similar weight to the US crisis, given the importance of contextual mechanisms such as the degree of regulatory oversight in the pharmaceutical industry.

Nonetheless, recent indications suggest a slight global average increase since the 1990s in opioid-related public health burden, led primarily by high-income countries, especially the US. The closest scenario to that in the US is neighbouring Canada, where estimates showed from 2005 to 2011 a 43.4 per cent increase in the dispensing of strong opioids, a rate which started to decline by 7.9 per cent from 2011 to 2012 (Fischer et al. 2014). Nevertheless, between 2016 and 2018, 10,337 apparent opioid deaths were recorded, the annual death rate increasing from 8.4 (2016), to 11.1 (2017), to 11.8 (2018) per 100,000 population (Special Advisory Committee on the Epidemic of Opioid Overdoses 2019).

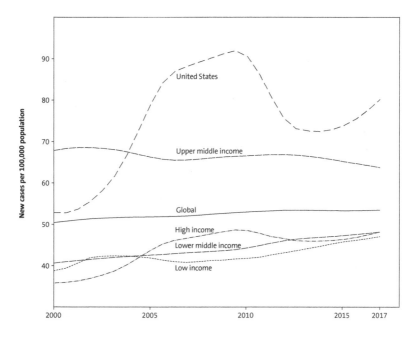

Figure 6.2 **Global incidence rates of opioid use, by income group, 1990–2017, compared to the US**
Source: IHME (2018)

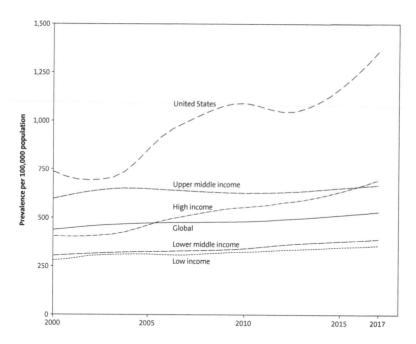

Figure 6.3 **Global prevalence rates of opioid use, by income group, 1990–2017, compared to the US**
Source: IHME (2018)

In Australia, during the period from 1990 to 2014, the dispensing of opioids increased from 4.6 to 17.4 defined daily doses per 1,000 population. The types of opioids dispensed also changed, with a seventeen-fold increase in the use of long-acting morphine and methadone and a substantial increase in the use of oxycodone, fentanyl, and similar substances between 2000 and 2011 (Karanges et al. 2016). From 2013 to 2017, approximately 1.9 million Australian adults were initiated on opioids yearly, 28.2 per cent of whom were prescribed opioids for non-cancer pain (Lalic et al. 2019).

Data from Israel suggests that, in the period between 2000 and 2008, consumption of strong opioid analgesics increased by 47 per cent: from 2.46 to 3.61 defined daily doses per 1,000 population per day (Ponizovsky et al. 2011). The rise persisted in the period 2009 to 2016, with a 68 per cent increase in consumption of five key opioid analgesics (Ponizovsky et al. 2018).

Opioid consumption in most European countries increased steadily from the mid-1990s, levelling off somewhat after the mid- to late-2000s (Bosetti et al. 2019). In Croatia (Krnic et al. 2015), Finland and Norway (Hamunen et al. 2009), France (Chenaf et al. 2019; Hider-Mlynarz et al. 2018), Scotland (Ruscitto et al. 2015), Slovakia (Hudec et al. 2013), Spain (García del Pozo et al. 1999; Garcia del Pozo et al. 2008), and the United Kingdom (Zin et al. 2014), the use of opioids, and strong opioids in particular, increased by

VAN RENSBURG *and* BRACKE

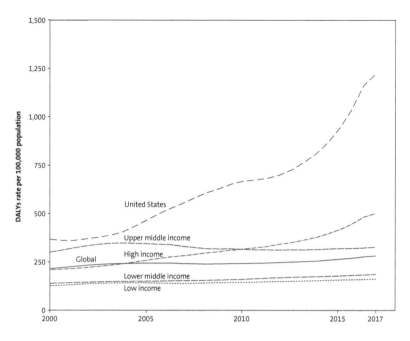

Figure 6.4 **Global rates of disability-adjusted life years related to opioid use, by income group, 1990–2017, compared to the US**
Source: IHME (2018)

percentages in the hundreds and into the thousands over various time periods beginning in the 1990s and early 2000s. There is of course variation in use patterns within the European region, with western and northern Europe showing rates of opioid use ten times higher than that of southern and eastern Europe (Bosetti et al. 2019). Fortunately, in many countries levels of use have plateaued or begun to decline in recent years (Bosetti et al. 2019).

The above-described findings are very much in step with global estimates. Global opioid analgesic use rose from 3.01 billion defined daily doses per annum during 2001-3 to 7.35 billion during 2011-13. This included substantial increases in North America, western and central Europe and Oceania, while opioid use in regions across Africa, Asia, Central and South America, and eastern and southeastern Europe remains relatively low (Berterame et al. 2016). In Brazil, for example, a cross-sectional survey suggested that opioid analgesics are used much less than in higher income settings, with a 0.5 per cent prevalence rate (da Silva Dal Pizzol et al. 2019).

Estimates from the above-mentioned Global Burden of Disease study help to put into perspective the weight of the opioid crisis in the US relative to the rest of the world. From 1990 to 2017, global opioid incidence increased from 50.4 per 100,000 population to 53.47 with a similar pathway across country income categories, a significantly smaller jump in new cases than

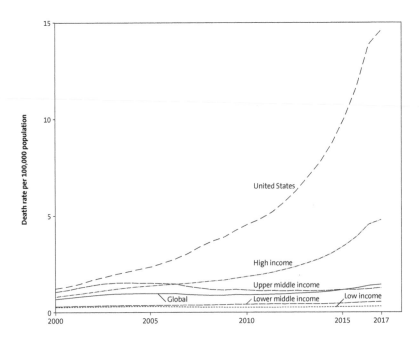

Figure 6.5 **Global death rates attributable to opioid use, by income group, 1990–2017, compared to the US**
Source: IHME (2018)

in the US (Figure 6.2). In terms of prevalence (Figure 6.3), a similar trend emerges: global cases per 100,000 population rose from 436.7 in 1990 to 529.87 in 2017, perhaps less dramatic than the near doubling of cases in the US over the same period, but still remarkable. Global and US differences in the DALYs rate are especially striking: while the global average went from 215.19 per 100,000 population to 281.21, the US DALYs rate in 2017 (1,220.23 per 100,000 population) was more than four times the global average and three times its own rate in 1990 (Figure 6.4). Finally, global opioid-related deaths on average doubled between 1990 and 2017 from 0.69 per 100,000 population to 1.43, while the US mortality rate linked with opioid use increased almost twelve-fold (Figure 6.5).

VAN RENSBURG *and* BRACKE

Politics and Power in the Governance of Opioid Use and Misuse

T his section briefly considers how politics and power have emerged in different ways in the opioid crisis, in line with health governance actors and the relations among them (Brinkerhoff and Bossert 2014). Accordingly, the focus turns to the ways in which service providers have added to the growing burden; relations between state actors and lobbyists in regulating the opioid market; and acts of resistance from citizens and clients to the pharmaceutical industry.

Political and promotion strategies to extend market reach among service providers

The US opioid crisis has drawn attention to the role of professional groups, pharmaceutical companies, and healthcare providers in the sharp increases in the public health burden. The American Pain Society, a professional membership organisation, was at the forefront in calling for pain to be acknowledged as the 'fifth vital sign' during the 1990s (the four being body temperature, pulse, respiratory rate, and blood pressure) (Dhalla et al. 2009). In 2001, this was cemented in the US Joint Commission for Accreditation of Healthcare Organizations' Pain Management Standards (updated in 2018), requiring healthcare providers to ask patients about their pain in order to battle the perceived underdiagnosis of pain among the American population. Accordingly, patients were routinely asked about their levels of pain, despite their reasons to seek care. This was measured in terms of a pain scale illustrated with levels of smiley faces from zero to ten. A response higher than five required a referral for a pain consultation (McGreal 2018). As a consequence, both ambulatory and hospital-based opioid prescribing increased considerably (Kolodny et al. 2015). The new requirement was significant since the Joint Commission is a gatekeeper for 20,000 health facilities in the US that require certification in order to access federal government funding. Pain management became a standard for accreditation, opening the way for companies such as Purdue Pharma to take on a new role, namely, to educate physicians in pain management, free of charge.

Training materials contained narratives that downplayed the addictive qualities of opioids and suggested that concerns about addiction, tolerance, and death were inaccurate and overstated. A central message was that 'opiophobia' led the medical community to confuse addiction with physical dependence (Kolodny et al. 2015). This kind of reorientation significantly impacted clinical culture, inculcating in new generations of health workers that pain management is a critical part of care. The American Pain Society and Purdue Pharma sought further to lobby the Federation of State Medical Boards (FSMB) in order to influence state-level health policy. Over a decade, the FSMB received almost US$2 million from the pharmaceutical industry to promote pro-opioid guidelines and a book (*Responsible Opioid Prescribing*) written by advocates for wider opioid-prescribing. The book was sold primarily to state medical boards and health departments for further distribution, the profits split between pharmaceutical partners and the FSMB. A context was created in which opioids were being prescribed widely and liberally (McGreal 2018).

In response to a growing body of critique, during the 2000s pharmaceutical companies invested heavily in lobbying efforts, backed by pharma-funded research, to ensure continued sales. Routine data were used as a tool by the pharmaceutical industry to target 'high-prescribers', physicians who liberally prescribed opioids, by heavily incentivising sales (van Zee 2009). Caution was therefore suppressed for several more years, and 200 million opioid prescriptions were produced by physicians in the US in 2010 alone (McGreal 2018). Indeed, a rationality underwritten by market-driven corporate benefit seems to be a key driver in the expansion of opioid use in the US and has increasingly influenced the governance of pain and pain management. Unlike the illegal heroin and fentanyl trade, prescription opioid use is very much in sync with an underregulated industry, a medical community amenable to influence, and questionable marketing practices (van Zee 2009).

In 2018, the Ranking Member's Office of the US Senate Homeland Security and Governmental Affairs Committee published a report investigating the relationship between pharmaceutical companies and pain advocacy groups (McCaskill 2018). From 2012 to 2017, five companies contributed almost US$9 million to fourteen groups working on chronic pain and other opioid-related issues, while from 2013 to 2017, individual physicians affiliated with these groups received more than US$1.6 million from the five companies (McCaskill 2018). Recent research has shown that physicians who received perks from pharmaceutical companies prescribed opioids an average of 9 per cent more in the following year, while physicians who did not take up any incentives prescribed fewer opioids in the following year (Hadland et al. 2018).

A change in the dominant discourse on pain management during the 1990s was facilitated by professional groups that used their capital as experts in the medical field to exercise influence over accepted standards for pain management. The investment in healthcare professionals' education and reorientation is a mainstream power way of inducing and manipulating actors that are essential in selling opioids to the public, with the second-stream power of medical expertise being exploited to further corporate interests (Scott 2001).

Efforts to reorient and reformulate opioid prescribing policy should ideally be rooted in scientific proof (Koplan and McPheeters 2004). The evidence used to promote the marketing of opioids since the 1990s has recently been called into question amid a slew of court cases against pharmaceutical companies by US states. At the time of writing, thirty-five states had filed court papers against pharmaceutical companies, who are facing more than 1,600 lawsuits from various actors including cities, Native American tribes, and counties. In Oklahoma, the state took three of the largest pharmaceutical companies to court, namely Purdue Pharma, Johnson & Johnson, and Teva Pharmaceutical Industries, accusing them of misrepresenting the addictive qualities of the opioids that they marketed to the public. While the cases against the latter two companies were ongoing at the time of writing, Purdue Pharma reached a US$270 million out-of-court settlement with the state that included establishing a foundation for addiction treatment and research and contributing to substance abuse treatment drugs, while Purdue's owners, the Sackler family, were ordered to pay US$75 million over five years (Bernstein and Zezima 2019). Further, the opioid manufacturer Indivior was accused by the Department of Justice in Virginia of deceiving healthcare providers and benefit programmes about the safety of Suboxone (an opioid drug used to treat opioid addiction) compared to other similar drugs. Though the case was not settled at the time of writing, the state's demand of US$3 billion in fines had a substantial negative effect on Indivior market shares (BBC 2019). These developments are a fitting example of command exercised by government and the courts by using the legitimate right to change opioid manufacturer practices (Scott 2001).

Regulating opioids in the US and beyond

In the US, drug policy is governed mainly on the federal level, and here the power of lobbying emerged as a critical tool to promote opioid use. In 2016, the Centers for Disease Control and Prevention launched federal guidelines that recommend limits on opioid prescriptions for chronic pain (Dowell et al. 2016), a federal response that reflects a growing reaction to overprescribing opioids (Harris and Huetteman 2016). Nonetheless, these guidelines were heavily criticised by most large pharmaceutical manufacturers (McCaskill 2018).

During the same year, the US Congress unanimously passed the Ensuring Patient Access and Effective Drug Enforcement Act of 2016, signed into law by then-President Obama. The Act essentially curbed one of the few federal agencies opposed to liberal opioid distribution, the Drug Enforcement Administration (DEA), by restricting its ability to seize suspicious narcotic shipments from drug manufacturers, thereby disabling a significant restraint on the distribution of opioids throughout the country. The power of the DEA and the Department of Justice to control pharmaceutical distribution has been systematically undercut by several of their officials 'switching sides'; since 2000, fifty-six officials went on to work for pharmaceutical companies and their legal firms. Using this form of capital, political action committees representing pharmaceutical lobby groups contributed US$1.5 million to the campaigns of twenty-three law-makers for the 2016 bill. In total, US$102 million was spent by the pharmaceutical industry to lobby Congress on the bill and associated legislation between 2014 and 2016. A senior DEA official in charge of federal drug regulation suggested that '[t]he drug industry, the manufacturers, wholesalers, distributors and chain drugstores have an influence over Congress that has never been seen before' (Higham and Bernstein 2017).

The growing legal backlash against the pharmaceutical industry–specifically focusing on the scientific basis for downplaying the addictive properties of opioids–has resulted in a downturn of market growth forecasts in the US, and there are fears that US-based pressures will push opioids such as OxyContin to the global stage. A 2017 letter signed by members of the US Congress to Margaret Chan, then-Director-General of the World Health Organization (WHO), called on WHO to prevent Mundipharma International, an arm of Purdue Pharma, from pursuing outside the US the same deadly strategy it used to market OxyContin in the US that 'helped spark a public health crisis that will take generations to fully repair'. The letter urges WHO to learn from the US experience and rein in such practices (Office of US Congressman Hal Rogers 2017).

While these fears seem valid, the global trend does not appear to be following the same pattern as it did in the US, as was shown in Figures 6.2-6.5. Legal and regulatory barriers to overprescribing opioids (Ponizovsky et al. 2012), as well measures to reduce the impact of marketing (Karanges et al. 2016), have been adopted in many countries. In Canada, for instance, the National Prescription Drug Use Strategy–a multisectoral package of measures aimed to address the drivers of unsafe opioid use–was launched in 2013 (Fischer et al. 2014), though its effects are yet to be fully evaluated.

Additional factors besides legal and regulatory barriers to opioid use are critical (Vranken et al. 2018). Research is lacking here, though it can be suggested that the predominantly free market health system, lax regulation of pharmaceutical development and distribution, and a strong lobbying sector in the US might have contributed to the sharp increase in the opioid use burden from the 1990s. Crucially, increasing public access to opioids does not necessarily lead to misuse; opioids provide relief and quality of life for millions of people suffering from pain. There needs to be a careful balance between excessively liberal availability and disproportionate control (Berterame et al. 2016). In terms of power and politics, there needs to be a balance between the coercion and command of governments (e.g. legislation and policy) and global governance bodies (e.g. international agreements held in place via the threat of sanctions), and the inducement and expertise used by pharmaceutical companies to distribute opioids to markets. Thus, as described in the next section, an important feature in regulating opioid development, distribution, and use is the role of clients and citizen groups that engage in activism to affect change.

Resistance among clients and citizens: civil protest and dissent

In February 2019, an activist group staged a protest in the Guggenheim Museum in New York City, aimed at the links between the Sackler family (which owns Purdue Pharma and OxyContin) and art museums such as the Guggenheim and the Louvre, to which the family has made substantial donations. The event's centrepiece involved people dropping thousands of fake prescriptions from the upper levels of the museum to imitate snow. This was in response to revelations from a lawsuit filed by the Massachusetts attorney general's office against Purdue that Richard Sackler, son of the founder of Purdue and current board member, had described OxyContin's launch as an event that would be 'followed by a blizzard of prescriptions that will bury the competition', and said, '[t]he prescription blizzard will be so deep, dense and white'. While this particular sentence was reported by many media outlets, its original source (Massachusetts Suffolk County Superior Court 2019) remains closed to the general public. The truth of this apparent statement is almost irrelevant; it became a powerful piece of discourse that spurred on protest action in a very public sphere. The outcome of the lawsuit–in which Sackler family members are accused of deception and fraud in promoting OxyContin despite concerns of its addictive properties–remains to be seen. It speaks to counteraction towards pharmaceutical groups on two fronts, namely in the court system and in the arts, both significant platforms and sources of power (Bourdieu 1986).

The protest was organised and coordinated by PAIN (Prescription Addiction Intervention Now), an activist group aiming to remove the Sackler family's presence in museums and universities and to address the opioid crisis. Among the group's demands are that key cultural institutions disavow the family and that Purdue Pharma rectify its alleged role in the opioid crisis by contributing financially to the public health response and to victim compensation (PAIN n.d.).

The fake prescriptions (see Box 6.2) were made out to Solomon Guggenheim (the creator of the Guggenheim Museum) from Richard Sackler, with an infinite number of refills for 80mg OxyContin, along with the instruction to '[i]ncrease prescriptions by convincing doctors that opioids provide "freedom" and "peace of mind"...make patients "more optimistic" and "less isolated"'. Parts of this phrase are taken from court documents in the Massachusetts vs. Purdue case detailing advice Purdue received from McKinsey, a global consultancy, to promote among doctors the idea that OxyContin leads to 'freedom' and 'peace of mind' and gives patients 'the best possible chance to live a full and active life' (Armstrong 2019; Massachusetts Suffolk County Superior Court 2019).

Whereas the work of investigative journalists exposing the politics of opioid manufacturing and marketing and the actions of Cameron Weiss's mother described earlier drew from counteraction power in the form of

Box 6.2 **PAIN fake prescription flyer**

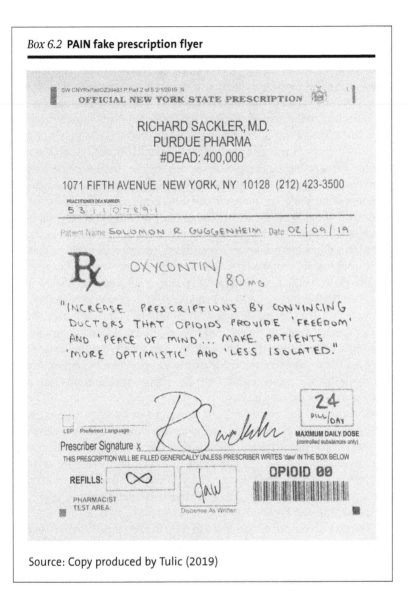

Source: Copy produced by Tulic (2019)

pressure, the actions of PAIN demonstrate the use of protest (Scott 2001). Indeed, PAIN's action seems to have had an effect, very likely in conjunction with the slew of court cases against Purdue and increasing pressure from mass media. While donations to prominent museums no doubt provided Purdue and the Sackler family a degree of legitimacy, several of their beneficiaries have started to cut ties. The US National Portrait Gallery cancelled a US$1.3 million donation from the Sackler Trust, while the Guggenheim and the Tate Museum both announced that they will not accept any future con-

VAN RENSBURG *and* BRACKE

tributions tied to the Sackler family (McGlone 2019). This is a good example of how citizens respond to the lack of responsiveness from politicians and policy-makers and an apparently destructive healthcare system (Brinkerhoff and Bossert 2014). Such mainstream power dimensions of protest and pressure are further embedded in legitimation sought by Purdue by making large donations to prominent cultural institutions.

Concluding Thoughts

This chapter has illustrated how politics influences the governance of health and well-being by drawing from examples in the protracted opioid use crisis. Within this period of accelerating complexity, the influences of a market-oriented rationality in health governance come to the fore. Health as a central subject of politics becomes commodified, and the driving force behind health governance becomes profit-driven processes that override the human rights and social justice values of healthcare, values not reducible to a cost-benefit ethic (Lukes 2008). The opioid crisis serves to illustrate how unregulated, multinational companies can profit from both addiction and rehabilitation. Well-being simply does not offer any incentive here, and misery becomes the catalyst for political engagement with governments, special interest groups, medical communities, and users themselves. This has no doubt been facilitated by global shifts from 'medicalisation' and professional power held by physicians towards privatisation and commercialisation, where '[h]ealth translates into a product that can be bought on the market, promises wellbeing and changes the citizen into a consumer' (Kickbusch 2007: 154).

It is critical to include a wide range of stakeholders during the whole policy process, especially clients and citizen groups; strong public participation was clearly lacking in initial efforts to reduce the expansion of the opioid epidemic in the US (Baker 2017). Health governance and policy has traditionally focused much more on content and structure than on the processes that lead to content and structure (Buse et al. 2009; Gilson and Raphaely 2008; Singleton and Rubin 2014). Policy-makers need to more carefully and systematically take politics and power relations into account. Only in this way can the broad range of interests be considered, helping to balance market-driven corporate interests with client and public health needs. Interagency taskforces focused on educating the public during policy-making and implementation are critical to involve and empower citizens with the technical knowledge required to fully participate (Alexander et al. 2017). To ensure good healthcare practice, the education of medical professionals needs to extend beyond merely providing training (e.g. to prescribe drugs more responsibly) towards changing curricula for medical, nursing, and allied health education to foster a deeper and more sustained change

(Samet and Kertesz 2018). As with all health policy and legislation, there also need to be robust monitoring and evaluation systems in place from the start, in order to pay close attention to unintended consequences: this was a critical misstep in the US experience in the roll-out of the Joint Commission's first Pain Standards (Baker 2017).

These suggestions mostly engage with mainstream forms of power; second-stream dimensions of power in healthcare are much harder to change, due to their inherent subtlety. Policy-makers are however urged to follow the core values of public health and to ensure that these are reflected in national and global reforms. Politics needs to be contemplated in conjunction with public health and science:

> Science, public health, and politics are not only compatible, but in conjunction, all three are necessary to improve the public's health. The progress of each area of public health is related to the strength of the other areas. The effect of politics in public health becomes dangerous when policy is dictated by ideology. Policy is also threatened when it is solely determined by science alone, devoid of considerations of social condition, culture, economics, and public will. (Koplan and McPheeters 2004: 2042)

Organised public action is one of few options available to citizens to resist disease-mongering (Wolinsky 2005), i.e. the informal alliances alleged to be formed between pharmaceutical companies, medical interest groups, and even patient advocates to promote the expansion of illness boundaries in order to increase market share for drugs and therapies (Moynihan and Henry 2006). Such public action is also critical in the promotion of human rights of the vulnerable, protecting those affected by the politics of health and illness. This, however, requires policy and legislation that allows for and protects the formation of organised civil society that can operate in relative independence from state and private sector influence. A strong, critical, independent media also goes a long way, as evidenced by the pivotal role investigative journalism played in uncovering the drivers behind the opioid crisis.

Finally, it is impossible to divorce a crisis such as the opioid epidemic from its socioeconomic roots, outlined in greater detail by Bambra in Chapter 3 of this Report. High levels of poverty, crime, and unemployment have been associated with higher use of opioid analgesics (Nordmann et al. 2013; Ruscitto et al. 2015). This suggests that complex challenges such as the opioid crisis are contingent on much more than health policy on its own. Rather, a multisectoral, wide-ranging approach is warranted that includes elements such as macroeconomic policy, health system design, housing, welfare, social development, and education. Ultimately, '[w]e all need to be strong advocates for good science, good public health, and good policies and the positive value that politics can provide for all three of these' (Koplan and McPheeters 2004: 2042).

VII. Healthcare as Social Investment

HANNA SCHWANDER

F or many citizens, policy-makers, and scholars, one of the biggest
achievements of our time is the welfare state. In modern societies, citizens in need of help turn to the state rather than begging on the street
or having to rely on charity. To protect citizens from harm, welfare states
have developed a broad range of policies and regulations and provide a variety of public services. As a socially constructed institution, the welfare state
not only addresses fundamental questions such as social fairness and the
basic notion of a good society but ultimately also reconciles democracy and
capitalism (van Kersbergen and Manow 2017). From a technical perspective,
a welfare state has been characterised by 'government-protected minimum
standards of income, nutrition, health, housing and education, assured to
every citizen as a political right, not charity' (Wilensky 1975: 1) or, following
Marshall (1950), as 'a democratic state that–in addition to civil and political
rights–guarantees social protection as right to citizenship' (van Kersbergen
and Manow 2017: 364).

One of the welfare state's most important aims is to compensate workers once they have suffered mischance, mostly by transferring cash benefits
to workers in need. Old-age or unemployment compensation benefits are
examples of passive compensation policies (Beramendi et al. 2015). Healthcare, by contrast, forms part of the increasingly relevant service dimension
of the welfare state, just like education, childcare, care for the elderly, and
active labour market policies. Healthcare is not only among the most popular branches of the welfare state, as shown later in this section, but also
among the most significant ones in terms of social spending. Public spending on healthcare is the second most extensive branch of social spending
in the Organisation for Economic Co-operation and Development (OECD)
countries, next to spending on old-age benefits, and far higher than spending on unemployment, as Figure 7.1 illustrates.

Within the OECD, spending on healthcare has followed an almost universal trend upwards. Before the global financial and economic crises of 2008-12,
healthcare spending rose faster than average economic growth in most countries. During the crises, however, many countries introduced strong austerity
measures such as cutting salaries or the number of employees in the health
sector[1], introducing additional out-of-pocket payments, or imposing restrictions on spending for pharmaceuticals. Since 2012, health spending has

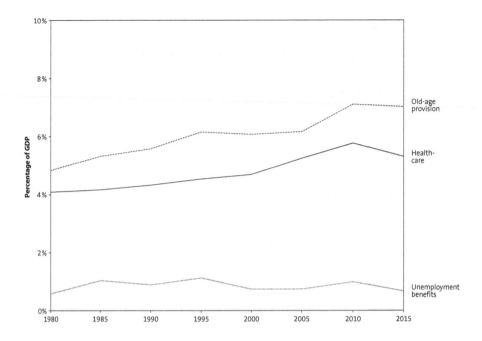

Figure 7.1 **Cross-national trends in public spending on healthcare, old-age benefits, and unemployment in the OECD as a share of GDP, 1980–2015**
Source: OECD (2019)

tended to follow economic growth more closely (OECD 2018a). Yet, despite a shift towards 'relative privatization' (Rothgang et al. 2010),[2] public finances still account for the bulk of health spending: according to the OECD (2018a), two-thirds of healthcare spending is financed by taxes and social insurance contributions. If no further cost containment measures are taken, private and public health expenditure across OECD countries are projected to almost double from around 6 per cent in the period 2006-10 to 12 per cent by 2060 (de la Maisonneuve and Martins 2015: 74).

Just as for the other branches of the welfare state, policy-makers consider this upward spending trend increasingly problematic given that the amount of resources to be poured into the healthcare system appears limited in times of 'permanent austerity' (Pierson 2001). Hence, since the late 1980s, when universal coverage of health risks was achieved in almost all OECD countries[3], the political debate in these societies has turned from the question of providing universal access to that of managing the cost side of healthcare provision. The debate focuses on controlling fees and general spending rather than excluding population segments or 'de-listing' once publicly covered benefits (Freeman and Rothgang 2010; Hacker 2004).

The upward trend in spending on health has several explanations. For one, technological progress makes medical services more expensive. In medical services, progress is defined by 'product' rather than 'process' innovation, meaning that innovation adds more products, resulting in higher costs rather than savings. Personal services such as medical attention are also much less subject to rationalisation than are material goods. Rather, they are characterised by the 'cost disease of personal services' (Baumol 1967) by which the price of personal services increases at a faster pace than average prices. Medical services become a luxury good for which demand increases with increasing wealth. This means that as people become wealthier their relative demand for material consumption goods such as cars, mobile phones, or clothing decreases, whereas their relative demand for medical services increases. In addition, the health market is characterised by uncertainty, risk aversion, and issue complexity, which empowers precisely those actors (i.e. medical doctors) that have an interest in high spending (Hacker 2004).

Spending for healthcare is also driven by the same demographic trends that drive spending on old-age pension benefits. The ageing of post-industrial societies in the OECD increases the number of multimorbid, chronically ill

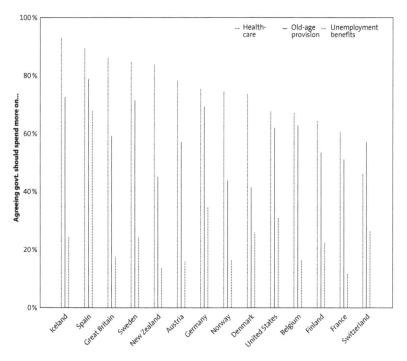

Figure 7.2 **Public support for higher government spending on selected welfare state branches**
Source: ISSP (2018)

patients in need of treatment, a factor that is exacerbated by the self-reproducing effect of successful treatment: successful treatment leads to more demand as survivors need further treatment or might need treatment in later stages of life (Freeman and Rothgang 2010).

Cost containment is further complicated by the popularity of healthcare among the population. Public provision of healthcare is among the most popular branches of the welfare state, arguably because of the universality of healthcare risks and the perception of the ill as deserving (van Oorschot and Roosma 2015). As shown in Figure 7.2, based on data from the International Social Security Programme (ISSP) Role of Government V (RoG V) module (2018), a majority of the public across the selected OECD countries demands more public spending on healthcare. Furthermore, in all but one country (Switzerland), the share of respondents in favour of more public spending on healthcare is higher than the share of citizens in favour of higher spending for old-age provision.

The twin pressures of rising demand and limited availability of resources are not unique to healthcare.[4] Other branches of the welfare state struggle to adapt to the new economic and social contexts as well. While earlier arguments expected international factors such as globalisation to lead to a downward pressure and welfare state retrenchment in the form of a 'race to the bottom' (Garrett 2001), the direction of social policy reforms rather points to a modernisation of the welfare state, a development best exemplified in the discussion about a social investment turn (Esping-Andersen 2002; Garritzmann et al. 2017; Hemerijck 2018; Jenson 2009). Social investment policies are 'policies that both invest in human capital development and that help make efficient use of human capital, while fostering greater social inclusion' (Morel et al. 2012: 2).

Reconsidering social investment's three functions (stock, flow, and buffer) and its emphasis on capacitating social justice, human capital development, and efficient use of human capital, this chapter argues that healthcare plays a crucial role in the new social investment welfare state. To underpin this argument, the next section outlines the position of healthcare within comparative welfare state research, emphasising that the literature proposed different explanations for the origins and cross-national variation of healthcare systems and of social protection systems. On that basis, the role of healthcare in the debate about a social investment welfare state is then explained. The final section summarises the argument for raising the profile of healthcare and highlights the implications it has for policy-making and governance.

Healthcare in Welfare State Research and Policy Analysis

The cross-cutting variation in the organisation of healthcare provision and the different underlying explanations for this variation are two reasons why the analysis of healthcare is still not fully integrated in the comparative welfare state research that underpins much policy-making and analysis (but see Bambra (2005) and Reibling (2010) for attempts to link healthcare and welfare typology research). To understand why this is significant, it is important to first review the main insights of the research field as it seeks to explain cross-national variation in social protection provision, highlighting its inherently political nature. Following is then a discussion of how these approaches apply to the analysis of healthcare and alternative explanations for cross-national difference in the provision of healthcare.

Esping-Andersen's (1990) classical typology of 'worlds of welfare capitalism' is based on three dimensions of welfare state analysis (decommodification, stratification, and primary provider of welfare[5]). As noted, the core explanation for this cross-regime variety is political: it is the result of conflict between social groups and their different political powers. Specific patterns of party competition and the power of political movements such as the labour or the women's movement closely correspond to the distinct worlds of welfare capitalism (Esping-Andersen 1990). More precisely, the dominance of liberal/conservative, social democratic, or Christian democratic parties in the respective political systems and their power in government are crucial in explaining why welfare states differ across countries (Allan and Scruggs 2004; Döring and Schwander 2015; Huber and Stephens 2001a; Manow et al. 2018a). Box 7.1 provides a brief overview of the main types of welfare states and political configurations that influence them.

Though highly influential in the analysis of welfare states and their origins, functions, and governance, the framework has not fully taken into account variation in how healthcare provision is organised (even though health risks are one of the oldest and most universal social risks) and the effect of this variation on access to healthcare and outcomes such as health inequalities. One explanation for this scant consideration is that the fundamental 'equality versus market' conflict on which the welfare state is centred in this framework does not directly apply to variations in healthcare systems.[6] How healthcare is organised does not affect distributive conflicts between social classes in the same way as the organisation of other social protection measures such as old-age pensions, unemployment compensation systems, or disability schemes does. In particular, it does not touch vested interests of traditional stakeholders such as trade unions and employer associations. This is seen as a reason why southern European countries with their strong and radical trade unions and left-oriented parties have developed universal, non-contributory but tax-

Box 7.1 **Main 'worlds of welfare capitalism'**

Liberal: Secular-liberal parties dominate party competition in the Anglo-Saxon world (e.g. Canada, the United Kingdom, and the United States), also because the majoritarian rules of electoral competition disadvantage the left (Döring and Manow 2017). The result is a residual system of social protection, which directs the middle class to search for market solutions. Accordingly, those who can afford it buy services such as education, healthcare, and other social protection in the form of private insurance on the market (Ansell and Gingrich 2013; Esping-Andersen 1990; Huber and Stephens 2001b; Iversen and Stephens 2008).

Social democratic: This type is the result of the hegemonic position of social democratic parties in the Scandinavian political systems, which built the welfare state according to egalitarian ideas with the support of strong trade unions. A mainly tax-financed welfare state not only pays out generous cash benefits but also offers comprehensive public services such as schooling and early childhood education and childcare. These encompassing public services were what guaranteed the support of the middle class for the welfare state and turned the welfare state into a highly legitimised 'people's home'.

Conservative: The conservative or corporatist welfare state, shaped by the pivotal Christian democracy in continental Europe (Huber and Stephens 2001b; Manow 2004), is a social insurance state, administered by a mix of private and public stakeholders and with a strong emphasis on cash transfers rather than public services to protect its citizens (Esping-Andersen 1990).

Southern Europe: Though not originally considered a distinct type, scholarly consensus (Bonoli 1997; Ferrera 1996; Guillen 2002; Leibfried 1993; Manow et al. 2018b) now sees the southern welfare regime as such for its strongly segmented labour markets and fragmented welfare states offering generous protection for insiders while providing little protection for others (Manow et al. 2018a). The patchy expansion of the welfare state is explained by the strong polarisation of the political system between a revolutionary left and a conservative Christian democracy, which made attempts to overcome occupational fragmentation in favour of universal social insurance schemes impossible (Ferrera 1996; Watson 2008). Universalism was implemented only where no vested worker interests were affected, namely, in healthcare.

financed national healthcare systems just as have liberal countries such as the UK or Canada where the left is historically much weaker (Manow 2015).

Accordingly, existing classifications of healthcare systems are not based on political power constellations or on their distributive implications but rather on the source of financing and the distinction between private or public ownership of facilities (Freeman and Rothgang 2010) or the number of payers combined with the ownership of facilities (Hacker 2004). Others include not only the financing but also the regulation and the type of providers of healthcare services (Reibling 2010; Wendt 2009, 2014). The most common typologies such as that differentiating between national health service systems, social insurance systems, and the rare type of private systems are therefore based on different criteria than the worlds of welfare capitalism typology. Furthermore, they cut across it, with national health services tending to be found in the countries of the Scandinavian type, southern Europe, and the UK, and social insurance in continental and central Europe, except Switzerland.

The second reason for the shadowy existence of health issues in analyses of the welfare state is that expansion and variation in healthcare provision are much less driven by political factors such as the strength of the labour movement or government partisanship that are at the heart of many conflict-based approaches. Thus, healthcare does not fit in the common theoretical frameworks.[7] As shown in Figure 7.3, based on data from the ISSP (2018) RoG V module, the traditional explanations for within-society variation do not seem to apply: support for more public spending on healthcare is much less stratified by educational attainment than is support for more spending on other typical social policy programmes such as old-age provision and unemployment benefits that have strong distributive implications. Rather, variation in healthcare systems is much more driven by institutional factors, in particular the extent to which veto players limit the decision-making power of governments, as historical institutionalists such as Immergut (1992) and Hacker (2004) highlight.

Immergut's seminal book (1992) on healthcare policy-making in France, Sweden, and Switzerland in the first half of the twentieth century starts from the observation that the government's ideological approach towards healthcare and the interests of the medical profession do not differ in the three countries. This rules out party-political factors and different demands of interest groups as explanations for cross-national differences. Instead, the conflict is between the governments that want available and affordable care for their citizens and the elite physicians who oppose state interference in their professional affairs, for instance regarding price controls. Thus, the variation in healthcare structures is attributed to the institutional power that the well-organised physicians have over the political process, in other words, their veto power or–in Immergut's terms–their 'access to veto points'. In Switzerland, for example, the availability of binding referendums provides physicians strong veto power. With the federal government's role in health

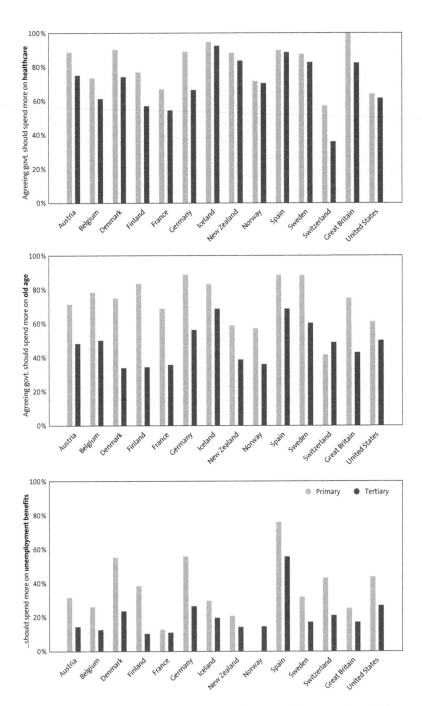

Figure 7.3 **Public support for additional spending on different welfare state branches according to education levels**

Source: ISSP (2018)

provision restricted, the original system of government subsidies to private insurance schemes to make them more affordable has remained in place, much to the advantage of the medical profession. France takes the intermediate position: the parliament of the Fourth Republic (1946-58, the decisive period in the construction of the healthcare system) was accessible to the lobbying efforts of interest groups resulting in a universal public insurance scheme with government-controlled fees for general practice and salaried hospital physicians. In Sweden, the strong concentration of political power within the executive branch isolated the government from interest group pressure, and elite doctors had no access to veto points once the decision to move towards a national health system had been decided.

If we generalise Immergut's argument, polities with a large number of veto points (such as federalism, the separation of power between the executive and legislative branches, or direct democratic institutions) will favour the opponents of government intervention in healthcare. It is therefore not surprising that no federal state has implemented a national health service and that the US as the 'most veto-point ridden polity of all rich democracies' has remained for a long time the only rich democracy without universal health coverage (Hacker 2004: 697).

Adding to the relevance of institutions is a phenomenon called path dependency (Pierson 1996, 2000) by which early institutional choices have long-term stabilising effects that are difficult to reverse. Most countries began to intrude into the doctor-patient relationship by subsidising non-governmental insurers, rather than financing services. These policies created important vested interests in a pluralist financing structure and reinforced doctors' preferences for fee-for-service payment. How extensive and long-lived these arrangements were had crucial effects on the types of systems countries retained (Hacker 1998). The longer it took the national government to replace private or occupational insurance, the more likely a country ends with a decentralised healthcare system in which private insurance plays a larger role: the delay allows the formation of a powerful interest group of private stakeholders (Hacker 1998). The case of the US illustrates the argument: since private insurance has essentially replaced public insurance, it became politically nearly impossible to expand public insurance at the expense of private insurance.

Hacker (2004) emphasises not only the structure of the political system but also the hierarchical versus decentralised financing structure of medical systems for the extent and type of change to healthcare systems. This is particularly true in the effort to contain costs. Structural cost containment reforms are most likely to be enacted in countries with concentrated executive power and no or a very limited number of veto points and with a hierarchical financing structure of the medical system, such as in the UK, Sweden, or Denmark. In countries with dispersed political authority, such as Germany or the US, it is highly difficult to overcome the veto points for major policy change; yet the fragmentation of the healthcare system may actually facilitate smaller-scale reform by leaving room for shifting coalitions of interest. Most difficult are reforms in countries with highly dispersed political authority and hierarchical financing structures, such as Canada, where neither the political system nor the medical system provides favourable conditions for change (Hacker 2004).

Although variation in healthcare systems is examined by some analysts, especially institutionalists like Immergut and Hacker, healthcare is still treated rather as an orphan in discussions on social protection (Hacker 2004). Yet, healthcare is an essential part of social protection. This is particularly evident in newer perspectives on the welfare state that do not consider social policy as 'politics against the markets' (Esping-Andersen 1985), that is, as extractions that had to be wrested from the forces of capitalism by the agents of organised labour in a political battle. Instead they see social policy as a productive factor for the economy that is in the interest of both employers and employees. This is the perspective that the social investment approach takes. The following briefly outlines the concept of social investment as well as its main goals and policy focus before elaborating on the role of healthcare within the social investment perspective.

Investing in a Healthy Population: Healthcare as Social Policy

As the advanced industrialised societies transitioned from the industrial to the post-industrial era, the traditional welfare state with its strong emphasis on protecting the income and job of the male breadwinner has taken flak from both neoliberal economists and progressive social scientists. While the neoliberal dogma rests on the belief that a generous welfare state implies efficiency loss and is irreconcilable with economic growth, proponents of a 'new welfare state' have taken issue with the dysfunctionalities of the traditional welfare state in terms of equality and economic efficiency (Hemerijck 2017). In a post-industrial society, the male breadwinner employment-based social insurance welfare state would increasingly foster suboptimal life chances among large parts of the population. Consequently, a new welfare state is needed (Esping-Andersen 2002).

These visions of a new welfare state are based on the presumption that social policy can be a 'productive force' if it invests in a competitive and productive population that is able to perform the complex tasks required by the knowledge economy (Jenson 2009; Vandenbroucke et al. 2011). Just as the traditional welfare state was built to ease the transition from a feudal to an industrial society by addressing social risks that would inevitably arise (van Kersbergen and Manow 2017), social investment policies help ease the transition from an industrial, Fordian economy to a post-industrial, individualised, and knowledge-based economy and the resulting new social risks (Bonoli 2007; Garritzmann et al. 2017; Hemerijck 2018; Jenson 2009). With their emphasis on human capital development, activation, and social inclusion (Bonoli 2014; Hemerijck 2015), social investment policies aim at 'preparing instead of repairing' (Morel et al. 2012). In terms of policy theory, social justice was reconceptualised from 'distributive fairness' in a Rawlsian sense (1971) to 'capacitating' social justice in the tradition of Sen (1992) and Nussbaum (2000) by which entitlements and services should enable individuals to act as 'autonomous agents' (Morel and Palme 2017). Hence the normative claim of social investment rests on concrete needs and capabilities for social participation, which is why social investment policies focus strongly on social inclusion and inclusive growth.

Health is an inherent part of social investment as some of the crucial aims of social investment are closely linked to health issues. Indeed, a vicious circle links poverty, education, and health. On the one hand, ill health leads to marginalisation, poverty, and–for children–lower learning outcomes. Investing not only in health but also particularly in reducing health inequalities consequently contributes to social cohesion and reinforces employability, thereby making active employment policies more effective and ultimately contributing to higher productivity and economic growth. Poverty, marginalisation, and low education, on the other hand, also lead to ill health (Bambra 2011a; McNamara et al. 2017; Nordahl et al. 2014; see also Bambra, Chapter 3 in this Report). More precisely, social investment fulfils three interdependent functions–stock, flow, and buffer (Hemerijck 2015)–along which the discussion of how healthcare is related to social investment policies is structured.

First, social investment policies raise the quality of the stock of human capital and capabilities. Investment in human capital development starts with early child development among pre-school children, continuing to universal access to high-quality school education, but also includes lifelong learning for adults with a job and and retraining for those in need of a new one. Access to healthcare is essential for a productive workforce and raises the quality of human capital and capabilities (Boyer 2002). Inequalities in health pose a significant challenge for social investment welfare states (Diderichsen 2016). This is particularly evident in the persistent and–given their traditions of social investment and relatively free and equal access to healthcare–surprisingly high health inequalities in the Nordic countries (Hurrelmann et al. 2011; Mackenbach 2012). Policies that attack health issues early on, such as the fight against child obesity, are therefore key to a social investment strategy. In Finland, for instance, social investment begins already before a child's birth and continues to adulthood: free maternity and child health clinics, free maternity packages, free or heavily subsidised daycare services, free meals from kindergarten to college, and free education from pre-primary school to university. Consequently, family background plays a smaller role in educational results in Finland than it does in many other European countries (Bouget et al. 2015).

The second function of social investment policies is to ease the flow between different labour market and life course transitions via activating policies. But such policies need to take into account that health inequalities are also about different consequences of being ill in terms of survival, disability, and participation (Diderichsen 2016). As such, activation policies should involve not only economic incentives and instruments for retraining and education but also efforts to revive functional abilities as well as to adapt the demands of working life to fit individuals' functional limitations, and thereby improve their ability to actually work (Diderichsen 2016). In the Nordic countries, for instance, the target groups for activation policies were expanded after the economic crisis of the 1990s to include now also people in need of disability benefits or with a variety of health and/or social problems (Dølvik et al. 2015; Pedersen and Andersen 2014). The disability scheme in Denmark was reformed in 2013 with the aim of giving people individual, tailor-made assistance to come back to work. These rehabilitation programmes could combine labour market activities, health treatment, and social help, and require close cooperation among these policy sectors and with the education sector (Pedersen and Andersen 2014). Such cooperation is all too often lacking, with recent reforms frequently increasing fragmentation rather than fostering coordination between the different actors.

Third, social investment also has a protective aim. Strong minimum income safety nets function as buffers, which are particularly relevant in fighting poor health outcomes as well as for preventing the negative outcomes of poor health for children. Family and general minimum income benefits are crucial safeguards to ensure that children of poor families lack no basic necessities and grow up in a secure and healthy environment in which they can develop (Bouget et al. 2015), thereby preventing particularly the intergenerational transmission of poverty. For instance, the Danish Social 2020 strategy seeks to extensively reform social, education, health, and employment policies as well as introduce targeted measures to improve conditions for people in vulnerable situations (Bouget et al. 2015). Regulative policies might also function as buffers to a certain degree: employment protection policies generally counteract labour market inequalities between healthy and unhealthy people, but in times of severe recession such as the 2008-12 period additional programmes are needed to protect vulnerable groups (Reeves et al. 2014).

Conclusion: A Case for Renewing Interest in Healthcare from a Distributive Perspective

This chapter argues that healthcare must be an inherent part of social policy, in particular in the social investment framework. The social investment perspective takes a more dynamic perspective on how social policy interacts with fertility, education, and labour decisions to enhance not only aggregate productivity but also well-being and life chances: unequal opportunities and unrealised human potential result in a waste of human capital and constitute a barrier to economic growth (Hemerijck 2017). Given its preparing orientation, the social investment welfare state tends to be more service-oriented than the old, industrial one and therefore better equipped to deal with the new social risks emerging in a post-industrial social and economic order (Morel et al. 2012). This can be seen in the main policy foci of the social investment approach: education, lifelong learning, upskilling and training, active labour market policies, and family policies to prevent child poverty and to reconcile work and family life. Reconsidering the three functions of social investment (stock, flow, and buffer) and its emphasis on capacitating social justice and the development and efficient use of human capital, the relevance of healthcare within the social investment framework is easy to see. In addition, fostering people's employability and bringing them into good, productive, and healthy work ease the financial pressure on healthcare systems by increasing the stock of active population contributing to financing the healthcare system.

Although health issues are often high on the agenda of policy-making discussions and healthcare is mentioned as a social investment policy in the academic literature, it is rarely considered in policy analysis. In some of the most recent academic volumes (Bonoli and Natali 2012; Hemerijck 2018; Midgley et al. 2017) on the new welfare state, healthcare is referred to only in passing, and none dedicates a chapter, or even a section within a chapter, to the analysis of healthcare governance, the effects of policy reforms on health outcomes, or similar questions. Hence, while the social investment approach adopts a life course perspective that emphasises the need for state intervention at transitional moments of an individual's life and the preventing dimension of state intervention, the literature has not fully considered the importance of healthcare to achieving the aims of social investment.

Universal access to high quality healthcare is a safety net not in the form of cash transfers for the weakest members of society but in the form of reducing health inequalities between social groups. Here, a social investment approach with its emphasis on preparing and educating might contribute to fighting health inequalities. Countries with high levels of income inequality also have lower average levels of population health (Hurrelmann et al. 2011). Yet, above a certain limit further increases in wealth have only a limited effect on the health of a country's population (OECD 2009: 6). In that case, a Matthew effect of increasing wealth takes place: only the already privileged groups achieve health benefits from increases in wealth, whereas the health of the less privileged improves only minimally. This means that, if economic growth intensifies existing income inequalities that translate into unequal life chances and health outcomes, social inclusion and capacitating social justice cannot be achieved. The limited effect of additional material resources on health outcomes suggests that other factors such as psychological, social, or cultural variables might be more relevant in affecting health outcomes (Hurrelmann et al. 2011; Ross et al. 2000). With its focus on cognitive and social development and education, the social investment state might well contribute to closing the gap and provide a route out of health inequality.

Endnotes

1   In Greece, one of the countries most drastically affected by the crisis, the salaries of the public healthcare workforce were cut by 15%, the thirteenth and fourteenth monthly salaries were abolished, and pension benefits were cut by 10% (Simou and Koutsogeorgou 2014).

2   Rothgang et al. (2005) also observe a convergence in spending patterns between advanced industrialised societies mainly due to a catch-up process of latecomer countries since the 1980s.

3   The US represents a partial exception insofar as, in light of the patchy and highly unequal access to a very expensive healthcare system, the political debate revolves around expanding access to healthcare as much as around containing costs.

4   Yet the debate about cost containment is not as loud as similar debates for old-age protection or unemployment compensation schemes, which is likely due to the popularity of the healthcare system (see Figure 7.2), the relative universal distribution of health risks (i.e. everyone anticipates needing healthcare later in life), and the fact that health risks are perceived to be outside an individual's control. Healthcare recipients are therefore deemed to be 'deserving' of need (unlike 'undeserving' unemployment or social insurance recipients) (van Oorschot 2006).

5   *Decommodification* denotes 'the extent to which individuals and families can maintain a normal and socially acceptable standard of living regardless of their market performance' (Esping-Andersen 1987), while *stratification* refers to the extent to which the welfare state interferes with the existing social order.

6   Generally, the 'worlds of welfare capitalism' typology suffers from an over-emphasis on cash benefits, which are relevant for protecting citizens. But welfare states are as much about the delivery of services, such as health, education, and social care, of which healthcare is among the most important (Bambra 2005). Moreover, health outcomes also cut across welfare state typologies (Hurrelmann et al. 2011).

7   Many sociologists and political scientists analysing the welfare state were mainly concerned with the redistributive capacity of the welfare state for different social classes and the impact on income equality, whereas economists focused on the economic cost associated with social protection.

VIII. Behavioural Insights for Health Governance

CHRISTIAN TRAXLER

T he traditional economic perspective on how to govern the health sector is based on the rational choice paradigm. In a world of fully rational and self-centred individuals that make well-informed, forward-looking decisions, economic incentives are a powerful tool to steer choices. Questions of optimal institutional design then turn into exercises of establishing the right incentives for different market participants, i.e. those who demand or provide health services.[1] In reality, however, it is humans–and not ultra-rational 'Econs' (Thaler and Sunstein 2008)–that make choices. And human decisions tend to be, well, human: influenced by limitations in attention, self-control, and willpower, i.e. 'bounded' in the degree of rationality, as well as by social norms, peer comparison, and conformity pressure.

If one proposes innovative and novel approaches to govern the health sector, one needs to properly test what works.

By now more realistic, richer (but also more complex) models of decision-making have found their way into the mainstream of modern economics.

The behavioural 'revolution' within economics (which was, in fact, a slow process that took several decades) produced a better, i.e. empirically more accurate, description of behaviour and–in the health sector–a better understanding of patients' and health professionals' choices. This, in turn, offered new views on health policy problems. Behavioural economics gave rise to novel policy approaches and instruments. The most prominent among these are 'nudges' (Thaler and Sunstein 2008), i.e. changes in the choice environment that aim at inducing behavioural change without resorting to economic incentives. However, there are many other ways beyond nudging in which behaviourally informed policy proposals differ from traditional economic approaches.

The idea of behaviourally informed policy-making quickly spread beyond the academic world. Already well before 2017, when Richard Thaler won the Nobel Prize in economics, many institutions were applying behavioural innovations. The front-runner and probably best known player in this industry is the United Kingdom's Behavioural Insights Team (BIT).[2] Their prolific health unit engages in many innovative projects with the National Health Service (NHS) and other important actors in the British health sector (see e.g. Hallsworth, Snijders et al. 2016).

In addition to relying on insights from the behavioural sciences, a key pillar of BIT's work is the rigorous testing of behavioural innovations using randomised controlled trials (RCTs). The strong emphasis on trialling (recall BIT's slogan 'test, learn, and adapt') is another–and, some might say, even more important–contribution of the behavioural turn: it arrived together with a stronger focus on evidence-based policy-making and relies on convincing impact evaluations. The motivation for this empirical focus is clear: if one proposes innovative and novel approaches to govern the health sector, one needs to properly test what works. While randomised evaluations are certainly not novel in some domains of health governance (where RCTs have been widespread for a long time), they provide credible new evidence in other domains.

There is now a vast number of institutions beyond BIT–academic and non-academic, governmental and private ones, national, international, but also local ones–which develop and test behavioural science innovations. The Organisation for Economic Co-Operation and Development (OECD) lists more than 200 institutions around the world that apply behavioural insights to policy-making.[3] Some of these units consist mostly of interdisciplinary teams of behavioural scientists (typically beyond behavioural economics) and focus exclusively on health topics, such as the Center for Health Incentives and Behavioral Economics at the University of Pennsylvania in the United States. The remainder of this chapter introduces some of the work and results produced by these institutions.

The next section describes several cases ranging from problems in preventive health to health plan choices that highlight the use (and limits) of nudges and other behavioural policy approaches to induce behavioural change among individual patients. Turning from the demand to the supply side of health services, the following section summarises studies illustrating the scope for applying behavioural insights to steer the provision of health services, i.e. to nudge clinicians or medical staff. The chapter concludes with a critical discussion of various concerns regarding the role of behavioural policy-making in the health sector.[4]

Behavioural Insights Applied to Consumers/Patients

The vast majority of behaviourally informed interventions focus on individual choices and decisions of those who demand services from or interact with the healthcare sector. This section reports lessons from different policy designs in this area.

Preventive health, check-ups, and screenings

One important insight from behavioural economics is that humans act in a present-biased manner: contemporary costs are systematically overemphasised relative to benefits that may be realised in the future (Ericson and Laibson 2019). This pattern has important implications in the domain of preventive healthcare, among many others. When present-biased individuals face the option to 'invest' in their future health, even small costs associated with (typically unpleasant) preventive care activities might cause them to delay such investments. This logic applies to a broad set of healthy behaviours, ranging from regularly exercising, avoiding fatty food, and the like, to utilising health services such as check-ups and early diagnosis screenings.

Altmann and Traxler (2014) explore the power of simple reminders in the context of dental check-ups. The study tests the effect of different reminders on patients' propensity to actively arrange and later attend a check-up appointment. Their RCT reveals a strong and, most importantly, long-lasting effect of reminders resulting in a sizeable increase in check-ups. However, reminders that provide additional information (e.g. about the benefits of preventive dental care) do not increase the basic impact of a reminder that simply asks, 'Please call to make an appointment'. In a follow-up project within the same institutional context, Altmann et al. (2017) examine the role of deadlines for contacting the dentist. Communicating relatively tight deadlines, i.e. imposing time pressure to respond to a reminder by calling the dentist, increases the frequency at which patients arrange check-up appointments in both the short and the long run. Interestingly, the deadline effect is observed both in a mere prompting treatment ('please call by...') as well as in combination with an economic incentive ('if you call by...you will get...'). The authors conclude that setting relatively tight deadlines (and thus reducing the scope for procrastination) is a particularly useful strategy when patients' attention is limited and a given task is only temporarily on top of mind (here: to arrange a check-up appointment).

A related set of studies explores strategies to bridge the gap between good intentions and actual actions. Results from this field point to the power of planning prompts, i.e. reminders that ask individuals very concretely about when, where, and how they will carry out a certain task. Milkman et al. (2011), for instance, investigate the effectiveness of using reminders to increase vaccination rates. Email reminders asking participants to note down the time and date of vaccination opportunities at on-site clinics significantly increase vaccination rates; however, asking participants to only note down the dates does not. In a related study, Milkman et al. (2013) examine whether intent-to-participate reminders increase colonoscopy screening rates among eligible adults. Email reminders that prompt individuals to plan their colonoscopy significantly increase completion rates for colonoscopies.[5]

While prompts seek to initiate active choices, another important theme in behavioural economics relates to individuals' inertia and inactivity (Thaler and Sunstein 2008). In line with this idea, Chapman et al. (2010) compare the effectiveness of default designs in increasing influenza vaccination rates, specifically by comparing automatically scheduled appointments (an 'opt-out' design) to interventions informing individuals about free vaccination possibilities and vaccination benefits (an 'opt-in' design). The study finds that the opt-out design significantly increases vaccination rates, suggesting that defaults and automatisms are more powerful nudges than reminders or other opt-in measures.

Complementary to the work on increasing patients' inclination to arrange a (new) check-up appointment discussed above, numerous studies examine means to increase attendance rates for scheduled appointments. Missed appointments constitute a major problem in modern health systems, as the underutilisation of new (expensive) technical equipment and medical teams is costly and implies an unnecessary delay for those on the waiting line. One study which tries to tackle this problem is Bos et al. (2005), who look at the effectiveness of reminders in this context by investigating attendance rates at a Dutch orthodontist. In an RCT, reminders do not significantly increase attendance rates, nor does the type of reminder being used. In more recent work on reminders, Hallsworth et al. (2015) test different SMS messages sent five days in advance of a hospital appointment on keeping this appointment in the UK. Relative to a default text that reminds patients about the date and time of the appointment, a social norms message ('9 out of 10 people attend') hardly lowers the number of missed appointments. However, an SMS that stresses the costs for the health sector ('Not attending costs NHS £160 approx.') proves effective and reduces the number of missed appointments by roughly 25 per cent.

Overall, these (and many similar) studies indicate that reminders, especially in combination with deadlines or planning prompts, can be a very cost-effective way (a) to stimulate the take-up of preventive health measures and (b) to reduce no-show rates. However, not every simple reminder achieves the objective, and it is crucial to trial what works before rolling out a policy or programme. While automated (digital) reminder systems have spread among many private and public actors from health sectors across countries, public sector regulators are slow in picking up on this trend. In many OECD countries, we still observe a vast array of regulatory approaches that aim at encouraging preventive health via (relatively weak) economic incentives rather than, for example, via enforcing mandatory reminder systems.

Medication adherence

Another hot-spot for behavioural health studies is problematically low medication adherence. Non-adherence implies incredibly large costs, with estimates for annual costs ranging from US$1 billion (Europe) to US$300 billion (the US) (Cutler et al. 2018). While researchers have tested a rich set of behavioural interventions focusing on increasing medication compliance, the evidence is slightly convoluted (partially due to the widespread use of compound treatments that bundle multiple behavioural ideas in one intervention), and the results on what works are rather mixed.

A first, relatively powerful approach to increase medical adherence builds on a trivial but important behavioural strategy: keep it simple! Patel et al. (2015) examine the effect of using fixed dose combinations of generic drugs (polypills) rather than separate medications (with different doses). Relying on self-reported medication adherence among Australian patients at high risk for cardiovascular disease, the authors find that the polypill simplification significantly increases adherence. (For a comprehensive survey on simplification effects, see Schedlbauer et al. 2010).)

Next, let us consider the scope for reminders. A promising result is reported in Dai, Mao, Volpp et al. (2017), who explore the impact of monthly reminder mailings on medication adherence during and after a three-month treatment period. In their RCT, interactive reminder messages (which for example prompted patients to commit to a self-determined adherence level) significantly increased adherence, measured as prescription refills, during as well as after the mailing period. Dai, Mao, Riis et al. (2017) further examine whether one could increase the impact of mailed reminders by sending them close to potential 'fresh-start' dates, in particular, birthdays or New Year's Day. This idea is motivated by a vast body of research documenting that humans use such life and calendar events to restart with healthy activities (see e.g. Cherchye et al. 2017). The results of their trial indicate, however, that referencing these events and sending reminders close to a fresh-start date do not increase medication adherence (relative to a control group with differently timed, basic reminders that would encourage patients to take their cholesterol, diabetes, or blood pressure medications).

One study that documents an increased reminder efficacy is Reddy et al. (2017), who investigate how (daily) reminders paired with (weekly) adherence feedback reports affect medication adherence. The study finds a significantly positive effect during the three-month intervention period. Three months later, however, these effects vanished, indicating that no habituation occurred. Interaction effects of reminders and economic incentives are rather mixed. Kimmel et al. (2016) document that pairing reminders with lottery incentives improves measured adherence. In contrast, Volpp et al. (2017) obtain a null result from an intervention that combines reminders with financial incentives or social support (considering both adherence and hospital readmissions as outcomes).[6]

Another strand of evaluations builds on the combination of reminders with newly available technologies (some of which are introduced in Gauld,

Chapter 10 of this Report). An earlier review that highlights the scope for automated, electronic interventions is Cutrona et al. (2010), who survey the effectiveness of different modes of delivering an intervention to improve adherence (to medications for cardiovascular disease or diabetes).[7] One important recent development is wireless-enabled or smart pill bottles, which allow for real-time monitoring of medication adherence. Working with such pill bottles, Reese et al. (2017) test different reminder interventions to increase immuno-suppression medication among kidney-transplant recipients. They find a significantly positive effect. Chan et al. (2015) examine the effect of using inhalers with audiovisual reminders on medication adherence in children in Auckland, New Zealand. Audiovisual reminders significantly increased use of preventive medication, improved morbidity scores, and decreased the number of school days missed. Kessler et al. (2018) investigate the effect of automated alerts and social support (via an individually elected 'medication adherence partner') on medication adherence rates. Feedback alerts, such as text messages or automated phone calls to patients that failed to take medication during the last two days, significantly increased medication adherence. Adding social support to the alert reminders, however, had no additional effect.

Overall, the evidence suggests that simplification of dosage schedules, reminders as well as automated, technology-enhanced feedback systems increase medication adherence. However, one should note that several studies document null results, in particular, regarding reminder effects.[8] Unfortunately, this mirrors null and mixed results obtained for other policy approaches in this domain.[9] The policy conclusions here seem to be twofold. On the one hand, to improve our understanding of what works in which context and which population, one should support further systematic testing of electronic prompting systems. On the other hand, one should not omit old-fashioned economic ideas: Priebe et al. (2016), for instance, assess whether financial incentives improve adherence to anti-psychotic medication among adults. Financial incentives significantly increased long-term anti-psychotic injectable medication for the duration of treatment, but these effects ceased after interventions stopped. Choudhry et al. (2011), who investigate the cost side of medication adherence, find that eliminating medication co-payments significantly increases adherence. Traditional economic motives are clearly an important driver of behaviour in this domain, and the behavioural turn does not imply that health governance should neglect the role of basic economic incentives.

Health insurance plans

The choice of health insurance plans has become one of the core areas of behavioural economic analysis informing health policy design.[10] Empirical research documents a vast gap between rational and human choices in these markets, where consumers have to choose among complex insurance schemes. Many patients make errors in active choices (i.e. they pick financially dominated insurance plans) and remain overly passive (i.e. they do not respond when changes in market and/or their own health conditions should lead them to switch insurance plans). In contrast to a rich body of evidence documenting these patterns, there is relatively little evidence on policy interventions that would improve outcomes (see e.g. Abaluck and Gruber 2016b; Bhargava et al. 2017).

Ericson and Starc (2016) study a health plan standardisation that was paired with improved, web-based information provision for consumers on the Massachusetts Health Insurance Exchange in the US. The reform has had a positive impact on patients' health insurance plan choices. A further case that highlights the stark contrast between behaviourally informed and traditional economic policy approaches is the work by Abaluck and Gruber (2016a), who investigate nudges that help patients to choose 'better' health insurance plans. Their results show that limiting choice sets (in particular, excluding the most disadvantageous health insurance plans) increases the quality of consumer choice. Hence, having fewer choices might be beneficial to consumers.

While these are prominent cases of behaviourally informed interventions on the US private health insurance market, it is important to stress that the welfare implications from nudges that aim at reducing frictions and consumer inertia may not necessarily be positive. Market responses, in particular, adverse section effects,[11] might make a well-intended nudge backfire (Handel 2013; Handel et al. 2019).

Behavioural Insights Applied to Healthcare/ Service Providers

Turning from the demand for health services to its supply, one encounters a smaller and slightly more segmented field of work. Recently, however, this area gained momentum, and many exciting new projects are on the way. Here only published studies are considered.

Default nudges and behavioural change of medical staff

Default rules constitute the most forceful nudge (in terms of steering behaviour). Within the health sector, the power of defaults is best known (and controversially discussed) in the context of organ donations (Johnson and Goldstein 2003). However, there seems to be plenty of scope to apply defaults to clinicians or medical staff. A neat illustration is provided by a study by Lehmann et al. (2016), who test an automatic enrolment design to increase vaccination rates among healthcare personnel. The control group faced an opt-in situation: they received a message prompting them to make an appointment for vaccination. The treatment group received a very similar message, but in an opt-out framing: healthcare workers had to cancel (or change) an automatically scheduled appointment. Among the latter group, appointments and thus vaccination rates almost doubled.

Patel, Day et al. (2016) assess the effect of nudging physicians towards prescribing generic alternatives for brand medications by offering brand medication as an option, not as the default. Exploring a health system-wide reform of prescription defaults in Pennsylvania, they document a massive impact of the default settings on the prescription rates for generic drugs. Unsurprisingly, prescription rates of generics remained persistently higher, even 2.5 years after the implementation of the new default (Olshan et al. 2019).[12] Default supply amounts on prescriptions, however, had mixed effects on prescribed quantities. Delgado et al. (2018) find that, although the total number of opioids prescribed did not decline during the experiment period, a higher proportion of prescriptions used the default supply amount. Their findings suggest that medical professionals tend to use defaults and that, when setting default quantities, the lowest amount should be the baseline.

Active choices and preventive health offers

Another strand of work tests behaviour strategies that target medical staff and clinicians to alter the way different health services are offered. Kim et al. (2018) examine a so-called active choice intervention. Rather than focusing on default settings, the idea behind such approaches is to 'force' individuals (in this case, physicians and medical assistants) to actively make a decision. More specifically, the intervention they examine prompts medical assistants to ask patients during check-in about influenza vaccination, while clinicians that subsequently see the patients receive vaccination order templates to apply during visits. The RCT results indicate that the intervention significantly increased vaccination rates. This finding is also consistent with observational studies (e.g. Patel et al. 2017). Patel, Volpp et al. (2016) test similar active choice interventions that aim at increasing orders for colonoscopy and mammography screenings among eligible patients. The prompt for medical professionals to accept or decline an order significantly increases orders and leads to higher completion rates for colonoscopies but not for mammography screenings.

Social norms messages and antibiotic prescriptions

One focus of behavioural interventions that gained a lot of attention concerns the question how to change high rates of antibiotic prescriptions, which contribute to the growing threat of antimicrobial resistance (see Besnier and Eikemo, Chapter 2, and Kickbusch and Liu, Chapter 5, in this Report for more on this challenge). In a high-profile study conducted by BIT, Hallsworth, Chadborn et al. (2016) test a mailing intervention among 1,581 British general practitioners (GPs) with high antibiotics prescribing rates (the top 20 per cent of their respective NHS Local Area Team). The mailing included, in addition to three simple, actionable steps to reduce antibiotics prescription, a social norms message: 'The great majority (80%) of practices in London prescribe fewer antibiotics per head than yours.' In contrast to a patient-focused intervention, the social norm mailings sent to GPs induced a significant drop in the rate of antibiotic items dispensed.[13]

Wickström Östervall (2017) investigates how reminders sent to thirty-one primary care facilities in Stockholm influence antibiotics prescribing during the flu season. Reminder nudges significantly decreased antibiotics use. Elango et al. (2018) document that clinicians' readiness to change affects the implementation of an intervention aimed at reducing unnecessary antibiotics prescribing. While these results are fairly promising, the persistence of the effects from this type of interventions remains unclear (e.g. Linder et al. 2017).

Hygiene behaviour

One objective of behavioural interventions concerns hygiene behaviour, in particular, washing one's hands, a key strategy to prevent healthcare-associated infections, which is often neglected in the context of a highly demanding and stressful workplace. Dai et al. (2015), for instance, document that compliance with hygiene protocols drops significantly during a typical twelve-hour working shift. This pattern is exacerbated by increased work load and mitigated by prolonged breaks.

While behavioural studies have explored interventions ranging from simple reminder messages (Grant and Hofmann 2011) to subtle 'olfactory priming' (for example, via a clean, citrus smell; see King et al. 2016), convincing evidence on successful nudge interventions is still scarce (Caris et al. 2018).[14] Neither the World Health Organization guidelines on hand hygiene in healthcare (see Section 18 in WHO 2009) nor a recent review (Gould et al. 2017) provide a clear picture of what works. There seems to be plenty of scope for more testing to identify how context matters for the success of an intervention. Policy-makers would be well advised to encourage more systematic trialling in this domain.

Intrinsic motivation and work norms

Another important theme from behavioural economics–the role of non-monetary incentives–naturally links up with the norms and values governing physicians' treatment decisions.[15] Kesternich et al. (2015) conduct a controlled experiment with prospective physicians and document how norms in the Hippocratic tradition shape behaviour. It thus seems natural to explore non-monetary policy tools that rely on these norms, or intrinsic motives more generally, to motivate physicians. An excellent example along these lines is studied by Kolstad (2013), who shows that information provided on quality 'report cards' exerts positive effects on the overall performance of cardiac surgeons in Pennsylvania. The report cards allow the disentangling of whether mortality rates are related to a surgeon's quality or to the underlying risks among the relevant patient population. The author exploits the fact that quality reports trigger changes in both extrinsic and intrinsic motivation, while patients' demand remained constant. The findings suggest that extrinsic financial incentives have only small positive effects. Kolstad argues that quality improvements are mainly due to social comparison effects, linked to changes in perceptions about one's own quality relative to the quality of a surgeon's peers.

Behaviourally Informed Health Governance

The previous sections have highlighted several cases of behaviourally informed applications to health problems. Table 8.1 offers an overview of 'what works' based on this brief glimpse at selected (but representative) work from a dynamically growing field, which constantly explores new areas and ideas for interventions. While not every nudge achieves the desired effect, the evidence discussed above makes clear that behavioural insights have significant potential for designing cost-effective policy interventions. In particular in combination with modern digital innovations, such as those introduced by Gauld in Chapter 10 of this Report, there is plenty of scope for using behaviourally smart tools to steer behaviour, on both the supply and the demand side of healthcare. Nudges and other behavioural policy approaches, however, are rarely uncontested and often polarise.[16] In fact, there is a long list of concerns and potential pitfalls to consider.

The most obvious concern relates to the potential abuse of (not-that-libertarian) paternalistic policy instruments. If nudges aim at 'improving decisions about health' (Thaler and Sunstein 2008), who decides what an improvement actually consists of? This concern is particularly relevant due to the less intrusive nature of nudges (as opposed to traditional policy tools), which renders opposition to hidden manipulation of choice more difficult.

Table 8.1 **Selected cases of behaviourally informed applications to health problems**

Target group	Field of application	Type of intervention	Evidence supporting effectiveness
Consumers/ Patients	Preventive health	Reminder/ prompt	Strong
		Default	Weak
		Financial incentive	Weak
		Social norms message	Weak
		Information provision	Mixed
	Medication adherence	Automated reminder	Strong
		Financial incentive	Weak
		Simplification	Weak
		Social support	Weak
		Reminder	Mixed
	Health insurance plans	Simplification	Weak
Healthcare/ Service providers	Behavioural change in medical staff	Default	Strong
	Antibiotics prescribing	Social norms message (peer comparison)	Strong
	Surgeons' performance	Information provision (peer comparison)	Weak
	Preventive health offers	Active choice	Mixed
	Hygiene behaviour	Monitoring	Mixed

Note: 'Weak' means that there is (so far) only little or limited experimental evidence in support of an effect of this type of intervention.

These concerns are well taken and make clear that any large-scale roll-out of nudging in the health sector must be accompanied by high ethical standards and transparency requirements.[17]

Expanding this line of reasoning, the paternalistic and technocratic thrust of many behavioural interventions should be accompanied by policy measures that strengthen individual capabilities. Boosting health literacy via education, information, and deliberation should be seen as a complement rather than a substitute to behavioural policy approaches. Even if these instruments will not mitigate, for example, patients' limitations in cognition, memory, or self-control (for that, one can think about a guiding choice architecture), it seems desirable to have decisions on health outcomes made by well-informed citizens, in particular in quickly ageing democracies.

A less obvious concern relates to what is typically considered a major advantage of nudging: its low cost. Obviously, this feature contributed to the popularity of this approach among policy-makers. However, if politicians and health sector managers become too optimistic about what can be achieved by low-cost interventions, this might result in unwise budgeting decisions. It is thus important to account for political economy pitfalls related to cost-cutting pressure. While a behaviourally smart policy can certainly contribute to lowering public and private health expenditures, expectations should be kept realistic.

There is a further political economy concern related to policy-makers' appetite for nudging: many behavioural innovations seem totally convincing (at least, when judged by the colourful presentations given by many nudging practitioners). So why not implement the idea straight away? As pointed out in the previous sections, not every good idea works in every context. The issue here is external validity, i.e. which context-specific features are important to render an intervention successful in a given set-up. For many domains and applications, the host answer is that we just do not (yet) know. This has a straightforward implication: strengthening the role of behavioural sciences in health governance is not simply achieved by a quick and naive adaptation of things that worked elsewhere. On the contrary, it is imperative to maintain a reasonable balance between testing (and replicating results!) and scaling.

Translated into the language of public policy-makers: while there are plenty of low-hanging fruits related to applying behavioural innovations in the health sector, harvesting these will take some time and requires patience. This also relates to a point rarely discussed in the academic community: dissemination and implementation support. Even if there is high-level policy support to 'test, learn, adapt' and even if there is ample evidence that a tested innovation achieves the desired effect, roll-out and widespread adaptation might nevertheless fail. Resistance to change and opposition to innovation are widespread phenomena, not least in the health sector. Turning innovations into large-scale policy change thus requires further policy support. The successful application of behavioural insights in health governance thus also depends on policy-makers' ability to generate structures of openness and support among the target points of innovation. Creating a culture of innovation requires support for (and also some pressure on) key actors–not only to trial, learn, and innovate, but also to implement new, unconventional instruments that have been tested successfully. This point, however, applies beyond behavioural innovations.

Endnotes

1   It should be stressed that this is, by no means, a trivial exercise. Many parts of the health sector are characterised by features that imply what economists refer to as 'market failure'. The outcome in such markets with, for example, asymmetric information or externalities is in general not efficient, and setting the 'right incentives' is a complicated task. Behavioural considerations further complicate this task (see Chandra et al. 2019).

2   Other influential behavioural science teams include the former Social and Behavioral Sciences Team in the US and BETA, the Behavioural Economics Team of the Australian Government.

3   See the updated references on this webpage: http://www.oecd.org/gov/behav ioural-insights.htm (last accessed 3 April 2019).

4   Neither the set of cases nor the set of topics covered in these sections is exhaustive. For example, the section on patients omits, among others, a vast body of behavioural economics work on healthy lifestyles, dieting, exercising, smoking cessation, and the like.

5   Another study on colonoscopy screening rates by Mehta et al. (2017) assessed the effectiveness of prompting designs and monetary incentives in increasing colonoscopy uptake. The results from this RCT show that (high) financial incentives might be more effective than prompts, but also much more costly to implement. This points to a more general issue: while the nudging literature mainly focuses on 'what works' and, at best, discusses cost-effectiveness (how much 'bang for the buck'), it hardly discusses welfare optimal behavioural interventions.

6   The findings in Volpp et al. (2017) are supported by A.E. Levy et al. (2018), who reviewed recent developments in fostering medication adherence among adults with coronary artery disease. Neither financial incentives nor social pressure significantly increased medication adherence rates in two large RCTs.

7   The authors categorise interventions into person-independent interventions (PII, i.e. mailed, faxed or hand-distributed) or delivered via electronic interface and person-dependent (PDI) interventions (non-automated phone calls, in-person interventions, etc.). Among PII studies, electronic interventions prove most effective; phone-based interventions are least effective. Among PDI studies, pharmacist interventions are the most effective. For further findings compare the more recent survey by Palmer et al. (2018), who review the effectiveness of mobile phone-based feedback interventions.

8   See, for instance, Kenyon et al. (2019), who examine the effectiveness of daily text message reminders on adherence to prescribed asthma medication among children. The intervention did not increase adherence.

9   One body of studies considers, for instance, different types of feedback processes (without explicitly focusing on reminder elements). One promising way to induce behavioural change seems to be providing information to physicians regarding their patients' adherence to prescribed medication. However, the review by Zaugg et al. (2018) finds no evidence that this type of feedback process increases adherence.

10   For a more comprehensive and more formal treatment, see Chandra et al. (2019).

11   Adverse selection refers to situations where demand and supply sides (here: of the insurance market) have different information. Specifically, if individuals choose between different health insurance plans and sort in a cost/risk-based manner across plans, adverse selection can then result in efficiency losses related to (i) individuals choosing the 'wrong' plans, (ii) risk-sharing losses when premium variability rises, and (iii) losses from insurers distorting their policies to improve their mix of insureds. Interventions that target the choices (the sorting) into different plans will, at least potentially, also trigger responses on the supply side, as insurance providers respond, anticipating the impact on the sorting process.

12   Note that these interventions are related to electronic health records (EHR), discussed in Gauld, Chapter 10 in this Report.

13   A successful patient-focused intervention is examined in Gerber et al. (2014). The authors run an RCT at eighteen community-based paediatric primary care practices. Clinicians' education and feedback on prescribing rates significantly reduce broad-spectrum antibiotics prescribing to children, but the effect does not persist.

14   Staats et al. (2017) document the effect from a more traditional monitoring and enforcement intervention that increased compliance with hand hygiene procedures among clinicians. However, this study also points out the risks of monitoring interventions.

15   An excellent survey on the use of economic experiments in behavioural health studies—a strand of work that is underrepresented in this chapter—is provided by Galizzi and Wiesen (2018).

16   It should be noted, however, that public opinion polls often document massive support for nudges. A lot of the polarisation in media and public discourse appears related to conflicting views on policy objectives rather than the instruments of policy (see e.g. Tannenbaum et al. 2017).

17   On this point, see, among many others, the contributions in Cohen et al. (2016).

IX. Innovative Governance and Health Reforms in Europe

ELLEN M. IMMERGUT, ANDRA ROESCU, *and* BJÖRN RÖNNERSTRAND

A paradigm shift in healthcare governance has occurred in Europe since the late twentieth century.[1] In the 1990s, ideas about New Public Management (NPM) and managed competition were highly influential in both western and eastern Europe. NPM proposed that government could be 'reinvented' by making it more like the private sector (Hood 1991; Osborne and Gaebler 1992). This meant abandoning central planning and rigid bureaucratic rules on purchasing and provision of services. Instead, competition amongst service providers and the creation of internal markets would allow better allocation of resources, and thus both higher efficiency and responsiveness. The guiding philosophical principles of NPM can be summarised as: market competition should replace command-and-control governance; market externalities must be internalised to market transactions; micro-purchasing decisions produce macro efficiency; markets should replace hierarchy.

By the mid-2000s, however, a new governance paradigm that placed greater focus on satisfying citizens, good governance, and transparency had started to emerge (Osborne 2006, 2010; Pollitt and Bouckaert 2011).

> *We can speak of a shift from market management to democratic management in healthcare governance.*

Although the nature of this post-NPM paradigm is still the subject of debate, the definition provided by Pollitt and Bouckaert (2011: 22) is very well suited to healthcare governance: 'To modernise the traditional state apparatus so that it becomes more professional, more efficient, and more responsive to citizens'. To be sure, one of the presumed benefits of market mechanisms is the satisfaction of demand, but in practice, NPM mechanisms in healthcare focused more on transactions between administrative purchasers and service providers than on the quality of healthcare and the satisfaction of demand (Bevir and Rhodes 2006). By contrast, the current wave of healthcare reforms shows a clear trend towards codifying patient rights, improving the quality of care, reducing corruption in healthcare, and increasing transparency. Thus, we can speak of a shift from market management to democratic management in healthcare governance.

This shift in governance paradigm is the result of political and administrative learning, as well as a change in the political dynamics of health politics. Debates about NPM–like earlier debates about establishing government healthcare programmes in the first place–were pitched largely in terms of partisan political competition on a left-right axis, and policy outcomes depended highly on whether veto points presented stakeholders with opportunities for blocking reforms. As health systems have matured and political stalemate has been overcome, however, parties have begun to compete on their competence to deliver high quality healthcare, and veto points–and even stakeholders–have become less important. Consequently, as we shall see, public opinion has become a key factor in current health-care politics and governance.

Health Politics and Reform Since the 1990s

Health politics has long been characterised by political conflicts about the balance between state and market in medicine. Calls for 'more government' versus 'more market' have fit the divisions of party politics very neatly and have provided fodder for party competition that can be the basis for appeals to the public in electoral campaigns. The staunch opposition of the Republican Party in the United States to the Affordable Care Act of 2010 (Obamacare) is just one example of this basic cleavage about healthcare financing and provision. In Europe, however, healthcare has increasingly become a 'valence' issue: most people support a strong role for government in health provision, universal health coverage, and high-quality services. Nevertheless, party competition on health issues remains high, and healthcare is a highly salient issue for voters. Consequently, parties must juggle between staking out partisan positions based on their ideological commitments and the pressure to show that their party is most competent to provide high-quality healthcare at a reasonable cost.

This state of affairs is the result of widespread efforts to radically reform healthcare governance using market mechanisms, as well as privatisation of healthcare financing and provision, during the late 1980s and throughout the 1990s in both western and eastern Europe. As this chapter will show, NPM reforms in western Europe were initially highly contested, but over time, market instruments developed greater cross-party support, often because of central-local government relationships and the pressures of voter opinion. In eastern Europe, too, reformers turned to markets–or their idealised beliefs of what a market could be–in order to transform state-run healthcare into more hybrid multipayer and multiprovider institutional complexes. As we will see, however, there are important differences regarding the success with which these transitions were mastered and how the costs of healthcare were divided.

IMMERGUT, ROESCU, *and* RÖNNERSTRAND

Furthermore, although market mechanisms and private provision gained in political acceptability, they also reached limits inherent to the effort to establish genuine markets in healthcare. For unless health provision is ultimately sold to the highest bidder–and withheld from those with no resources–healthcare may be more aptly considered as a 'fictitious' commodity and can never be fully marketised (Polanyi 1944). Consequently, current healthcare governance has turned increasingly to more centralised financial levers and stronger governmental guidelines, coupled with more decentralised decision-making and empowerment of patients, a new paradigm that has alternately been termed New Public Governance (Osborne 2010) or Neo-Weberian Management (Pollitt and Bouckaert 2011).[2]

The New Public Management revolution in Western Europe

New Public Management began both as a political statement and as an administrative approach to public sector management. Reliance on market mechanisms was based on the idea that efficiency gains and better allocation of resources could be achieved by decentralised decision-making on healthcare purchasing. In the United Kingdom, schemes such as the Thatcher government's internal market based on the purchaser-provider split, general practitioner (GP) fundholders, and National Health Service (NHS) trusts relied on micro-efficient purchasing decisions to provide macro-efficiency at the system level and to reinternalise externalities. In addition, market mechanisms were thought to allow much greater diversity in healthcare provision than in a command-and-control management approach (Immergut 2011). For example, if doctors had a fixed budget for purchasing pharmaceuticals, they would be able to decide to purchase very expensive medications for precisely those patients most likely to benefit, rather than following a blanket prescription policy for all. Thus, the internal market was logically connected to the Conservative Party's pro-market ideology.

The idea was that efficiency gains and better resource allocation could be achieved by decentralised decision-making.

Not surprisingly, the Labour Party opposed the internal market, and in the 1997 election campaigned on a promise to '"save" the NHS' (Labour, cited in Gingrich and Greer forthcoming). However, when the Blair government took office, it maintained the purchaser-provider split and many aspects of the internal market, while committing to expand NHS resources. Furthermore, in the event, many of the theoretical ideals of the internal market could not be put into practice because there were not always sufficient providers for market competition, especially for hospital services (Gingrich and Greer forthcoming). Consequently, the partisan divide over managed competition eventually led to a cross-partisan acceptance of a watered-down managed competition approach that ultimately culminated in the abandonment of national control over the health service and to devolution, which provided an opportunity to end the internal market in Scotland and Wales and for an increased focus on quality of care, public health, and patient rights (Gingrich and Greer forthcoming).

Much of the same pattern can be seen in Sweden. Coming into power in 1991 after an eternity in opposition, Swedish conservatives and liberals latched onto NPM as a way to radically renew and trim the Swedish public sector. Laws were passed to allow regional health authorities to contract out health and social services to private providers and to encourage the establishment of private medical practice. Although the Social Democrats objected to this privatisation of medical provision, they themselves had embraced some NPM principles by charging local governments (responsible for nursing care and at-home elder care) a high daily rate for long-term care provided by regional hospitals. By internalising the externalities, this reform changed the cost equation for the municipalities, and as a result they began expanding their nursing and home care services at a rapid pace. Furthermore, at the subnational level, even Social Democratic-governed regions experimented with internal market reforms.

The move to mixed public-private healthcare provision in Sweden culminated in the Primary Care Choice Act, passed in 2009, which required county councils to provide patients with a choice of providers, including private physicians and privately-owned health centres–even though care would be publicly funded. Although criticised by the left-wing parties, this legislation was left intact following changes in government. In addition, the rise of private-patient-only specialist care paid for largely by private supplemental health insurance provided by employers was tolerated by both left and right governments. Thus, the public-private mix in Sweden may be viewed as an example of 'constrained partisanship' in which parties seek to put their own spin on the balance between government and markets, but without seeking to radically change or dismantle the existing healthcare governance structures. Instead, there is increasing emphasis on quality of care and patient rights, which allows political parties across the political spectrum to appeal to voters (Blomqvist and Winblad forthcoming).

In Spain as well, partisan conflicts between left (Spanish Socialist Workers' Party, PSOE) and right (People's Party, PP) over managed competition and public-private partnerships in the 1990s eventually gave way to a compromise position based on allowing the autonomous communities to experiment at the regional level (Chuliá forthcoming).

The British, Swedish, and Spanish reforms of the 1990s took place in a context of tax-funded national health services and entailed mainly increased scope for private provision and market mechanisms, although there has also been some increase in private payment. In several continental systems, there has been more focus on private insurance financing. In the

Netherlands, for example, the 2005 health reform resolved decades of stalemate regarding public versus private insurance. With income levels set such that about one-third of the population was privately insured and with lax regulation of private insurance rate hikes, the private sector had long been viewed as driving up the costs of both public and private health insurance in the Netherlands. After many years of efforts to use corporatist negotiations to reduce costs in the public system, the influential 1987 Dekker report proposed a merger between the public and private insurance systems and application of NPM principles by fostering greater competition amongst insurance carriers.

Attitudes towards this merger were divided along partisan lines. While the liberal People's Party for Freedom and Democracy (VVD) preferred the transfer of health insurance to the private sector, the social democratic Labour Party (PvdA) fought for public insurance and significant protection of patients and providers against rising healthcare costs. The fall from government of the pivotal Christian Democratic Appeal (CDA) and electoral victory for the liberal VVD proved a turning point, as the CDA rethought its social market position in health insurance and the VVD was in a key position to press for a private insurance solution. This broke the decades-long logjam of partisan and stakeholder conflicts on the direction of Dutch healthcare reform. The 2005 health reform merged social health insurance carriers with private insurance companies to establish a mandated private health insurance system, financed both by taxes and privately paid premiums. Strong regulations on pre-existing conditions and benefits, as well as subsidies for low-income persons, ensured health security. As in the countries with national health services, after the passage of this large-scale structural reform, Dutch health politics has settled back into valence politics, based on corporatist management of costs through budget agreements, but also a focus on quality of care and patient rights (Anderson and van Druenen forthcoming).

Switzerland's health system has been significantly shaped by the many veto points in its political system, and in particular the ability of opponents to block legislation via popular referenda. Throughout the twentieth century, referendum vetoes blocked the introduction of compulsory health insurance, and even the threat of veto was sufficient to block major expansions of public health provision. Consequently, the Swiss healthcare system developed with relatively low public financing and high levels of private insurance financing–quite similar to the US. Nevertheless, in the 1990s popular initiatives were used to put the issue of compulsory health insurance back on the agenda, which this time resulted in a compromise between left and right on compulsory mandated private insurance (Immergut 1992; Rüefli forthcoming).

In France and Ireland, as well, the relationship between private voluntary health insurance and public health coverage has been on the agenda.

French policy has been to subsidise private voluntary insurance for low-income persons so as to reduce their out-of-pocket costs. Although left and right parties disagreed on whether costs should be constrained through increased user charges or caps on medical prices, the historical roots of voluntary health insurance in the French mutual societies allowed for cross-party approval for this expansion. At the same time, top-down budget constraints have been promoted by a technocratic elite that cuts across party lines (Brunn and Hassenteufel forthcoming). In Ireland, high out-of-pocket charges have been moderated by voluntary health insurance coverage and the gradual introduction of free access to tax-financed medical care for the young and the elderly (Devitt forthcoming).

All in all whether regarding private provision or payment, the party and stakeholder conflicts about healthcare governance of the 1990s have since been toned down, and the focus has shifted to the provision of high quality services and citizen satisfaction.

Conflicts about health-care governance of the 1990s have been toned down, the focus shifting to citizen satisfaction.

One partial exception may be Germany, where left-right conflicts about the merger of public and private insurance into a citizens' insurance (the left's position) versus converting the statutory health insurance system into premium-based individual health insurance policies (the liberal-conservative position) was abandoned when an electoral impasse led to the formation of a grand coalition government in 2005. This government introduced a compromise structural reform that pooled social health insurance contributions and allocated them to the statutory sickness insurance funds based on risk-weighted formulas. But the issue of public versus private medicine has not been laid to rest and continues to flare up periodically. At the same time, however, there is evidence of an increasing focus on valence aspects of healthcare provision, such as patient rights, waiting time guarantees, quality, and anti-corruption measures (Immergut and Wendt forthcoming).

Privatising state-run systems

In Eastern Europe, the transition to capitalism and democracy brought with it a drive to replace state-run communist era health services with social health insurance, private medical practice, and, in some countries, private hospitals. In contrast to many western European cases, in which veto points were activated to block the expansion of public health insurance and state regulation of private providers, in some eastern European transition scenarios, veto points have played the opposite role, as they have sometimes been deployed to stop privatisation rather than the introduction of government programmes.

The Czech Republic is a case in point. With anti-communist reformers convinced that social health insurance as well as private medical provision were the keys to reform, social health insurance was introduced in 1991, with provisions that encouraged ample scope for competition amongst insurance carriers, medical practitioners, and hospitals, with fee-for-service payment as an incentive system for doctors. In practice, however, this initial smooth sailing on enactment of a full-scale health reform foundered on financial problems created by a spiralling supply of health services related to privatisation and fee-for-service payment methods, as well as cutthroat competition amongst insurance carriers that mitigated against risk-sharing. Consequently, subsequent reforms introduced measures to stabilise the situation through regulation of insurance competition and replacement of open-ended fee-for-service payment with preferred-provider schemes, as well as changes to hospital payments and salaries.

Political disputes over plans to stabilise health insurance finances by increasing user fees and later about the conversion of hospitals into joint stock companies spanned many changes in Czech government and, as in Western Europe, were characterised by left-right partisan positions. In the end, however, the Constitutional Court blocked a large increase in hospital fees, which the Social Democratic Sobotka government seized as an opportunity to eliminate user fees altogether. Consequently, the Czech Republic came through the transition period with a highly universal system based on social insurance, after a political learning process on the need for market regulation. Nevertheless, there is substantial debt in the healthcare system, and owing to increases in uncovered pharmaceutical charges, out-of-pocket payments and unmet need amongst lower income groups are on the increase (Popic forthcoming a).

In contrast to the pattern in other transition counties, Slovenia had maintained the social health insurance that had been introduced while it was part of the Habsburg empire. In lieu of adopting the Soviet single-payer *Semashko* model, Communist Party leaders gradually expanded coverage throughout the post-World War II period. Consequently, there was no need to introduce social health insurance or to break away from a centralised state-planning model. Instead, the first post-communist DEMOS coalition government confirmed the compulsory contributory system, which was to be governed by elected boards and financed by payroll contributions. This government introduced user fees and co-payments and provided for the opening of the primary care sector to private practitioners, but under restrictive conditions.

On top of the compulsory contributory system, a subsequent social liberal (Liberal Democracy of Slovenia, LDS) government established voluntary complementary health insurance paid by a flat-rate, community-based premium with a risk-equalisation scheme. Although controversial, as the premiums are not dependent upon income and the insurance is private, the long period of stable LDS government and the high take-up rate of voluntary insurance (80 per cent of the Slovenian population is covered), as well as the solid support of trade unions for the complementary scheme, blocked efforts by left-wing parties to merge private voluntary insurance with the compulsory health insurance scheme. Thus, rapid decisions at the transition, subsequent stable governments, and corporatist social partnership arrangements resulted in one of the more successful post-communist health systems that enjoys relatively low unmet need and low levels of out-of-pocket payments (Popic forthcoming b).

In Estonia, as well, decision-making on the post-transition health system went relatively quickly and produced a largely universal social health insurance system, albeit a more state-centred one. In the early transition, policy ideas quickly coalesced on the German social insurance system as a model. Even though there were some disagreements, the transition government introduced a decentralised compulsory health insurance system based on payroll contributions set at a high level (13 per cent), legalised private medical practice, and revoked the civil service status of hospital employees so that they could be employed under private contracts. As in the Czech Republic, there was a conviction that health institutions should be private and regulated by private law. Over time, however, steps were taken to centralise the social health insurance system and to increase national planning powers. At the same time, legislation such as that allowing families to choose their GP aimed to reduce over-dependence on hospital care, a typical legacy of the Soviet *Semashko* era.

Debates about the initial introduction of social health insurance as well as reoccurring issues such as user fees and the status of voluntary health insurance were not politicised or a focus of party politics in Estonia. Relative political stability and the lack of a left-right political cleavage favoured a more technocratic approach to health politics and an emphasis on central steering, which together have resulted in relatively low cost and distance barriers to healthcare access (though in recent years waiting times have dramatically increased as a result of austerity measures). Furthermore, Estonia has neither taken the Czech route of prohibiting user fees, nor adopted Slovenia's focus on voluntary health insurance to share the costs of user fees. As a result, the percentage of out-of-pocket financing of the healthcare system remains high. Nevertheless, Estonia has the third highest level of public financing in eastern Europe (following the Czech Republic and Slovakia), and its record on healthcare outcomes and public satisfaction with the health system is very positive when compared to the other Baltic countries (Ainsaar et al. forthcoming).

In these three transition countries, largely universal coverage could be established through social health insurance, even though there are important differences remaining in the generosity of financing and the weight of user fees. In several other transition countries, the social insurance sector was never fully institutionalised and was slowly brought back under central state control. In Latvia, for example, efforts to expand voluntary health insurance failed completely, and social health insurance was slowly re-incorporated into central state budgets, while health provision remained entrenched in local bureaucracies. With insufficient tax funding, however, ever larger proportions of healthcare costs have been financed by out-of-pocket payments. As politics tends to revolve around nationalism and anti-corruption issues, better coverage for healthcare has not been an election issue (Eihmanis forthcoming). Similarly, in Bulgaria, out-of-pocket payments are used to compensate for the lack of tax revenues and voluntary insurance. Here, too, the transition to social health insurance was never completed, and tax financing remained insufficient and ineffective. High levels of corruption make the situation even worse. In contrast to Estonia and Latvia, there is a left-right cleavage in party politics in Bulgaria, which might have led to pressure for better healthcare coverage, but in the event, unstable governments led to delayed and incoherent healthcare reforms (Stolarova-Demuth forthcoming).

The Public-Private Mix in Health

As a result of the NPM reform efforts of the 1990s and early 2000s, many health systems experienced rather large transformations in their financial governance structures. As shown in Figure 9.1, most European countries experienced an increase in privately financed health-care, with eastern European countries undergoing a large and abrupt shift from largely state-based to significant private financing. By contrast, the few countries that experienced an increase in the proportion of financing classified by the Organisation for Economic Co-operation and Development (OECD) as 'public' are–with the exception of the US–in western Europe. Large shifts occurred in the Netherlands and Switzerland (as well as the US) through the introduction of mandated health insurance provided by private insurance carriers. These reforms increased compulsory health insurance coverage and included provisions for regulation of benefits and coverage, as well as tax subsidies for low-income earners. As compulsory contributory insurance is classed by the OECD as 'public' these shifts appear in Figure 9.1 as increases in public financing for Switzerland, the Netherlands, and the US, although one could argue that mandating represents a hybrid model between public and private.[3]

A higher public sector share of expenditures has been associated with lower total healthcare costs and a greater ability for governments to allocate health resources (Béland and Gran 2008; Wendt 2015). However, for health security, the proportion of individual out-of-pocket payments in total health spending is arguably more important than the proportion of private payments. As Figure 9.2 shows, most European healthcare systems

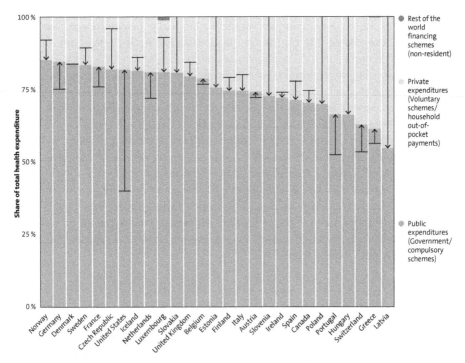

Figure 9.1 **Public and private medical expenditure, 2016, with 1989 as reference**

Source: OECD (2018b)

Notes: The marker lines represent the share of government/compulsory schemes in 1989 (France: 1990; Belgium: 1995). The arrows illustrate the difference between 1989 and 2016.

are financed with larger proportions of out-of-pocket payments than even in the US–with Greece, Hungary, Latvia, Lithuania, Portugal, and Switzerland all at above 25 per cent. One should not forget, however, that this proportion does not indicate how high a burden out-of-pocket payments place on individuals; it is simply a measure of the proportion of total health expenditures financed by out-of-pocket payments. Further, the impact of the out-of-pocket share on health inequality depends upon other factors, such as per capita income. A high level of out-of-pocket payments can be more easily shouldered in high-income Switzerland, where it is also a result of individuals' increasing preference for managed competition health insurance policies with lower premiums and correspondingly higher deductibles. Thus, Switzerland is an exception amongst the countries with a high share of out-of-pocket payments. In most other cases, the proportion of out-of-pocket payments is a good first indicator of the prevalence of health insecurity.

Both compulsory contributory and private voluntary health insurance can be used to reduce out-of-pocket payments. As discussed above, policy

IMMERGUT, ROESCU, *and* RÖNNERSTRAND

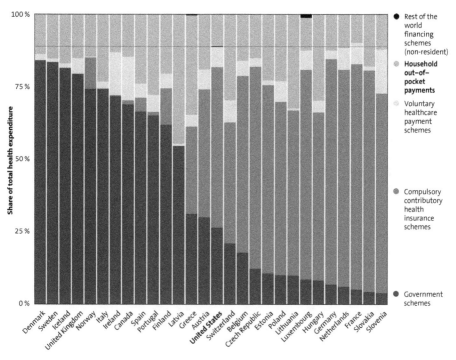

Figure 9.2 **Financing sources of healthcare expenditures in selected OECD countries, 2016**

Source: OECD (2018b)

Note: The dotted line represents the share of US out-of-pocket payments as a benchmark.

decisions were made to expand private voluntary health insurance coverage in France and Slovenia, and to eliminate user fees for children and elderly persons in Ireland. In addition, the take-up rate of private insurance in Ireland is high. As we can see from Figure 9.2, all three countries have lower levels of out-of-pocket payment and substantial levels of private voluntary health insurance. Thus, private health insurance can be effective in reducing the proportion of expenditures left to out-of-pocket payments.

By contrast, many eastern and southern European health systems do not cover this gap through either tax-based services, mandatory insurance, or voluntary insurance coverage. Consequently, a higher proportion of healthcare expenditures is financed by out-of-pocket payments. If one estimates the impact of informal payments (bribes) as part of the total cost, the individual risk burden is even higher (Ensor 2004). This is an area of concern, as out-of-pocket payment has been linked to higher levels of subjective unmet medical need, and in particular to levels of income inequality in subjective unmet need (Kaminska and Wulfgramm 2018; Fjær et al. 2017; Schneider et al. forthcoming; Schokkaert et al. 2017; Allin and Masseria 2009). Indeed, as Figure 9.3 shows, respondents in Italy, Latvia, Romania, and Greece all report rates of unmet need owing to costs at near or above 5 per cent.

Furthermore, Figure 9.4 indicates a positive relationship between out-of-pocket payment and cost-based unmet need–although of course this is only a bivariate plot. There are, however, some puzzling outliers. In Lithuania and Hungary, respondents report much lower levels of unmet need than one would predict based on their high out-of-pocket costs. (This is also the case in Switzerland, which has already been discussed as a rich outlier.) Health experts in both Hungary and Lithuania consider the high levels of out-of-pocket payment to be a barrier to access to the health system (Földes forthcoming; Murauskiene forthcoming). But those surveyed seem to accept this state of affairs. At the same time, there are countries such as Italy and (especially) Greece, in which respondents report higher levels of unmet need than one would predict from their high levels of out-of-pocket financing. This may be related to the distribution of out-of-pocket costs across

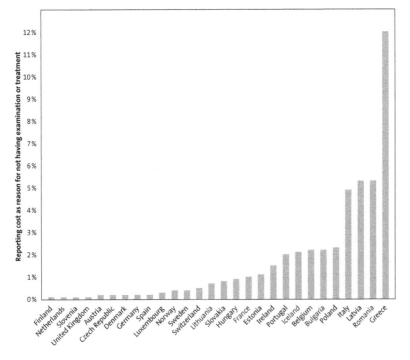

Figure 9.3 **Unmet need due to cost, 2016**

Source: Eurostat (2019) [hlth_silc_14]

Notes: Survey question: 'What was the main reason for not having a medical examination or treatment?' Graph displays per cent of respondents (as calculated and provided directly by EUROSTAT) answering 'Could not afford to (too expensive).' The data for hlth_silc_14 were downloaded using the Stata package EUROSTATUSE.

IMMERGUT, ROESCU, *and* RÖNNERSTRAND

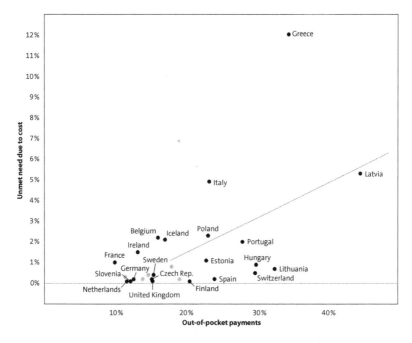

Figure 9.4 **Unmet need due to cost versus out-of-pocket payments, 2016**
Source: Eurostat (2019) and OECD (2018b)

individuals, such that even with a similar proportion of health costs paid by out-of-pocket payments at the system level, individuals may be more highly burdened in systems where the costs are unevenly distributed. For example, in the US, the proportion of out-of-pocket financing is comparatively low, but individuals may face extremely high access barriers based on their individual health insurance situation.

Valence Politics and New Public Governance of Healthcare

As we saw, over time, partisan political conflicts regarding the public–private mix in health became more moderate, as politicians, policy-makers, and healthcare stakeholders gained experience with NPM. Left parties began to accept some aspects of market competition, while centre-right and liberal parties accepted a clear role for government in health. Consequently, by the mid-2000s, politicians and policy-makers increasingly began to emphasise patients' freedom of choice, patient rights, quality of services, and transparency. This new focus on citizens cut across the left-right divide in many party systems and allowed centre-right parties to compete on healthcare issues. Thus, we can speak of a turn to valence politics in the healthcare field. Parties increasingly compete on their ability to deliver excellent healthcare, rather than on the positional issue of whether health financing and delivery should be public or private. Of course the public-private issue has not been eliminated entirely; yet, it is much less central today than it was in the 1990s, a decade in which nearly all health systems in Europe experimented with market reforms.

Improving patient rights

One key valence issue is the surge of interest in patient rights. This development can be observed in both eastern and western Europe, as shown in Table 9.1. Since 1990, there have been a total of sixty-six legislated patient rights reforms amongst the twenty-seven countries covered, or an average of 2.8 per country. The average number of reforms in western Europe was 2.8 per country, while in eastern Europe it was 1.9 for this period.

These reforms covered a range of issues. First, patients' right to information about their health status and treatment, their personal health records, and their ability to make choices about their treatment have been adopted in various laws and charters in most European countries. A second aspect of patient rights is the introduction of formal complaint procedures and ombudsmen to act as conduits for receiving complaints and representing patients. Third, a number of governments have introduced waiting time guarantees for outpatient and hospital services.

In Denmark, for example, waiting time guarantees come with the proviso that should timely hospital treatment not be provided by the local regional authority, patients will have access to more distant public hospitals, and even in some cases to for-profit providers (Vrangbæk forthcoming). In this way, the issue of patient rights has been linked to increased patient choice in some health systems. Increased choice generally started with the option of choosing outpatient or inpatient providers from different regions, but is increasingly including private and for-profit providers–an issue that caused the incumbent Finnish government to lose the 2019 election, which was seen as a referendum on the choice issue (Koivusalo et al. forthcoming). Thus choice is linked to the older debates about public and private, but is now much more framed as increased freedom or choice as opposed to less state or more markets.

A number of patient rights reforms go beyond valence issues and edge into the area of morality issues, and may therefore be more controversial. Rights for the mentally ill or the right to palliative care for the dying are broadly supported, but other rights, such as coverage for in vitro fertilisation or, especially, euthanasia can be highly conflictual. In Luxembourg,

Table 9.1 **Patient rights in Europe**

Country	Reforms extending patient rights	Year(s) of passage
Western Europe		
Austria	1	2006
Belgium	2	1990, 2002
Denmark	8	1993, 1998, 1999, 2002, 2005, 2010, 2012, 2014, 2016, 2016 (reform reversed)
England	2	1991, 2009
Finland	2	1992, 2004
France	1	1996
Germany	1	2015
Italy	2	1995, 2010
Luxembourg	3	2009 (2), 2014
Netherlands	3	1996, 2013, 2015
Norway	8	1990, 1996, 1999 (3), 2014 (2), 2015
Portugal	4	2008 (2), 2009, 2014
Scotland	2	2003, 2011
Sweden	5	1991, 2005, 2010, 2011, 2014
Switzerland	0	
Wales	1	2011
Eastern Europe		
Albania	0	
Bulgaria	1	2009
Czech Republic	2	2011 (2)
Estonia	0	
Hungary	1	1997, 2006, 2010 (reform reversed)
Latvia	3	1997 (2), 2009
Lithuania	8	1994, 1995, 1996 (2), 1997, 2004, 2009, 2017
Poland	1	2008
Romania	1	2003
Slovakia	1	2004
Slovenia	2	2003, 2008

Source: Immergut et al. (forthcoming)

Note: Each reform counts as +1, except for reversed reforms abolishing patient rights which count as −1.

for example, the Law on Euthanasia required a constitutional change for passage, as the Grand Duke refused to authorise the law, but only to sign it (Leist forthcoming).

Fighting corruption in health

A second valence issue that is currently receiving increasing attention is corruption. In Sweden, to name just one example, opposition Member of Parliament Margareta Larsson challenged Social Democratic Party Minister for Health and Social Affairs Annika Strandhäll with a parliamentary question about institutional corruption in the pharmaceutical industry shortly before the 2018 election.[4] Even though the Social Democratic Party traditionally 'owns' the healthcare issue in Sweden's left-right competition, corruption has allowed the opposition to shift party politics into valence mode and to compete on an even playing field.

Corruption in healthcare is increasingly recognised as a significant

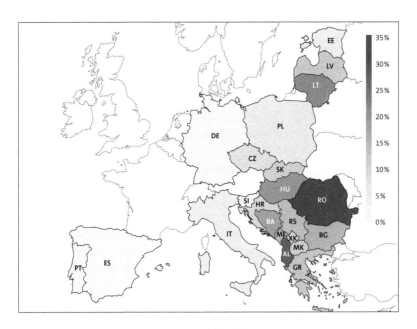

Figure 9.5 **Bribery in selected European health systems, 2016**
Source: Transparency International (2016)
Notes: Survey question: 'Have you or another member of your household paid a bribe to any one of eight public services in the past 12 months?' One of the eight services was 'Public health system'. Base: People that came into contact with the public health system, excluding missing responses. No data were available for countries without shading.

IMMERGUT, ROESCU, *and* RÖNNERSTRAND

threat to healthcare systems. Losses due to corruption within health systems are estimated to comprise more than 7 per cent of healthcare expenditures globally (Bruckner 2019). Even in Europe, corruption is a significant problem. As Figure 9.5 shows, the payment of bribes for healthcare service delivery is a severe problem in many eastern Europe countries (darker shading) and to some extent in southern Europe. Throughout both eastern and western Europe, large-scale scandals regarding improper billing, procurement, and pharmaceutical prescriptions are receiving increasing public attention (Day 2018; Jain et al. 2014).

Generally speaking, corruption is defined as the use of public positions for personal gain. Healthcare systems are viewed as being particularly vulnerable to this aspect of poor governance, as healthcare transactions create opportunities for abuse and opportunistic behaviour (Holmberg and Rothstein 2011; Savedoff 2011; Savedoff and Hussmann 2006; Vian 2008). One factor often highlighted is asymmetric information. More specifically, the funders of medical services, such as public agencies, insurance companies, or the patients themselves, cannot know for sure if the treatment suggested by physicians or other health professionals is motivated by medical considerations or a desire for private benefits (Holmberg and Rothstein 2011; Savedoff and Hussmann 2006). The existence of an influential market of vendors and pharmaceutical firms creates a risk of bribery, and the discretion that health professionals have in deciding what medicines are needed, and in what quantities, increases the opportunity for abuse. For instance, an older study of corruption in the Bulgarian pharmaceutical procurement process (Meagher 2006) pinpointed the procedures for getting drugs placed on the positive list of approved prescription drugs for social health insurance reimbursement and the procurement patterns of hospitals as weak points in the system. Comparison of Bulgaria's positive list with World Health Organization lists and those of neighbouring countries showed an overabundance of newer, more expensive drugs and the absence of some older, less expensive drugs. Hospital purchasing decisions were marred by faulty bidding procedures for procurement such as the manner of ranking of bids, discretionary exemptions for documentation requirements, and post hoc price adjustments, as well as practices such as providing free samples of pharmaceuticals to get the bid (Meagher 2006).

Corruption and poor governance have been shown to negatively impact public health campaigns against antibiotic resistance and antibiotic misuse (Collignon et al. 2015; Rönnerstrand and Lapuente 2017). There are several possible causal pathways connecting corruption to antibiotic abuse. First, corruption may erode the implementation of treatment guidelines and enforcement of laws and regulations regarding the dispensing of antibiotics, which may spur overprescribing and overconsumption (Collignon et al. 2015; Mueller and Östergren 2016). Second, doctors may become both psychologically and economically dependent on pharmaceutical companies as a result of gifts, and doctors may 're-pay' by prescribing the products of those companies. And third, patients who pay bribes may feel entitled to a quid pro quo and therefore demand prescriptions for antibiotics from physicians that have taken bribes (Rönnerstrand and Lapuente 2017).

A report prepared for the European Commission (Ecorys 2013) identifies a broad range of different types of corruption practices prevalent in European Union member states: bribery in medical service delivery, procurement corruption, undue reimbursement claims, as well as fraud and embezzlement of medicines and medical devices. Recommendations on policy measures to combat corruption are hampered by the fact that different types of corruption may stem from very different types of market failures and that a range of context factors affect the extent of corruption. Depending upon whether corruption is understood as a principal-agent problem or collective action problem, the policy recommendations will differ. For a principal-agent problem, monitoring in the form of both 'policy patrols' (frequent surveillance) and 'fire alarms' (procedures for alerting authorities) may be effective. But if the issue is widespread corruption stabilised by collective action problems, monitoring will be next to useless (Marquette and Peiffer 2018; Persson et al. 2019).

Recommendations on anti-corruption measures for healthcare call for strengthening bottom-up accountability of healthcare providers to the communities and patients they serve (Bruckner 2019). The voice of the patient is viewed as an essential part of health sector governance, such that policies that involve community members in local accountability are gaining recognition (Björkman Nyqvist et al. 2017). This connects approaches to good health system governance with the increasing trend towards the empowerment of patient involvement and patient rights, but also to the politicisation of health corruption notable in some parts of Europe.

The voice of the patient is viewed as an essential part of health sector governance, such that policies that involve community members in local accountability are gaining recognition.

Particularly in eastern Europe, corruption has played an important role in party politics (Eihmanis, forthcoming). Corruption was a major factor in the rejection of e-health measures in Latvia and Lithuania, whereas lack of corruption was critical for the progress in the Estonian e-health programme (Ainsaar et al. forthcoming). More broadly, public opinion scholars have found informal payments to influence public satisfaction with the provision of healthcare. Findings are not fully conclusive, but generally, informal payments seem to reduce satisfaction with the healthcare system and the provision of healthcare. Furthermore, corruption has consequences for the governance of healthcare systems because it limits healthcare service access, violates universalistic norms of healthcare systems, and decreases healthcare service efficiency (Clausen et al. 2011; Habibov 2016; Nikoloski and Mossialos 2013).

IMMERGUT, ROESCU, *and* RÖNNERSTRAND

Public Satisfaction with Healthcare Systems

N ew Public Governance measures increasingly focus on citizen empowerment and seem to be associated with valence politics. But how has this affected public opinion? As we see in Figure 9.6, satisfaction with health services has increased throughout Europe since 2002. If we break this down, we see that the trend is stronger in western Europe than in eastern Europe, but that it is nevertheless present. One reason for this regional difference may be that in eastern Europe patient rights are often not backed by the same legal guarantees and procedures as in western Europe. In addition, as noted above, corruption reduces satisfaction, and corruption is more prevalent in eastern Europe than in western Europe. Moreover, there are a multitude of different factors that may affect patient satisfaction, ranging from the adequacy of healthcare funding and delivery to general satisfaction not only with the government but with life in general.

Indeed the relationship between citizen-friendly policies and public

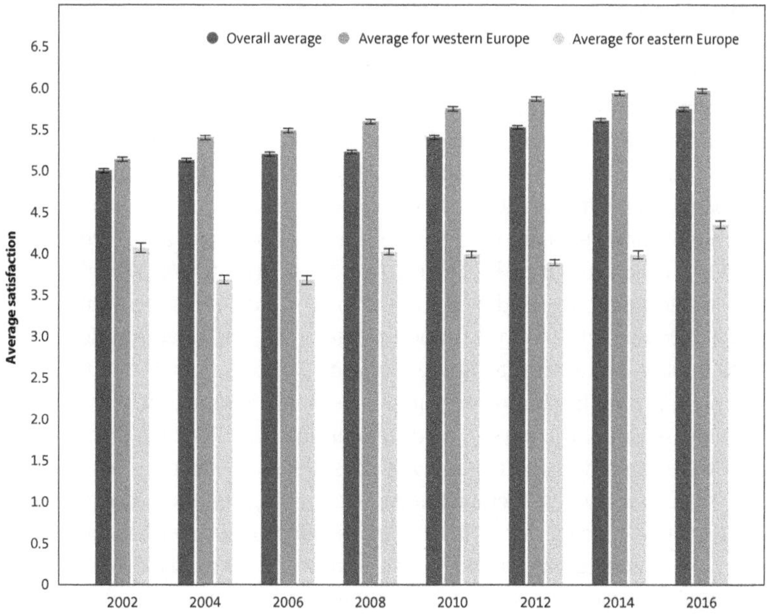

Figure 9.6 **Public satisfaction with the state of health services, 2002–16**

Source: European Social Survey Cumulative File, ESS 1-8 (2018)

Notes: Survey Question: 'Please say what you think overall about the state of health services in [country] nowadays?' Rating on scale of 0 to 10, where 0 is extremely bad, 10 is extremely good. Design and population size weights applied in estimating the average satisfaction per wave in all European countries available in ESS.

satisfaction may be simply spurious. In order to determine whether this is the case, a matched comparison of survey respondents before and after the introduction of waiting time guarantees in Germany and Sweden was conducted. The results demonstrated a causal impact of the waiting time guarantee on satisfaction (Burlacu et al. 2018). Of course, further research would be needed to establish that this is a general trend in either western or eastern Europe. Nevertheless, attitudes of eastern Europeans about their health systems have started to converge with those in western Europe as their health institutions become more similar (Schneider and Popic 2018).

Conclusion

This chapter has argued that political learning has resulted in a shift from polarised political conflict about public versus private medicine to an emphasis on better management of health systems through a citizen-centred focus and patient involvement that may be termed a New Public Governance paradigm.

The earlier NPM revolution has indeed had some positive effects on healthcare financing and delivery in Europe. More private provision and increases in private health insurance have increased patients' choices and provided incentives for increased healthcare provision and thus increased health capacities in some countries. At the same time, unless accompanied by tax subsidies and regulations to ensure universal coverage and access, privatisation and marketisation bring with them a risk of reduction in health equity. In systems characterised by the dominance of the public sector and where efficiency reforms have been supplemented with enforceable patient rights and quality guarantees (as in the Scandinavian countries and in the UK), light privatisation has improved public satisfaction and quality of care.

In eastern Europe, the keys to a successful post-Cold War healthcare transition were rapid decision-making and consolidation of a social health insurance system, including adequate financing. Again, given the context of a completely state-centred public healthcare system, some privatisation of provision and financing has had a positive impact on the availability and quality of health services. However, where public funding is insufficient and provision inefficient, extremely high out-of-pocket payments threaten universal healthcare provision. Patient rights and anti-corruption policies have been introduced on paper, but often lack enforcement mechanisms and institutions for good governance.

Governments' increasing focus on citizen involvement offers hope for further development of effective patient rights and sanctions for corruption. Rising public satisfaction with healthcare seems to show that New Public Governance is moving in the right direction. Further analysis would

be required in order to determine whether governments' increasing attention to the demands of citizens is indeed producing an increase in their
satisfaction.

Endnotes

1   This overview is based on the Welfare State Futures HEALTHDOX study, which
    examined healthcare politics from 1989 to 2017 in thirty-six countries, NORFACE
    Grant Number 462-14-070, ERA-Net Plus Grant Number 618106.

2   The usage in this article is closer to Pollitt and Bouckaert (2011), but the term New
    Public Governance is used as it is more inclusive.

3   When the OECD updated its categorisation of private health insurance in the US
    to reflect the fact that the Affordable Care Act declared health insurance to be
    compulsory, the proportion of voluntary health expenditure fell from 39.5% (data
    accessed in 2017) to 6.9% (data accessed in 2019). The difference (32.6 percent-
    age points) is now almost completely included under compulsory schemes, which
    were previously at 22.8% and are now at 55.2%. Similarly, the share of 'public'
    expenditures in current expenditure on health increased from 48.8% in 2013 to
    81.4% in 2014. Some of this increase is also attributable to expanded enrolment
    in Medicaid (the US public assistance healthcare programme), which was enabled
    by the ACA but not always implemented by the states.

4   Sveriges Riksdag 2017/18:400 Institutionell korruption inom läkemedelsbranschen,
    available at: https://data.riksdagen.se/fil/483498FC-AF8F-4590-88C4-7EE8CB7FA4
    88.

X. Digital Health: Key Challenges

ROBIN GAULD

B roadly defined, digital health refers to use of computer-based technology. This includes the wide range of internet-based and other technologies that provide and help analyse information, assist with organisational issues, provide specific healthcare service delivery solutions, and generate data that may be used for a variety of purposes (Mackert et al. 2016; Widmer et al. 2015; Zhang et al. 2018). Digital health, therefore, is provided via personal and other computers, purpose-built devices, 3D printers and other technologies, and mobile phones–all of which are connected to the internet.

As an evolving field, digital health is extremely promising, with many predictions of how it will improve healthcare delivery and access. It also presents constant questions around how technologies will be used and who will have access to these technologies, and around issues of ethics and control which lie at the centre of many digital health and technology developments (Gauld and Williams 2009; West 2005). For example, traditionally, healthcare has been developed and provided in a relatively one-way, hierarchical manner, with clinicians controlling knowledge around diagnosis and treatment, the processes of how care is delivered, and what care is most appropriate for a patient and condition. Due to information asymmetries, patients have had limited capacity for influence and have been relatively passive recipients of care. Digital health has disrupted this one-way clinician-to-patient model in multiple ways, giving patients and the public access to information and an unprecedented ability to influence everything from diagnosis through to the care they receive (Tang and Ng 2006).

> *Digital health has disrupted the one-way clinician-to-patient model in multiple ways.*

Following this, the field of digital health is obviously very broad and ever-expanding as new technologies and applications of technology emerge. In the area of mobile healthcare delivery alone, there are tens of thousands of applications available with constant additions (Hamine et al. 2015; Müller et al. 2016). Most are focused on new uses of data, such as data that help patients and healthy individuals better monitor and manage their health, or on methods for improving access to and utilisation of services. This includes systems that require service providers to align their activities into a single system that gives patients the potential to monitor service performance and gain information on when different services have been provided. An example would be when a patient has been referred from a primary care provider to a hospital-based specialist service, and when tests or other diagnostic services have been required. The application would provide real-time information to the patient on booked appointments, any delays with or changes to these appointments, when test or other results are available, and any range of related clinical information. There are multiple such applications within countries and health systems as well as globally, developed in-house by public providers or offered in the marketplace by private developers, creating complex governance problems. For example, a governing board and service leaders may need to work through ensuring that data can be easily transferred between different systems, that products are providing value for money and high-quality services, and that patient data are appropriately handled with patient privacy protected.

Many of the present challenges with population health and personal healthcare delivery, involving questions of how to improve health and health systems in the face of demographic change and ageing and development of multimorbidity, are being tackled with digital health solutions (Hall et al. 2014). Indeed, there are considerable investments in digital health from all sectors–government, non-governmental organisations, and private businesses. The promise is that digital health will transform how healthcare is delivered and by whom, the locations for healthcare delivery, and peoples' interactions with the healthcare system. It is also providing new ways for patients to learn about and better manage their own health and healthcare needs.

Governments around the world are investing in digital health and developing ambitious plans for digitally-enabled health system transformation, involving all sectors of the economy and society. Examples range from government-issued social security cards that give users access to services and providers access to patient data, through to mobile phone applications that give patients access to information about their health and health services. Historically, the potential for involving all sectors in the process of improving population health as well as personal health and coordinating their activities has never existed. Yet governance of digital health remains in an embryonic state, with the issues in focus constantly changing. This chapter outlines the developmental agenda, the key issues this poses, and a series of governance questions of concern. The chapter concludes by offering a charter for digital health governance for use across the health sector.

The Digital Health Agenda

As noted elsewhere, including in this Report, health systems are complex and often highly confusing; health systems are blamed for harming patients, whose care is vulnerable to system-induced error, and noted for being inefficient (Baker et al. 2008; Gauld 2009; Institute of Medicine 2001). The complexity is related to the nature of healthcare and healthcare needs. Many services and needs are best provided for in community settings by primary care providers. These providers might be medically qualified, or they might be allied professionals such as nurses or therapists. Who a patient sees will depend on their specific needs. This will differ over time and between healthcare encounters. Patients with more complex needs, such as those with chronic or acute conditions, will usually require more specialised care. This normally means visiting a specialist medical practitioner who may be based in a clinical or hospital setting. It may also mean being referred for tests and other diagnostic services. Specialists often refer patients to one another, again depending on the patient's condition. In-hospital services for patients with unusual or uncertain conditions often require involvement of multiple professionals across different specialities and departments. Thus, a patient's journey through the health system can be extremely convoluted. For the patient, this can be the cause of confusion and frustration. Health professionals can, similarly, find the system frustrating when seeking information or services from different parts of the system for a patient. Medical errors, which persistently affect a significant percentage of patients and often result in permanent disability and even death, are frequently the result of system failures (Department of Health 2000). This includes imperfect information being passed from one professional to another, such as prescribing errors, diagnostic errors, or simple communications between professionals on different rosters around a patient's progress and treatment regime (Leape et al. 2009).

The challenges facing population and personal health today are widely noted. In brief, these are associated in part with rapid population ageing in most wealthy countries and related healthcare needs, particularly for those living longer. The challenges include increasing incidence of multimorbidity, also referred to as multiple chronic disease, such as among older patients who suffer from combinations of diseases, for example, chronic heart failure along with respiratory illness, arthritis, depression, and diabetes (Barnett et al. 2012; see also Besnier and Eikemo, Chapter 2 in this Report for more detail on these trends). Sedentary lifestyles and overconsumption add to the challenges, with multimorbidity also being associated with overweight and inattention to personal health and well-being. Alcohol consumption and smoking further fuel multimorbidity (Hanlon et al. 2018).

How to promote better health and well-being, change people's behaviours in order to improve their health, and provide better information for them around their health status are important questions for policy-makers and health service providers. In the face of the increasing social and economic burden of disease in many countries, the key concerns are the financial costs of providing care as well as the many other required resources, including the supply of health professionals (Bähler et al. 2015; McPhail 2016).

Digital health solutions for health systems

Digital health holds considerable promise for solving many of the above health system challenges. Digital solutions are frequently cited as a foundation for service integration (Nicholson et al. 2013). Integrated care requires a strong professional focus on building better systems, including professionals working collaboratively and sharing resources to ensure that, where possible, services are seamless from the patient perspective. In practice, this would mean that patients experience a health system in which they perceive all professionals are working for the same system, with their activities and information, particularly patient records and treatment plans, routinely available and agreed to.

Electronic health records (EHRs) and personal health records (PHRs) are important facilitators of integration, with high hopes pinned on such solutions (Burton et al. 2004; Clarke and Meiris 2006; Raymond et al. 2015). EHRs are electronic versions of the traditional paper patient file, including medical history and prescribed drugs, and are crucial to health professionals. A robust EHR system, dependent on software design and sophistication, enables sharing of records in real time across a health system, with different professionals able to update a patient's file. EHRs routinely incorporate electronic-prescribing, which has been shown to reduce prescribing errors, a common source of patient harms, and to improve safety and system efficiency. A good e-prescribing system will provide information on medicines for professionals at point of prescribing, incorporate checks and balances so that it is not possible to prescribe an accidental overdose, indicate possible interactions between medicines, and interface seamlessly with a dispensing pharmacist (de Moor et al. 2015; Westbrook et al. 2012).

A large global industry has developed around EHRs, with many multinational software developers securing sales and ongoing business with providers in multiple countries. This may mean a vendor supplies and supports EHRs for a proportion of providers and patients across different health systems and contexts. Usually, this requires EHR adaptations for local context or some changes in how services are provided in order to align with EHR functionality. It also means there are usually multiple, potentially competing EHRs in use within a country and health system. Of course, some countries and systems develop and maintain their own bespoke EHRs. There are advantages and disadvantages of both vendor-supplied and in-house EHR development.

Furthermore, there are multiple advantages of EHRs over traditional paper records. For one, a robust EHR requires professionals to work together in agreeing on the sorts of information accessible to one another and on levels of access to information. For example, agreements will be needed on issues such as patients' sexual and mental health histories, which could have implications if accessible more broadly across a health system than with just the patient's provider of these specific services. This, as well as privacy and protection of confidential patient information, highlights a key governance issue.

Many EHR systems are able to be accessed and contributed to by patients, a function that is often a goal of EHR development. Patient EHR access brings the care recipient to the forefront of care system design, which is frequently a driver of better integration. With better and real-time information, patients are empowered to demand improved care; the simple process of opening record access to patients orients health professionals and provider organisations towards them and their needs. EHR access and patient-focused functionality can facilitate patients' ability to book and change appointment times, to have a role in coordinating their own care with different providers, to retrieve a wide range of information related to their conditions, and, of course, to provide feedback on the care process and systems. EHR access can include immediate access to test and other diagnostic results simultaneous with professional access, as well as routine reminders to book follow-up appointments or to comply with a treatment regime (for more on how such reminders work, see Traxler, Chapter 8 in this Report). It often also includes capacity to exchange emails directly with health professionals and video-enabled consultations (Chen et al. 2009). Indeed, the latter is fast becoming a model of care delivery in itself, with online providers competing with traditional, local service providers (de la Torre-Díez et al. 2015).

Looking into the future, developments in areas such as 3D printing promise to revolutionise how healthcare is delivered. Early trials indicate that, in due course, prescriptions will be dispatched for printing directly to a 3D printer, perhaps in a patient's home, circumventing a need to collect medicines from a pharmacy (Trenfield et al. 2018). Predictions are that virtual reality will eventually develop to a point in which experiences will be 100 per cent real. If so, this could mean health professionals and patients will no longer need to be present in the same room. Doctors will be able to examine patients and undertake a wide range of medical and even surgical interventions, perhaps with assistance of robots dispatched to the home.

Digital health solutions for population and personal health and well-being

Personal health records (PHRs), while less commonly used, are widely available, often via software vendors, and might be considered an important foundation for driving patient attention to personal health and well-being, in conjunction with access to an EHR. PHRs generally offer capacity to gather personal health and other information that may assist the owner to monitor health and track personal and other health goals (Greenberg et al. 2017). Users may input a range of information, from basic statistics such as weight and fitness levels, through to food and other health plans. Increasingly sophisticated smart-phones and other devices enable data collection from daily activities and monitoring of health and other indicators, drawing these data into the PHR. A PHR might link with systems of external services such as personal health and fitness trainers. There is potential to also draw in all sorts of health-related data, such as food and alcohol purchases, although automation and integration of data along these lines are presently not available. A PHR can function, in some ways, like a healthcare diary and may be linked with an EHR, giving potential to help professionals better understand patient behaviours and goals and changes in these over time. In this regard, a PHR may be used in partnership with health professionals in order to help a user comply with medical advice, particularly around health behaviour change. Again, the range of PHRs available creates governance challenges, including around regulation of the PHR industry, data collection, storage standards, privacy issues, how to educate patients on the use of PHRs, and which products are likely to provide the best performance and value for money.

Beyond PHRs, multiple other digital supports for health and well-being exist. The myriad of mobile phone applications offer help with everything from sleep to food consumption and preparation to exercise regimes. Wearable devices aid health monitoring, while gaming and other activities offer methods for motivating users and providing reminders about the need to focus on health and its improvement. For older people, some types of digital solutions, including robots, can be particularly beneficial (Robinson et al. 2014). Robots, for example, can assist with medication dispensing and provide other forms of support. Evaluations have found older people to be favourable toward robots helping in this way (Demiris et al. 2008; Mann et al. 2015). Digital solutions are also enabling 'smart' housing for older, isolated, or disabled people, improving safety and connectivity. Sensors, for example, will send messages to monitoring and emergency services if a lack of movement is detected; reminders will also provide alerts for differing reasons.

An industry is starting to emerge, and will likely spread more broadly, around digital solutions for physical and other health problems (Penno and Gauld 2017). This includes exoskeletons that support the wearer, perhaps an older, frail, or disabled person, giving them higher functionality, including ability to walk long distances and lift heavy items. Bodily enhancement technologies, similarly, promise to restore movement and extend physical ability. Predictions also include the development of nanobots and related technologies that will be ingested by patients to undertake a range of internal procedures that traditionally require a surgical or other procedure. This includes correction of cell and DNA defects that are the cause of ill health and disease, such as cancers.

At the same time, an industry is emerging around precision medicine and health, i.e. medical treatments and medicines that are designed specifically for individuals based on their personal characteristics and the predictive value of particular therapies (Love-Koh et al. 2018). Precision medicine deploys a combination of diagnostic tools, including genetic tests and analysis, and data analytics with therapies designed for the individual. The implication is that some individuals may be identified through genetic and other testing as having higher risk of certain conditions, for example, early-onset dementia. Increasingly, such predictions for risk of all sorts of conditions and diseases will be possible. The results and processes involved will be digital and form part of a patient's lifetime data set and could be used by different parties for different purposes. On the upside, precision medicine can mean that medicines and other interventions are adjusted and designed for individuals with a much better fit and likelihood of producing results, in much the same way as clothing is when personally tailored.

In summary, digital health initiatives offer substantial scope for health system improvement. EHRs, PHRs, and other digital technologies have the potential to shift the focus of healthcare away from professionals toward individual patients and communities. They also increase the capacity both for patients to take control of their healthcare and care needs and for holding patients to account for health improvement, including adhering to health professional advice and instructions. Very importantly, digital health, the internet, and the use of cloud data collection and storage enable data collection and accessibility in ways not previously possible. All data are potentially available everywhere, accessible by anyone connected to the internet. The capacity for analysis through big data techniques, which can draw and manipulate data from anywhere data are collected, is unprecedented. The ways in which data may be used are also multifaceted. Analyses may be of communities and their behaviours, or of individuals, involving data generated over time and in different places. Following the discussions in the previous paragraphs, digital health raises important governance dilemmas that require consideration, the answers to which will vary across health systems, countries, and cultures.

> *Digital technologies have the potential to shift the focus of healthcare away from professionals toward individual patients and communities.*

Digital Health Issues and Governance Questions

The way in which healthcare is delivered today in most health systems and countries is based on historic and traditional approaches to modern medicine. The traditions around how services are organised–across often siloed medical specialty lines and divided into community or hospital care settings–have been relatively resistant to change (Freidson 2001; Gauld 2009; Gauld et al. 2014; Kuhlmann et al. 2015b; WHO 2008). These institutional arrangements are solidified by the nature of health professional training and regulation, with professional educators and registration bodies tending to be divided along professional lines.

By contrast, digital health, as described in this chapter, has recently emerged with few historically-determined boundaries or developmental limits. Digital tools interface with and support traditional models of care delivery, such as mobile phone applications designed to improve post-surgical recovery and outcomes, but also cut across processes and systems such as EHRs, data collection and analysis, and new emerging technologies. This raises multiple issues and questions, overviewed below, that require sound governance and responses.

Data

Perhaps the most pressing set of issues surrounds digital data in the broadest sense. As described earlier, data collection and potential for use are now pervasive with few people in developed countries not affected. For the most part, individuals can take comfort that their care is improving due to data collection, availability, and analysis. Yet there is scope for widespread harm which hinges on the extent to which the governance of data is robust. Questions that demand addressing include how and from where data are collected. If from individuals at point of healthcare service, such as data entered into EHRs, then data security and privacy are of fundamental importance (Vayena et al. 2018). Most EHRs have very high levels of encryption and require authorisation, providing access only to those so authorised. Many EHR systems will routinely report inappropriate access, such as by health professionals not assigned to a case, creating additional protection for patients.

Questions such as what sorts of data should form the core of an EHR are also fundamental. As noted earlier, mental and sexual health are two areas that require particular attention, with additional authorisation needed to access such records. The same is true with precision medicine where personal genetic traits are predictive of disease development. All such cases have deep implications for individuals if data are incorrectly accessed, shared, or leaked (Iyengar et al. 2018; Papacharissi 2018; Vayena et al. 2018). Employers, for example, might use such data to justify dismissal or not offering employment. Very importantly, in countries where medical insurance forms the backbone of funding, data may be used to deny coverage, placing certain communities and individuals at a disadvantage often when they have no means of reversing the health conditions or circumstances.

Data ownership and individual control over data and its governance come to the fore in all of the aforementioned cases. Most EHRs are designed with professional control in mind. Good governance will also involve patients, who often have very different perspectives from professionals, in the design and authorisation processes and their development. For example, indigenous people are known to have particular concerns around the use of data outside of their tribal or home areas and a desire to retain ownership over health data and, therefore, authority over any data usage (Reid et al. 2018). This implies a need for involvement in governance and consultation around data usage.

An area often not considered is posthumous data (Hoeksema et al. 2017). Key questions involve how individuals and families gain control over data, effectively a person's 'health bio', at time of and after death. This includes how and whether these data are stored in perpetuity, for example, through pledging that data will be donated on death, as one would their organs, and subsequently used. Also of concern is how an individual's data are drawn together from multiple sources, including data that may be collected and stored via various websites, social media, and other forums.

Software vendors and other businesses involved in EHRs and the range of other data points revolving around healthcare also require robust regulation and governance (Gauld and Goldfinch 2006). Most countries rely on a range of different regulatory mechanisms as well as industry self-regulation. The complex landscape of multiple EHR vendors, often competing with one another, and individual vendors often selling different versions of EHR software to different providers along with other digital offerings makes governance and self-regulation challenging. Industry standards have often been driven by conversation between regulators, health service providers and professionals, and industry. In this regard, collaborative approaches, aimed at ensuring that systems intersect and that data transported and shared between systems are uncorrupted, are crucial. This means that competing products can offer different functions and user interfaces–as Apple and Android phone operating systems do–but that the same standards and protocols are used for data transfer and for achieving interoperability. One example of this is HL7 (Health Level 7), the internationally-agreed standard for encrypted healthcare messaging. With HL7 and interoperability, messaging and data transfer systems are supposed to 'talk' perfectly with one another.

Equal access

As with access to the internet and computers, a divide in access to and use of digital health technologies exists. Studies indicate that the divide is along socioeconomic, age, and ethnicity lines (Estacio et al. 2017; Gauld and Williams 2009). This means some groups and individuals have superior access to digital technologies and, by implication, better healthcare than others. How to address this situation is a key concern for policy-makers and health service providers, particularly in jurisdictions where goals for healthcare include that it is universally accessible and that equity of access and outcomes is fundamental. Underscoring the challenges with the digital divide are questions around access to technologies and facilitators of usage, such as fast computers and mobile phones and unlimited access to broadband internet and 3G or 4G mobile phone networks. Beyond this, and perhaps more fundamentally, are questions around how to ensure that the population are skilled in digital health technology use. Last are issues around ensuring that data focused on healthcare and process improvement are made available to patients in usable and user-friendly formats. Simple issues such as a complicated login process can be enough to put the unenthusiastic patient off digital technology use.

Cross-border issues

As with other digital technologies, digital health is integrally linked to the internet and therefore has few potential borders. This poses various challenges with related regulatory and other concerns. For regulators and governments, concerns revolve around how to ensure data collected within borders are secure, how data are accessed across borders and by whom, and how to deal with digital technology providers, including data collection and storage services, that are based in different and often multiple jurisdictions. This means data and services can be broadly distributed and easily linked to other forms of data. Again, questions of privacy, access, and secondary data use—use of data collected for one purpose being used for other purposes or by other parties—come to the fore. Of course, regulators must focus on public and private data, as multiple points of data collection, provision, and storage sit outside of direct public sector control. As such, regulators must interact closely with and monitor the activities of a wide range of private companies with global operations or globally accessible services, from large multinational corporations through to the numerous small businesses involved in developing and servicing digital health applications and technologies. Self-regulation and public accountability for data usage are important. This is particularly so in the context of data leaks, data-sharing when individuals and communities have not necessarily given approval for this, and when hackers have obtained personal information held by a business or government agency.

An issue that has frequently been central to high-cost health information system failures is digital systems and services developed for a particular health system and context. Health information system providers tend to be global corporations, offering relatively generic products and systems that require adaptations for different health systems and contexts. When systems developed for a particular country or context are purchased or used by another, fundamental differences in how care is funded and delivered can mean the need for considerable software adaptations. For example, EHRs and other patient and service management information systems are often developed within a United States or European context, with an emphasis on financial management since the focus in the US and several European systems is on capacity to generate billing and other information required by health insurance agencies. The US, of course, has had privately-provided insurance as the dominant form of funding, while in Europe in some areas private hospitals may dominate service provision with social insurance as the funding mechanism. Other countries and hospitals purchasing information systems with financially-oriented features, or features that support particular clinical service designs, can find that systems are not a perfect fit. The result can be financially demanding and organisationally costly, and often result in cost overruns, poor health professional and patient uptake through systems being difficult to navigate and clumsy to use, and, in turn, a level of system failure. Routinely, implementation of such health information systems requires unforeseen, ongoing investments in system upgrades and adaptations that were not incorporated in initial purchase agreements, the costs of which are borne by the purchaser. The accountability of vendors, working globally, to specific countries and health systems is often minimal. Yet there continues to be limited information on failures and related accountability questions collated and distributed for global consumption in order to increase vendor accountability and performance and to improve purchaser understanding of the risks around large-scale projects (Gauld 2007; Sligo et al. 2017).

The demand for expertise

Digital health demands new levels of expertise beyond that of health professionals, and the demands are growing as the industry and digital capabilities evolve. A key challenge for the future will be ensuring a sufficient workforce with specific expertise. An example is precision medicine. As noted, this requires expertise in genomics as well as in artificial intelligence (AI), algorithms, and other areas of computer science such as machine learning (Love-Koh et al. 2018). Added to this is an understanding of healthcare. Ideally, digital health needs to be incorporated into health professional training programmes, woven throughout and fundamental to how healthcare is understood and organised and conditions diagnosed and treated. Some training and professional registration bodies recognise this need. However, there is also a need more broadly to be aware of workforce supply issues.

Beyond technology that supports medical practice and healthcare delivery is the demand for expertise in health technology assessment (HTA). HTA is the process of evaluating the effectiveness and contribution to improvements in quality of life of clinical interventions, medical devices, prescribed drugs, and other technologies (Olberg et al. 2017). Many countries have agencies and initiatives dedicated to HTA, such as the National Institute for Health and Care Excellence in the United Kingdom, Patient-Centered Outcomes Research Institute in the US, and Pharmac in New Zealand (Chalkidou et al. 2009; Gauld 2014). HTA processes can result in denials of funding for particular technologies, as there may be insufficient evidence in support of them, or recommendations for patients and providers to consider before use. Digital health as described in this chapter adds a further dimension to HTA. For example, as more data become available over time around the efficacy of an intervention, or an algorithm becomes more effective through ongoing adjustment, this will require periodic HTA. There will be a requirement for those with digital health expertise to be increasingly involved in HTA, in order to ensure robust understanding of this dimension of care. At the same time, there will be a demand for health professionals and patients affected by increasing knowledge of different healthcare pathways (determined by algorithms and data) to be involved in evaluating evidence and consequent service design recommendations. Further research into how digital technologies should be evaluated is needed (Love-Koh et al. 2018). Of course, HTA is also important in terms of evaluating new digital health initiatives that may incur considerable cost to ensure that promised benefits are likely to be delivered.

A Charter for Digital Health

The discussions above have provided summary insights into digital health and related governance questions. Given the constantly evolving yet relatively embryonic state of digital health and myriad issues raised, it is unlikely that any one country or health system would be able to develop a digital governance model that would be sustained over time without need for periodic adjustment. It is also unlikely that a global governance model would suffice for an individual country's needs and would encompass the multiple cross-border and cross-sector activities and questions that digital health brings into stark relief.

Following this, there is arguably a need for policy-makers within and across health systems to develop a digital health charter to guide the governance development process and to provide a framework for areas on which to focus governance activities (Pollitt 1994). Because of the ubiquitous nature of digital health, charter development should be led by the global community, ideally through the World Health Organization.

The points outlined below, summarised in Box 10.1, offer a starting point for digital health governance charter development.

Data collection and ownership

With data coming from multiple sources, yet almost always drawn from patients, questions of data ownership are fundamental. These questions include whether patients and the public should retain control over all data and any requests for usage, as well as questions over how data are used in practical situations and for decision-making. Obviously, it can be difficult attempting to gain consent from individuals each time their data may be used. Therefore, assurances may be needed that patients are informed about how data may be used and by whom, the limits to data usage, how data are governed, how and when data may be shared, and their right to withdraw consent at any stage. Following this, principles of ethics sit at the heart of any digital health charter.

Public and patient rights to participation in digital health development

The public needs to be at the centre of all discussion around digital health development and related policy and practices. This demands deliberative processes (Wiklund 2005). The challenge lies in how to engage the public, which, in a deliberative context, can involve a range of approaches and be complex (Dryzek 2002). Traditional methods such as appointees on committees, focus groups, eliciting feedback on developmental processes, and public meetings will remain critical channels. Digital health must also be an important enabler, including use of AI and other channels for gathering and analysing public perceptions, preferences, and views. Yet the public also needs to be involved in how these technologies are used for such purposes, along with all other healthcare related purposes. Open standards for digital health development need to be supported and promoted. This will enable improved capacity for the digitally-able public to both participate in developmental processes and disseminate information on implications and data usage. Any charter, ideally, should commit to giving the public the potential to control how data are used, including changing the activities of commercial as well as public entities. It should prioritise ethical considerations around data and technology usage and standards for data-sharing over profitability. While such a focus on public control for a charter is important, it has implications for the private sector, particularly in terms of managing risks around investments, the costs of unacceptable use, and shareholder demands. Public participation, very importantly, brings a level of accountability to digital health developments otherwise not present.

Data protection, storage, and usage

Following the previous point, with data at the centre of digital health, a charter should outline data storage, usage, and contribution expectations. This includes security, who can access data, how they are shared, and when and by whom changes are made to data. Given the fluidity of data, a charter may set expectations for technologies such as blockchain to be used. This may apply to personal health data, meaning that data origins and changes would be clearly recorded. Use of blockchain could, in turn, assist with security and auditable documentation of a person's lifetime health bio, including posthumous use (Mettler 2016). This is particularly important in order to facilitate processes of donating data upon death to be accessible for research or other purposes. Some expectations also need to be created for how the characteristics of data sets are explained to the public and service providers.

Standards for data-sharing

A key concern, as noted, is around how data are shared and the mechanisms for this. For the public to have confidence in data-sharing, a charter should define standards and expectations. This includes technical standards that support interoperability from software development through to data exchange. It also includes standards that support machine learning, in which data are drawn from multiple sources, systems, and locations. Such standards must ensure that systems are secure and promote the required sharing and interactions that will lead to better machine learning and AI. Standards must also incorporate consideration of what sorts of data can be shared and where limits on sharing need to be enforced. Again, standards must reassure the public, be responsive to concerns, and involve public input. In the spirit of building global agreement, standards for digital health governance also need to be openly shared.

Ethics and expertise

How questions of ethics associated with AI and data are handled is fundamental to a charter. Given the discussion above, the balance between ensuring that digital health developments will make for better healthcare with a goal of being ethically and morally appropriate and generating return on investment needs to be carefully monitored, analysed, and debated. Of course, there is also a need for expertise in horizon-scanning, ensuring capacity to keep abreast of new and emerging developments and analysis of their implications.

A charter must also detail the expertise that is needed for robust digital health governance. Any governance process–the process of establishing governance arrangements–or issue that requires oversight and scrutiny demands specific expertise. Governance structures, in a traditional sense, often consist of individuals who shift from one industry to another with generic skills in running organisations and building strategy. With digital health, the generic skill set needs also to include computer science and associated areas such as algorithm development.

Accountability and audit

Last, but not least, a charter must detail expectations for accountability and audit. This includes accountability of policy-makers for setting digital health parameters and their impacts, of industry, and of the public and accountability for data collection and usage. For data collection and usage, accountability is likely to involve all of the aforementioned parties in a complex set of arrangements. Accountability can involve requirements for reporting on specific issues as well as in-depth examination of particular cases. This is where audit can play an important role with periodic spot checks of activities. There may also be commitment to disseminating for public consumption the outcome of such processes. This must be in lay terms, with goals of improving digital health transparency as well as building public confidence.

Conclusion

Clearly, the digital health agenda is broad, rapidly evolving, and complex. It affects all components of health systems and services, as well as individuals and populations. The potential for improvements in how services are designed and delivered and for innovation is large. So too is the potential for better understanding and changing health behaviours, but also for negatively impacting on individuals and communities through misuse and misunderstanding of digital technologies and data. For these reasons, effective governance is fundamental to digital health development.

However, as this chapter has outlined, governance in the digital context is underdeveloped with a need to attend to various tenets. A charter is demanded to ensure that governance is balanced and focused on key issues that require an effective and robust response. As noted elsewhere in this Report, governance is the process of setting directions and standards and ensuring that these are upheld and that service providers are accountable for their practices and performances, including ensuring that these do not harm patients and the public or infringe on their rights. The challenge is for healthcare leaders, including policy-makers, professionals, and industry actors, to forge governance arrangements, underpinned by principles captured in a charter as outlined in this chapter.

Effective governance is fundamental to digital health development.

XI. Health Governance Challenges and Recommendations: A Summary

Mujaheed Shaikh, Claus Wendt, *and* Klaus Hurrelmann

In the introductory chapter of this Governance Report we began by enumerating several current and future challenges to healthcare and by outlining the relevance of effective governance in tackling these challenges. Owing to the increased demand for healthcare services, changing demography, increasing role of technology in service delivery, evolving disease landscape, and a massive rise in healthcare costs, healthcare systems today are by far the most expensive sector. It remains a major challenge for healthcare governance to implement effective cost containment measures without compromising quality of care.

Despite several efforts, reorganisation of this important sector is marred with global and national economic and political challenges. The chapters in the Report present an overview of many of these issues at a global, national, and regional level, discuss the nature of health governance, and provide suggestions and recommendations to effectively meet the needs of the healthcare system and the people served by and working within it.

This Report's concluding chapter summarises the governance challenges touched upon in the individual chapters, their implications, and the strategies that governance actors can adopt for instituting effective governance models for successfully delivering future healthcare. Specifically, we provide recommendations keeping in mind the multilevel nature of governance, i.e. global actions and national and regional measures, and the role of the individual in the delivery and receipt of care.

We focus on five major governance challenges the individual chapters have highlighted:

- The unequal level and distribution of health;
- The national and transnational security of healthcare;
- The interrelation between healthcare and social welfare;
- The patient-centred delivery and receipt of healthcare;
- The digitalisation of delivery and receipt of healthcare.

The Unequal Level and Distribution of Health

As Elodie Besnier and Terje Andreas Eikemo point out in Chapter 2, significant progress in the level of health has been made over the last decades: life expectancy and healthy life expectancy have shown a remarkable increase worldwide. However, as the global burden of communicable diseases is decreasing, the burden of non-communicable diseases is growing. In high-income countries, the burden of the demographic transition and ageing population is putting a strain on healthcare systems.

As a consequence, progress is slowing down in certain areas, and disease-specific burden is continuing to pose a threat. For example, several neglected diseases are affecting mortality, HIV/AIDS-related illnesses are adversely affecting disability-adjusted life years, the number of years in poor health has increased due to a faster increase in life expectancy relative to health-adjusted life expectancy, and progress in reducing neonatal mortality has been extremely slow.

Above all, important inequalities persist within and between countries. Clare Bambra mentions in Chapter 3 that the unequal distribution of health is still a forgotten relative in this context. The evidence presented shows that stark inequalities exist both between and within countries in several health outcomes. While some inequalities can be explained by economic development, gender, age, and income, others remain unexplained. The unequal availability and receipt of healthcare eventually has adverse implications on the health status of different groups of the population. As a consequence there are enormous differences in life expectancy and healthy life expectancy of groups with high and low socioeconomic status. Obviously, inequity of healthcare in the long run results in costs for the whole society and its economy.

The evidence presented in Besnier and Eikemo's and Bambra's chapters thus shows that high-income countries as well as low-income countries are facing unprecedented challenges to sustain the progress made so far. They all will face heavy new challenges to health. Recognising and accepting these issues and placing global concerns over short-term political ones are necessary.

Recommendations

We cannot improve what we do not know. The collection and analysis of timely and accurate assessments of population health to measure progress and identify areas of improvement are thus a natural first step in ensuring sustainability of health achievements and reducing inequalities. As pointed out by Besnier and Eikemo, subjective measures often contrast with objective measures of health and in some cases might even lead to differential policy implications. Therefore, developing new and accurate measures of health and improving existing ones must be considered an ongoing task. Measuring the progress made in an accurate fashion is essential to inform global health governance and to develop, implement, and evaluate relevant policies.

Significant effort has been put into identifying the level and trends of existing and potential threats to health globally. The identification of the impact of these threats, whether global or local, should be emphasised in the global governance agenda. In particular, identifying the differential impact of these threats on different socioeconomic groups is crucial to pull the right policy levers to tackle the problem of inequality.

Bambra highlights the importance of targeting some of the proximal determinants of inequality such as access to health services, better housing, and personal and community capabilities (e.g. access to education, income, and social protection). Clear, earmarked, and explicit strategies in terms of goals and outcomes go a long way in realising gains from policies. Appropriate target-setting with effective and plausible action can reduce inequalities and improve overall health.

Support from the state at the community and individual levels is effective in tackling deprivation and health inequality. Initiatives such as raising the minimum wage, increasing public spending, and engaging in area-based public interventions along with regulatory mechanisms, social policy tools, and improved access to social welfare schemes have been shown to be effective in different contexts. However, one must recognise that policies such as these often involve multiple actors, most of which are outside the health system. Coordinated and coherent actions by government actors, international players, private entities, and citizens thus are crucial to fostering and maintaining a holistic approach to health.

As Besnier and Eikemo suggest, an approach such as Health in All Policies (HiAP) to measure the health impact of policies could be a way to engage different levels of government and call for a multisectoral approach to health and well-being. Global or multilateral initiatives such as the Sustainable Development Goals and European Union (EU) and WHO EURO strategies have contributed significantly to the progress achieved over the last thirty years, recognising the fact that health challenges have to be addressed through global, national, and transnational governance.

The National and Transnational Security of Healthcare

S uerie Moon and Anna Bezruki (Chapter 4) as well as Ilona Kickbusch and Austin Liu (Chapter 5) clearly demonstrate that the nature of global health threats and shared health challenges have led to a growing understanding that these issues have to be addressed through global governance mechanisms. Governance for health and well-being thus has not only become more global but also more multisectoral, reflecting a wider understanding of health as both a driver and a consequence of sustainable development.

Despite an overall decline of the burden of disease, the threat of communicable diseases persists, as has been mentioned in the previous section. New infectious threats grow globally while other well-known diseases spread or reappear (e.g. Ebola, Severe Acute Respiratory Syndrome (SARS), measles, polio, HIV/AIDS).

Outbreaks of infectious diseases threaten global health security and have significant economic and social implications. Due to the transnational nature of these outbreaks, global governance along with national and subnational capacities form an important line of defence. As Moon and Bezruki demonstrate with the examples of the SARS and Ebola crises, despite the necessity of effective global coordination and effort, governance gaps remain. In particular, weak country commitment, ineffective and sluggish knowledge-sharing platforms, research and development concerns related to accessibility and affordability, and financing and accountability concerns remain.

Recommendations

Disease threats often emerge, spread rapidly in resource-constrained settings, and quickly become global phenomena. International assistance and cooperation thus become critical. Global actors must emphasise visible and measurable country commitments in the form of service delivery, containment efforts, and financing. Assessment and external peer review of the disease situation must be agreed upon as a primary objective of global cooperation.

A comprehensive and systematic monitoring framework engaging all stakeholders including private players such as pharmaceutical companies needs to be developed, and efforts to gather data not only on the scale of the outbreak but also on government responses must be made. Upon assessment, an overarching framework of knowledge-sharing and coordination must be developed to ensure the success of global health security. In particular, timely and transparent sharing of disease data and results, lab samples and clinical trial data, vaccination efforts in terms of successes and failures,

SHAIKH, WENDT, *and* HURRELMANN

and combined global surveillance systems can go a long way to ensure efficient handling of any outbreak.

At a more local level, community participation and training are key to breaking transmission chains and curbing the spread of outbreaks. However, national will is important in terms of financing such community initiatives where governance must reconcile efforts to increase outbreak capacity with efforts to achieve universal health coverage. Thus, operational (improving national capacity) and constitutional (signaling outbreak management as high priority) preparedness is paramount to the success of global healthcare security.

The Interrelation between Healthcare and Social Welfare

Healthcare, although acknowledged to be an integral part of social protection, has not occupied a prominent place in the welfare state literature. As André Janse van Rensburg and Piet Bracke (Chapter 6) as well as Hanna Schwander (Chapter 7) point out, this is surprising insofar as sickness and accidents belong to the earliest social risks to be covered in the historic development of social protection systems, and spending on healthcare amounts to a substantial part of the gross national income.

Protection of citizens and promotion of their health and well-being are, as shown by Kickbusch and Liu (Chapter 5), important functions of state and other governance actors. The governance of health is extremely political in nature and involves strategic interaction between different players within and outside the governance discourse. Incorporating all such actors in the governance discourse and ensuring that all overt and hidden interests are given due consideration is anything but trivial.

While welfare state proponents argue for a supportive role and social investment by the state to ensure citizen well-being, as Schwander demonstrates, neoliberal thinking commodifies health and turns the focus on individual responsibility and agency of users. The role of national governments and transnational organisations such as the EU to strengthen greater social investment thus merits attention. A social investment approach takes into consideration that healthcare fulfils a double function in the welfare state. On the one hand, having a healthy population is essential for a productive labour force and thus essential for growth in capitalist societies. On the other hand, healthcare is a social policy in the sense of preventing poverty and enabling individuals to participate socially and economically.

Recommendations

A welfare state that invests in transforming its population into a competitive and productive force through social investment is necessary given economic and political changes. As noted earlier, health interacts with multiple dimensions of an individual's life such as educational achievement, employment, productivity, and knowledge. The welfare state should thus focus on investments that raise the stock of human capital–preparing young adults for the labour market, increasing health literacy, and improving productivity and knowledge, among other things.

In fact, governance discourse must propose implementing policies throughout the life course of the population, particularly during early childhood, when individuals are most vulnerable to adverse events but also most amenable to public policies. Social investments such as income safety nets, employment protection policies, and general minimum income benefits function as buffers and have a strong protective role. Continuation of such investments, increasing them when necessary, and implementation of new affirmative schemes for vulnerable people especially during difficult times are important.

The interaction between governance actors, politicians, and private enterprises often requires a careful understanding of the motives and actions of each party. Health advocates and policy-makers must therefore focus on acquiring advanced diplomatic and negotiation skills in order to successfully influence and implement governance agendas. Providing citizens with a voice and a prominent role in the governance process so as to break the politics-health nexus is imperative. Promotion of human rights and protecting the ill affected by health politics require organised public action and legislation that allows formation and functioning of non-governmental organisations and other such independent public interest organisations.

While it may be difficult to separate welfare politics from health politics, the ultimate aim should be to allow for a welfare state whose politics promote population and individual health and well-being. Although welfare states such as the Scandinavian ones are well established to reduce social inequalities, they seem to be less successful in the reduction in health inequalities. Governance measures need to take care that social policies and social investments are, in combination with health policies, better equipped to reduce health inequalities.

SHAIKH, WENDT, *and* HURRELMANN

The Patient-centred Delivery and Receipt of Healthcare

As Ellen Immergut, Andrea Roescu, and Björn Rönnerstrand state in Chapter 9, despite vast efforts, almost all countries in the world–high-income as well as low-income countries–have not yet succeeded in reorganising the healthcare sector and implementing an effective user-oriented and user-centred structure. In fact, the highly complex and fragmented healthcare systems are primarily geared toward the requirements, constraints, and imperatives of the professional actors in the healthcare system. The system concentrates on the people and institutions that provide care. An innovative healthcare system instead focuses on the demands, needs, preferences, and value orientations of citizens, patients, and users. As Christian Traxler describes in Chapter 8, formulating appropriate incentives and establishing mechanisms that engage both the patient and the provider are necessary steps towards successful and patient-oriented delivery and receipt of care.

Recommendations

What we need are healthcare systems strictly related to medical needs and patient rights. Incorporating insights from behavioural science to develop patient-oriented approaches to deliver care can be a way forward, as Traxler is able to demonstrate. On the demand side, i.e. at the patient level, preventive medicine, medication adherence, and choice of health insurance plans are important areas with significant scope for behavioural intervention on the part of the policy-maker. Gentle reminders for appointments, soft deadlines, self-reporting of medication adherence, and integrating simple technology in care programmes are examples for possible behavioural intervention. On the supply side, i.e. the provider level, behavioural techniques and interventions that nudge medical staff to change prescription behaviour, actively offer preventive services, engage in personal hygiene at the workplace, and improve quality through social norms messages should be repeatedly tested and considered.

At a more system level, patient rights are increasingly gaining foothold in political debates and the policy arena (see Table 9.1 in Immergut, Roescu, and Rönnerstrand's chapter for related reforms). Individual rights to information about health, illness, and treatment options and the ability to make choices cannot be emphasised enough. Improving choice of providers such as in the United Kingdom and waiting time guarantees such as in Denmark and the UK provide examples of such approaches.

Integrated care and multiprofessional health centres that are easily accessible are being increasingly demanded by patients. One solution is to offer a comprehensive range of outpatient health centres, some of which can develop from today's medical care centres. The establishment of an appropriate infrastructure must ensure that all patients can reach these decentralised health centres. More and more people need services from members of all health professions. The tasks and functions of the non-physician health professions have to be expanded. Communication, coordination, and cooperation have to be promoted urgently in specialist medical care.

Such approaches will naturally change the role of the hospital as well. The hospital of the future will be geared to the needs of patients. Outpatient pre- and post-treatment, as far as it corresponds to the needs and well-being of patients, will be expanded. Irrespective of inpatient stays or emergency care, outpatient care services will be set up in hospitals to complement the existing infrastructure of outpatient health centres. Since the hospital is located at the interface with other care areas, above all with outpatient healthcare, health and social care, and palliative care, a cross-sector contact point for patients and their relatives is necessary to ensure further care, treatment, and monitoring. The initial contact point, the health centres, and cross-sectoral hospital care will ensure continuity of healthcare in all sectors of the health system.

The Digitalisation of Delivery and Receipt of Healthcare

D igitalisation and the role of technology in the delivery of healthcare have never been more topical than now. Digital health offers considerable promise to solve many of the coordination and delivery issues–globally through the exchange of timely information in the event of a health crisis, nationally at the health system level through implementation of electronic health records, and individually through personalised health records involving the patient in the care pathway. To this end, digital wearable devices, precision medicine, robotics, and big data provide substantial scope for health improvement.

However, digital health raises important governance dilemmas due to its very nature, as Robin Gauld notes in Chapter 10. Besides patient data protection, ownership, and individual control, other challenges include resistance on the part of providers, accessibility to digital technologies, cross-border regulatory concerns, global fit of locally developed digital solutions, and need for expertise to operate technology.

SHAIKH, WENDT, *and* HURRELMANN

Recommendations

Gauld highlights the need for a digital governance charter that outlines rules of expected behaviour, including keeping the best interests of the public in focus and not necessarily those of the industry. Considering the immense variation in the issues faced in digital health both spatially and temporally, a digital charter should incorporate multiple cross-border and cross-sector activities and questions pertinent to the role of technology in healthcare.

A digital health charter as a starting point must adopt a patient-centred approach with control in the hands of the patient. Engaging patients and the larger public by means of traditional methods such as public meetings and focus groups, while important, must be complemented with newer forms of engagement with the help of artificial intelligence to gather feedback and preferences. Promotion of open standards for digitalisation of health and enabling accessibility to digital health are key to the participation of the patients in the digital revolution of health.

Patient data and information are what makes digital solutions workable. Therefore, data storage, usage, and protection cannot be emphasised enough in a digital health charter. Clearly recording origins and changes, particularly for personal health data, is crucial. Blockchain technology can be utilised to assist with security and auditable documentation of individual health bios, keeping in mind data security and storage concerns. Standards and expectations regarding data-sharing must be unambiguously defined, involving the public at every stage and not only listening to them but also incorporating their feedback in the digitalisation process.

Expertise in digital health mapping and ensuring up-to-date technology in line with new developments are also crucial. Detailing the specific expertise requirement in oversight and scrutiny, and adequate training if necessary, must be conducted. Finally, accountability and audit are imperative to ensure that these guidelines are followed. For this, it is important to forge a governance agenda including government leaders, policy-makers, the industry, and patients.

Conclusion

While *The Governance Report 2019* aims to provide a diverse set of recommendations and best practices for policy-makers, analysts, and individuals in governance positions, it does not aim to be a one-stop shop. Instead, it serves as a starting point for them to ponder over (a) the many challenges facing health; (b) the multidimensional nature of health governance in terms of both the objectives and the players involved; and (c) the propositions and recommendations by experts that have contributed to this Report so that the concept of governance assumes a pivotal role in designing and implementing future policies.

Health governance has been defined in the introductory chapter as the set of processes, mechanisms, and actions of all decision-makers in politics, science, business, and civil society that aim to protect and promote the health of the population and the individual. As we have pointed out, this includes interprofessional approaches on the basis of interdisciplinary cooperation and requires action in many systems, sometimes with and sometimes without the involvement of the health sector.

Kickbusch and Liu mention in Chapter 5 that health was one of the first areas for which an international governance structure was developed in the new world order that was beginning to emerge in the mid-nineteenth century. Since then a wide array of institutions, mechanisms, and actors have emerged as the world moved from international to global health. They all offer the opportunity to better address the determinants of health and reduce disparities between and within countries in the global burden of diseases and injuries. They all follow a more holistic approach to health and well-being–a multisectoral approach framed as Health in All Policies (HiAP), understanding health as an investment and a tool for sustainable development.

As the chapters in this Governance Report demonstrate, the resulting challenges are enormous. These include the tasks of optimising the ratio of resources to outcomes and developing a new approach to health with a strong emphasis on health maintenance, well-being, and quality of life. Testing new ethical standards for health systems and care, new priorities for care, and new forms of funding is also critical. Therefore, new healthcare governance models are required to cope with the simultaneous challenges of ageing populations, growing demand, shortage of healthcare personnel, and limited scope for increasing healthcare spending.

The Hertie School offers excellent conditions for the implementation of such a differentiated and comprehensive concept of health governance. Among the School's thirty professors, several work directly in the field of health research, and nearly a dozen others are active in the adjacent fields of demography, family, social affairs, labour, economy, culture, and other health-related, relevant research areas of policy. Through cooperation between the research areas, it is possible for the Hertie School faculty to put the concept of HiAP into practise in concrete terms.

References

Aaby, A., Friis, K., Christensen, B., Rowlands, G., and Maindal, H. T. (2017). 'Health Literacy Is Associated With Health Behaviour and Self-reported Health: A Large Population-based Study in Individuals With Cardiovascular Disease', *European Journal of Preventive Cardiology*, 24(17): 1880–8.

Abaluck, J., and Gruber, J. (2016a). 'Evolving Choice Inconsistencies in Choice of Prescription Drug Insurance', *The American Economic Review*, 106(8): 2145–84.

Abaluck, J., and Gruber, J. (2016b). Improving the Quality of Choices in Health Insurance Markets. NBER Working Paper 22917. Cambridge, MA: National Bureau of Economic Research.

Abe, K., Ishibashi, N., Matsumura, H., and Suzuki, Y. (2019). 'Securing Resources for Health Emergencies Management', *Health Systems & Reform*, doi: 10.1080/23288604. 2019.1594546.

Ainsaar, M., Roots, A., and Kõre, J. (forthcoming). 'Estonia', in E. M. Immergut, K. M. Anderson, C. Devitt, and T. Popic (eds), *Health Politics in Europe: A Handbook*.

Aizenmann, N. (2019) [website]. *Ebola Responders Face 2 Problems. The Solution to One Could Make the Other Worse*. Retrieved from https://www.npr.org/sections/goats andsoda/2019/03/19/704765877/what-needs-to-be-done-to-end-congos-ebola-crisis (accessed 23 March 2019).

Alexander, G. C., Frattaroli, S., and Gielen, A. (2017). The Opioid Epidemic: From Evidence to Impact. Baltimore, MD: Johns Hopkins Bloomberg School of Public Health.

Allan, J. P., and Scruggs, L. (2004). 'Political Partisanship and Welfare State Reform in Advanced Industrial Societies', *American Journal of Political Science*, 48: 496–512.

Allen, K. (2019) [website]. *World Bank's 'Pandemic Bonds' Under Scrutiny After Failing to Pay out on Ebola*. Retrieved from https://www.ft.com/content/c3a805de-3058-11e9-ba00-0251022932c8 (accessed 17 April 2019).

Allin, S., and Masseria, C. (2009). 'Unmet Need as an Indicator of Health Care Access', *Eurohealth*, 15(3): 7–10.

Altmann, S., and Traxler, C. (2014). 'Nudges at the Dentist', *European Economic Review*, 72: 19–38.

Altmann, S., Traxler, C., and Weinschenk, P. (2017). Deadlines and Cognitive Limitations. IZA Discussion Papers 11129. Berlin: IZA.

Anderson, K. M., and van Druenen, R. J. (forthcoming). 'The Netherlands', in E. M. Immergut, K. M. Anderson, C. Devitt, and T. Popic (eds), *Health Politics in Europe: A Handbook*.

Anderson, P. (2015). 'Tackling Alcohol-related Harms', in D. McDaid, F. Sassi, and S. Merkur (eds), *Promoting Health, Preventing Disease: The Economic Case*. Maidenhead: Open University Press, 81–100.

Ansell, B., and Gingrich, J. (2013). 'A Tale of Two Trilemmas: Varieties of Higher Education and the Service Economy', in A. Wren (ed), *The Political Economy of the Service Transition*. Oxford: Oxford University Press, 195–224.

Argimón, S., Abudahab, K., Goater, R. J. E., Fedosejev, A., Bhai, J., Glasner, C., Feil, E. J., Holden, M. T. G., Yeats, C. A., Grundmann, H., Spratt, B. G., and Aanensen, D. M. (2016). 'Microreact: Visualizing and Sharing Data for Genomic Epidemiology and Phylogeography', *Microbial Genomics*, 2(11), doi: 10.1099/mgen.0.000093.

Armstrong, D. (2019) [website]. *Oxycontin Maker Explored Expansion Into 'Attractive' Anti-addiction Market*. Retrieved from https://www.propublica.org/article/oxycontin-purdue-pharma-massachusetts-lawsuit-anti-addiction-market (accessed 15 April 2019).

Arrow, K. J. (1963). 'Uncertainty and Welfare Economics of Medical Care', *The American Economic Review*, 53(5): 941–73.

Asaria, M., Ali, S., Doran, T., Ferguson, B., Fleetcroft, R., Goddard, M., Goldblatt, P., Laudicella, M., Raine, R., and Cookson, R. (2016). 'How a Universal Health System Reduces Inequalities: Lessons From England', *Journal of Epidemiology and Community Health*, 70(7): 637–43.

Ayotte, K., Bera, A., Brooks, S., Cameron, B., Davis, S., Dybul, M., Frieden, T., Gerberding, J. L., Glassman, A., Greenert, J., Greenwood, J., Ham, C., Hamburg, M., Hofmann, K., Inglesby, T., Katz, R., Kolker, J., Morrison, J. S., Reynolds, C., Wormuth, C., Young, T., and Zarate, J. (2019). *Harnessing Multilateral Financing for Health Security Preparedness*. Retrieved from https://healthsecurity.csis.org/articles/harnessing-multilateral-financing-for-health-security-preparedness/ (accessed 17 April 2019).

Bähler, C., Huber, C. A., Brüngger, B., and Reich, O. (2015). 'Multimorbidity, Health Care Utilization and Costs in an Elderly Community-dwelling Population: A Claims Data Based Observational Study', *BMC Health Services Research*, 15: 23.

Baker, D. W. (2017). 'History of The Joint Commission's Pain Standards: Lessons for Today's Prescription Opioid Epidemic', *JAMA*, 317(11): 1117–8.

Baker, G. R., MacIntosh-Murray, A., Porcellato, C., Dionne, L., Stelmacovich, K., and Born, K. (2008). *High Performing Healthcare Systems: Delivering Quality by Design*. Toronto: Longwoods Publishing Corp.

Bambra, C. (ed) (2019). *Health in Hard Times: Austerity and Health Inequalities*. Bristol: Policy Press.

Bambra, C. (2016). *Health Divides: Where You Live Can Kill You*. Bristol: Policy Press.

Bambra, C. (2013). 'In Defence of (Social) Democracy: On Health Inequalities and the Welfare State', *Journal of Epidemiology and Community Health*, 67(9): 713–4.

Bambra, C. (2012). 'Reducing Health Inequalities: New Data Suggest that the English Strategy Was Partially Successful', *Journal of Epidemiology and Community Health*, 66(7): 662.

Bambra, C. (2011a). 'Health Inequalities and Welfare State Regimes: Theoretical Insights on a Public Health "Puzzle"', *Journal of Epidemiology and Community Health*, 65: 740–5.

Bambra, C. (2011b). *Work, Worklessness, and the Political Economy of Health*. Oxford: Oxford University Press.

Bambra, C. (2005). 'Cash Versus Services: "Worlds of Welfare" and the Decommodification of Cash Benefits and Health Care Services', *Journal of Social Policy*, 34: 195–213.

Bambra, C., and Eikemo, T. A. (2009). 'Welfare State Regimes, Unemployment and Health: A Comparative Study of the Relationship Between Unemployment and Self-reported Health in 23 European Countries', *Journal of Epidemiology and Community Health*, 63(2): 92–8.

Bambra, C., Fox, D., and Scott-Samuel, A. (2005). 'Towards a Politics of Health', *Health Promotion International*, 20(2): 187–93.

Bambra, C., and Garthwaite, K. (2015). 'Austerity, Welfare Reform and the English Health Divide', *Area*, 47(3): 341–3.

Bambra, C., Garthwaite, K., Copeland, A., and Barr, B. (2016). 'All in It Together? Health Inequalities, Welfare Austerity and the "Great Recession"', in K. E. Smith, S. Hill, and C. Bambra (eds), *Health Inequalities: Critical Perspectives*. Oxford: Oxford University Press, 164–76.

Bambra, C., Garthwaite, K., and Hunter, D. (2014). 'All Things Being Equal: Does It Matter for Equity How You Organize and Pay for Health Care? A Review of the International Evidence', *International Journal of Health Services: Planning, Administration, Evaluation*, 44(3): 457–77.

Bambra, C., Munford, L., Brown, H., Wilding, A., Robinson, T., Holland, P., Barr, B., Hill, H., Regan, M., Rice, N., and Sutton, M. (2018). Health for Wealth: Building a Healthier

Northern Powerhouse for UK Productivity. Newcastle: Northern Health Science Alliance.

Barnes, M. C., Gunnell, D., Davies, R., Hawton, K., Kapur, N., Potokar, J., and Donovan, J. L. (2016). 'Understanding Vulnerability to Self-harm in Times of Economic Hardship and Austerity: A Qualitative Study', *BMJ Open*, 6(2): e010131.

Barnett, K., Mercer, S. W., Norbury, M., Watt, G., Wyke, S., and Guthrie, B. (2012). 'Epidemiology of Multimorbidity and Implications for Health Care, Research, and Medical Education: A Cross-sectional Study', *The Lancet*, 380(9836): 37–43.

Barr, B., Bambra, C., and Whitehead, M. (2014). 'The Impact of NHS Resource Allocation Policy on Health Inequalities in England 2001-11: Longitudinal Ecological Study', *BMJ Clinical Research Edition*, 348: g3231.

Barr, B., Higgerson, J., and Whitehead, M. (2017). 'Investigating the Impact of the English Health Inequalities Strategy: Time Trend Analysis', *BMJ Clinical Research Edition*, 358: j3310.

Barr, B., Kinderman, P., and Whitehead, M. (2015). 'Trends in Mental Health Inequalities in England During a Period of Recession, Austerity and Welfare Reform 2004 to 2013', *Social Science & Medicine*, 147: 324–31.

Barr, B., Taylor-Robinson, D., Stuckler, D., Loopstra, R., Reeves, A., and Whitehead, M. (2016). 'First, Do No Harm: Are Disability Assessments Associated With Adverse Trends in Mental Health? A Longitudinal Ecological Study', *Journal of Epidemiology and Community Health*, 70(4): 339–45.

Baumol, W. J. (1967). 'Macroeconomics of Unbalanced Growth: The Anatomy of Urban Crisis', *American Economic Review*, 57: 415–26.

BBC (British Broadcasting Corporation) (2019) [website]. *Indivior Shares Plunge on 'Shameful' Opioid Drug Scheme*. Retrieved from https://www.bbc.com/news/business-47879868 (accessed 10 April 2019).

Beatty, C., and Fothergill, S. (2016). The Uneven Impact of Welfare Reform: The Financial Losses to Places and People. Project Report. Sheffield: Sheffield Hallam University.

Beatty, C., and Fothergill, S. (2014). 'The Local and Regional Impact of the UK's Welfare Reforms', *Cambridge Journal of Regions, Economy and Society*, 7(1): 63–79.

Béland, D. and Gran, B. (eds) (2008). *Public and Private Social Policy: Health and Pension Policies in a New Era*. Basingstoke: Palgrave Macmillan.

Benton, A., and Dionne, K. Y. (2015). 'International Political Economy and the 2014 West African Ebola Outbreak', *African Studies Review*, 58(1): 223–36.

Beramendi, P., Häusermann, S., Kitschelt, H. and Kriesi, H. (eds) (2015). *The Politics of Advanced Capitalism*. New York: Cambridge University Press.

Bernstein, L., and Zezima, K. (2019) [website]. *Purdue Pharma, State of Oklahoma Reach Settlement in Landmark Opioid Lawsuit*. Retrieved from https://www.washingtonpost.com/national/health-science/purdue-pharma-state-of-oklahoma-reach-settlement-in-landmark-opioid-lawsuit/2019/03/26/69aa5cda-4f11-11e9-a3f7-78b7525a8d5f_story.html (accessed 16 April 2019).

Berterame, S., Erthal, J., Thomas, J., Fellner, S., Vosse, B., Clare, P., Hao, W., Johnson, D. T., Mohar, A., Pavadia, J., Samak, A. K. E., Sipp, W., Sumyai, V., Suryawati, S., Toufiq, J., Yans, R., and Mattick, R. P. (2016). 'Use of and Barriers to Access to Opioid Analgesics: A Worldwide, Regional, and National Study', *The Lancet*, 387(10028): 1644–56.

Bevir, M., and Rhodes, R. A. W. (2006). *Governance Stories*. London: Routledge.

Bhargava, S., Loewenstein, G., and Sydnor, J. (2017). 'Choose to Lose: Health Plan Choices From a Menu With Dominated Option', *The Quarterly Journal of Economics*, 132(3): 1319–72.

Biehl, J. (2016). 'Theorizing Global Health', *Medicine Anthropology Theory*, 3(2): 127.

Birn, A.-E. (2014). 'Philanthrocapitalism, Past and Present: The Rockefeller Foundation, the Gates Foundation, and the Setting(s) of the International/Global Health Agenda', *Hypothesis*, 12(1): e8.

Björkman Nyqvist, M., Walque, D. de, and Svensson, J. (2017). 'Experimental Evidence on the Long-run Impact of Community-based Monitoring', *American Economic Journal: Applied Economics*, 9(1): 33–69.

Blakely, T., Tobias, M., and Atkinson, J. (2008). 'Inequalities in Mortality During and After Restructuring of the New Zealand Economy: Repeated Cohort Studies', *BMJ Clinical Research Edition*, 336(7640): 371–5.

Blomqvist, P., and Winblad, U. (forthcoming). 'Sweden', in E. M. Immergut, K. M. Anderson, C. Devitt, and T. Popic (eds), *Health Politics in Europe: A Handbook*.

Bollyky, T. J. (2019) [website]. *The Future of Global Health Is Urban Health*. Retrieved from https://www.cfr.org/article/future-global-health-urban-health (accessed 10 April 2019).

Bollyky, T. J. (2018). *Plagues and the Paradox of Progress: Why the World Is Getting Healthier in Worrisome Ways*. Cambridge, MA: The MIT Press.

Bonoli, G. (2014). *Social Investment Policies in Times of Permanent Austerity: Paper for the XVIII ISA World Congress of Sociology, Yokohama 13-19 July 2014*. Yokohama, Japan.

Bonoli, G. (2007). 'Time Matters: Postindustrialization, New Social Risks, and Welfare State Adaptation in Advanced Industrial Democracies', *Comparative Political Studies*, 40: 495–520.

Bonoli, G. (1997). 'Classifying Welfare States: A Two-Dimension Approach', *Journal of Social Policy*, 26: 315–72.

Bonoli, G., and Natali, D. (2012). *The Politics of the 'New' Welfare State*. Oxford: Oxford University Press.

Bos, A., Hoogstraten, J., and Prahl-Andersen, B. (2005). 'Failed Appointments in an Orthodontic Clinic', *American Journal of Orthodontics and Dentofacial Orthopedics*, 127(3): 355–7.

Bosetti, C., Santucci, C., Radrezza, S., Erthal, J., Berterame, S., and Corli, O. (2019). 'Trends in the Consumption of Opioids for the Treatment of Severe Pain in Europe, 1990–2016', *European Journal of Pain*, 23(4): 697–707.

Bouget, D., Frazer, H., Marlier, E., Sabato, S., and Vanhercke, B. (2015). Social Investment in Europe: A Study of National Policies. Brussels: European Commission.

Bourdieu, P. (1986). 'The Forms of Capital', in J. G. Richardson (ed), *Handbook of Theory and Research for the Sociology of Education*. Westport: Greenwood Press, 241–58.

Bourdieu, P., Wacquant, L. J. D., and Farage, S. (1994). 'Rethinking the State: Genesis and Structure of the Bureaucratic Field', *Sociological Theory*, 12(1): 1–18.

Boyer, R. (2002). *La Croissance, début de siècle*. Paris: Albin Michel.

Brinkerhoff, D. W., and Bossert, T. J. (2014). 'Health Governance: Principal–Agent Linkages and Health System Strengthening', *Health Policy and Planning*, 29(6): 685–93.

Broniatowski, D. A., Jamison, A. M., Qi, S., AlKulaib, L., Chen, T., Benton, A., Quinn, S. C., and Dredze, M. (2018). 'Weaponized Health Communication: Twitter Bots and Russian Trolls Amplify the Vaccine Debate', *American Journal of Public Health*, 108(10): 1378–84.

Brown, T. M., Cueto, M., and Fee, E. (2006). 'The World Health Organization and the Transition From "International" to "Global" Public Health', *American Journal of Public Health*, 96(1): 62–72.

Browne, J., and Levell, P. (2010). The Distributional Effect of Tax and Benefit Reforms to Be Introduced Between June 2010 and April 2014: A Revised Assessment. IFS Briefing Note BN108. London: Institute for Fiscal Studies.

Bruckner, T. (2019). The Ignored Pandemic: How Corruption in Healthcare Service Delivery Threatens Universal Health Coverage. London: Transparency International.

Brunn, M., and Hassenteufel, P. (forthcoming). 'France', in E. M. Immergut, K. M. Anderson, C. Devitt, and T. Popic (eds), *Health Politics in Europe: A Handbook*.

Buck, D., and Dixon, A. (2013). Improving the Allocation of Health Resources in England. London: King's Fund.

Burci, G. L. (2018) [website]. *Global Health Disruptors: WHO Framework Convention on Tobacco Control*. Retrieved from https://blogs.bmj.com/bmj/2018/11/28/global-health-disruptors-who-framework-convention-on-tobacco-control/ (accessed 10 April 2019).

Burke, J. (2018) [website]. *Wave of Rebel Attacks Leads to Surge in DRC Ebola Cases*. Retrieved from https://www.theguardian.com/world/2018/oct/25/wave-of-rebel-attacks-leads-to-surge-in-drc-ebola-cases (accessed 21 March 2019).

Burlacu, D., Immergut, E. M., Oskarson, M., and Rönnerstrand, B. (2018). 'The Politics of Credit Claiming: Rights and Recognition in Health Policy Feedback', *Social Policy & Administration*, 52(4): 880–94.

Burton, L. C., Anderson, G. F., and Kues, I. W. (2004). 'Using Electronic Health Records to Help Coordinate Care', *The Milbank Quarterly*, 82(3): 457-81.

Buse, K., Dickinson, C., Gilson, L., and Murray, S. F. (2009). 'How Can the Analysis of Power and Process in Policy-making Improve Health Outcomes?', *World Hospitals and Health Services*, 45(1): 14.

Busse, R., Blümel, M., Scheller-Kreinsen, D., and Zentner, A. (2010). *Tackling Chronic Disease in Europe: Strategies, Interventions and Challenges*. Copenhagen: European Observatory on Health Systems and Policies.

Byatnal, A. (2018) [website]. *'Tax for TRIPS' Deal Altered UN Declarations on NCDs, TB*. Retrieved from https://www.devex.com/news/exclusive-tax-for-trips-deal-altered-un-declarations-on-ncds-tb-93580 (accessed 10 April 2019).

Calado, D. (2018) [website]. *Traditional Chinese Medicine as a Bridge to BRI*. Retrieved from http://www.chinadaily.com.cn/a/201808/13/WS5b70ea94a310add14f385632.html (accessed 10 April 2019).

Caris, M. G., Labuschagne, H. A., Dekker, M., Kramer, M. H. H., van Agtmael, M. A., and Vandenbroucke-Grauls, C. M. J. E. (2018). 'Nudging to Improve Hand Hygiene', *The Journal of Hospital Infection*, 98(4): 352–8.

Castells, M., Bouin, O., Caraça, J., Cardoso, G., Thompson, J. and Wieviorka, M. (eds) (2018). *Europe's Crises*. Cambridge UK: Polity Press.

CDC (Centers for Disease Control and Prevention) (2015) [website]. *African Union and US CDC Partner to Launch African CDC*. Retrieved from https://www.cdc.gov/media/releases/2015/p0413-african-union.html (accessed 7 March 2019).

CDC (2011). 'Vital Signs: Overdoses of Prescription Opioid Pain Relievers—United States, 1999–2008', *MMWR Recommendations and Reports*, 60(43): 1487–92.

CDC (n.d.) [website]. *SEDRIC: System for Enteric Disease Response, Investigation, and Coordination*. Retrieved from https://www.cdc.gov/foodsafety/outbreaks/investigating-outbreaks/sedric.html (accessed 19 January 2019).

Chalkidou, K., Tunis, S., Lopert, R., Rochaix, L., Sawicki, P. T., Nasser, M., and Xerri, B. (2009). 'Comparative Effectiveness Research and Evidence-based Health Policy: Experience From Four Countries', *The Milbank Quarterly*, 87(2): 339–67.

Chan, A. H. Y., Stewart, A. W., Harrison, J., Camargo, C. A., Black, P. N., and Mitchell, E. A. (2015). 'The Effect of an Electronic Monitoring Device With Audiovisual Reminder Function on Adherence to Inhaled Corticosteroids and School Attendance in Children With Asthma: A Randomised Controlled Trial', *The Lancet Respiratory Medicine*, 3(3): 210–9.

Chandra, A., Handel, B., and Schwartzstein, J. (2019). 'Behavioral Economics and Healthcare Markets', in B. D. Bernheim, S. Della Vigna, and D. I. Laibson (eds), *Handbook of Behavioral Economics: Foundations and Applications, Volume 2*. Amsterdam: North Holland, 460–502.

Chapman, G. B., Li, M., Colby, H., and Yoon, H. (2010). 'Opting in vs Opting out of Influenza Vaccination', *JAMA*, 304(1): 43–4.

Chen, C., Garrido, T., Chock, D., Okawa, G., and Liang, L. (2009). 'The Kaiser Permanente Electronic Health Record: Transforming and Streamlining Modalities of Care', *Health Affairs*, 28(2): 323–33.

Chen, L., and Yang, M. (2018). 'New Opportunities for China in Global Health', *The Lancet Global Health*, 6(7): e722–3.

Chenaf, C., Kaboré, J.-L., Delorme, J., Pereira, B., Mulliez, A., Zenut, M., Delage, N., Ardid, D., Eschalier, A., and Authier, N. (2019). 'Prescription Opioid Analgesic Use in France: Trends and Impact on Morbidity–Mortality', *European Journal of Pain*, 23(1): 124–34.

Cherchye, L., Rock, B. de, Griffith, R., O'Connell, M., Smith, K., and Vermeulen, F. (2017). A New Year, a New You? Heterogeneity and Self-control in Food Purchases. Working Papers ECARES 2017-46. Brussels: Université Libre de Bruxelles.

Chorev, N. (2012). *The World Health Organization Between North and South*. Ithaca: Cornell University Press.

Choudhry, N. K., Avorn, J., Glynn, R. J., Antman, E. M., Schneeweiss, S., Toscano, M., Reisman, L., Fernandes, J., Spettell, C., Lee, J. L., Levin, R., Brennan, T., and Shrank, W. H. (2011). 'Full Coverage for Preventive Medications After Myocardial Infarction', *The New England Journal of Medicine*, 365(22): 2088–97.

Chuliá, E. (forthcoming). 'Spain', in E. M. Immergut, K. M. Anderson, C. Devitt, and T. Popic (eds), *Health Politics in Europe: A Handbook*.

Chung, C. P., Dupont, W. D., Murray, K. T., Hall, K., Stein, C. M., and Ray, W. A. (2019). 'Comparative Out-of-hospital Mortality of Long-acting Opioids Prescribed for Non-cancer Pain: A Retrospective Cohort Study', *Pharmacoepidemiology and Drug Safety*, 28(1): 48–53.

Cicero, T. J., Ellis, M. S., and Kasper, Z. A. (2017). 'Increased Use of Heroin as an Initiating Opioid of Abuse', *Addictive Behaviors*, 74: 63–6.

Clarke, J. L., and Meiris, D. C. (2006). 'Electronic Personal Health Records Come of Age', *American Journal of Medical Quality*, 21(3_suppl): 5S–15S.

Clausen, B., Kraay, A., and Nyiri, Z. (2011). 'Corruption and Confidence in Public Institutions: Evidence From a Global Survey', *The World Bank Economic Review*, 25(2): 212–49.

Clegg, S. (1989). *Frameworks of Power*. London: SAGE.

Clift, C. (2013). The Role of the World Health Organization in the International System. Centre on Global Health Security Working Group Papers: Working Group on Governance 1. London: Chatham House.

Cohen, I. G., Lynch, H. F. and Robertson, C. T. (eds) (2016). *Nudging Health: Health Law and Behavioral Economics*. Baltimore: Johns Hopkins University Press.

Collignon, P., Athukorala, P.-C., Senanayake, S., and Khan, F. (2015). 'Antimicrobial Resistance: The Major Contribution of Poor Governance and Corruption to This Growing Problem', *PloS One*, 10(3): e0116746.

Commission on Macroeconomics and Health (2001). *Macroeconomics and Health. Investing in Health for Economic Development. Report of the Commission on Macroeconomics and Health*. Geneva: World Health Organization.

Commission on Social Determinants of Health (2008). Closing the Gap in a Generation: Health Equity Through Action on the Social Determinants of Health. Final Report of the Commission on Social Determinants of Health. Geneva: World Health Organization.

Cutler, R. L., Fernandez-Llimos, F., Frommer, M., Benrimoj, C., and Garcia-Cardenas, V. (2018). 'Economic Impact of Medication Non-adherence by Disease Groups: A Systematic Review', *BMJ Open*, 8(1): e016982.

Cutrona, S. L., Choudhry, N. K., Fischer, M. A., Amber Servi, A., Liberman, J. N., Brennan, T. A., and Shrank, W. H. (2010). 'Modes of Delivery for Interventions to Improve Cardiovascular Medication Adherence: Review', *The American Journal of Managed Care*, 16(12): 929–42.

Cyber Security Policy (2018). Securing Cyber Resilience in Health and Care: Progress Update October 2018. London: Department of Health and Social Care.

da Silva Dal Pizzol, T., Turmina Fontanella, A., Cardoso Ferreira, M. B., Dâmaso Bertoldi, A., Boff Borges, R., and Serrate Mengue, S. (2019). 'Analgesic Use Among the Brazilian Population: Results From the National Survey on Access, Use and Promotion of Rational Use of Medicines (PNAUM)', *PloS One*, 14(3): e0214329.

Dahn, B., Mussah, V., and Nutt, C. (2015) [website]. *Yes, We Were Warned About Ebola*. Retrieved from https://www.nytimes.com/2015/04/08/opinion/yes-we-were-warned-about-ebola.html (accessed 10 April 2019).

Dai, H., Mao, D., Riis, J., Volpp, K. G., Relish, M. J., Lawnicki, V. F., and Milkman, K. L. (2017). 'Effectiveness of Medication Adherence Reminders Tied to "Fresh Start" Dates: A Randomized Clinical Trial', *JAMA Cardiology*, 2(4): 453–5.

Dai, H., Mao, D., Volpp, K. G., Pearce, H. E., Relish, M. J., Lawnicki, V. F., and Milkman, K. L. (2017). 'The Effect of Interactive Reminders on Medication Adherence: A Randomized Trial', *Preventive Medicine*, 103: 98–102.

Dai, H., Milkman, K. L., Hofmann, D. A., and Staats, B. R. (2015). 'The Impact of Time at Work and Time off From Work on Rule Compliance: The Case of Hand Hygiene in Health Care', *The Journal of Applied Psychology*, 100(3): 846–62.

Day, M. (2018). 'Top Italian Public Health Official Faces Allegation of Failing to Disclose Pharma Links', *BMJ Clinical Research Edition*, 363: k5325.

de la Maisonneuve, C., and Martins, J. O. (2015). 'The Future of Health and Long-term Care Spending', *OECD Journal: Economic Studies*, 2014: 61–96.

de la Torre-Díez, I., López-Coronado, M., Vaca, C., Aguado, J. S., and de Castro, C. (2015). 'Cost-utility and Cost-effectiveness Studies of Telemedicine, Electronic, and Mobile Health Systems in the Literature: A Systematic Review', *Telemedicine Journal and e-Health*, 21(2): 81–5.

de Maeseneer, J., van Weel, C., Daeren, L., Leyns, C., Decat, P., Boeckxstaens, P., Avonts, D., and Willems, S. (2012). 'From "Patient" to "Person" to "People": The Need for Integrated, People Centered Health Care', *International Journal of Person Centered Medicine*, 2(3): 601–14.

de Moor, G., Sundgren, M., Kalra, D., Schmidt, A., Dugas, M., Claerhout, B., Karakoyun, T., Ohmann, C., Lastic, P.-Y., Ammour, N., Kush, R., Dupont, D., Cuggia, M., Daniel, C., Thienpont, G., and Coorevits, P. (2015). 'Using Electronic Health Records for Clinical Research: The Case of the EHR4CR Project', *Journal of Biomedical Informatics*, 53: 162–73.

Delgado, M. K., Shofer, F. S., Patel, M. S., Halpern, S., Edwards, C., Meisel, Z. F., and Perrone, J. (2018). 'Association Between Electronic Medical Record Implementation of Default Opioid Prescription Quantities and Prescribing Behavior in Two Emergency Departments', *Journal of General Internal Medicine*, 33(4): 409–11.

Deloitte (2019). 2019 Global Health Care Outlook: Shaping the Future. Sydney: Deloitte.

Demiris, G., Oliver, D. P., Dickey, G., Skubic, M., and Rantz, M. (2008). 'Findings From a Participatory Evaluation of a Smart Home Application for Older Adults', *Technology and Health Care*, 16(2): 111–8.

Department of Health (2009). Tackling Health Inequalities: 10 Years on. A Review of Developments in Tacking Health Inequalities in England Over the Last 10 Years. London: Department of Health.

Department of Health (2008). Tackling Health Inequalities: 2007 Status Report on the Programme for Action. London: Department of Health.

Department of Health (2000). An Organisation With a Memory. Report of an Expert Group on Learning From Adverse Events in the NHS. London: The Stationery Office.

Devitt, C. (forthcoming). 'Ireland', in E. M. Immergut, K. M. Anderson, C. Devitt, and T. Popic (eds), Health Politics in Europe: A Handbook.

Dhalla, I. A., Mamdani, M. M., Sivilotti, M. L. A., Kopp, A., Qureshi, O., and Juurlink, D. N. (2009). 'Prescribing of Opioid Analgesics and Related Mortality Before and After the Introduction of Long-acting Oxycodone', CMAJ Canadian Medical Association Journal, 181(12): 891–6.

Dhatt, R., Kickbusch, I., and Thompson, K. (2017). 'Act Now: A Call to Action for Gender Equality in Global Health', The Lancet, 389(10069): 602.

Dicker, D., Nguyen, G., Abate, D., et al. (2018). 'Global, Regional, and National Age-sex-specific Mortality and Life Expectancy, 1950–2017: A Systematic Analysis for the Global Burden of Disease Study 2017', The Lancet, 392(10159): 1684–735.

Diderichsen, F. (2016). 'Health Inequalities – A Challenge for the Social Investment Welfare State', Nordisk välfärdsforskning | Nordic Welfare Research, 1: 43–54.

DiSARM (n.d.) [website]. DiSARM – Disease Surveillance and Risk Monitoring: Data-Driven Decision Making Platform for Malaria Elimination. Retrieved from https://www.disarm.io/ (accessed 15 January 2019).

Dølvik, J. E., Fløtten, T., Hippe, J. M., and Jordfald, B. (2015). The Nordic Model Towards 2030. A New Chapter? Oslo: Fafo.

Döring, H., and Manow, P. (2017). 'Is Proportional Representation More Favourable to the Left? Electoral Rules and Their Impact on Elections, Parliaments and the Formation of Cabinets', British Journal of Political Science, 47(01): 149–64.

Döring, H., and Schwander, H. (2015). 'Revisiting the Left Cabinet Share: How to Measure the Partisan Profile of Governments in Welfare State Research', Journal of European Social Policy, 25(2): 175–93.

Dowell, D., Haegerich, T. M., and Chou, R. (2016). 'CDC Guideline for Prescribing Opioids for Chronic Pain – United States, 2016', MMWR Recommendations and Reports, 65(1): 1–49.

Dryzek, J. S. (2002). Deliberative Democracy and Beyond: Liberals, Critics, Contestations. Oxford: Oxford University Press.

Dugarova, E., and Gülasan, N. (2017). Global Trends: Challenges and Opportunities in the Implementation of the SDGs. New York: United Nations Development Programme, United Nations Research Institute For Social Development.

Dyakova, M., Hamelmann, C., Bellis, M. A., Besnier, E., Grey, C. N.B., Ashton, K., Schwappach, A., and Clar, C. (2017). Investment for Health and Well-being: A Review of the Social Return on Investment From Public Health Policies to Support Implementing the Sustainable Development Goals by Building on Health 2020. Health Evidence Network Synthesis Report 51. Copenhagen: WHO Regional Office for Europe.

Ecorys (2013). Study on Corruption in the Healthcare Sector. HOME/2011/ISEC/PR/047-A2. Luxembourg: Publications Office of the European Union.

Ehrlich, C., and Kendall, E. (2015). 'Integrating Collaborative Place-based Health Promotion Coalitions Into Existing Health System Structures: The Experience From One Australian Health Coalition', International Journal of Integrated Care, 15(4), doi: 10.5334/ijic.2012.

Eihmanis, E. (forthcoming). 'Latvia', in E. M. Immergut, K. M. Anderson, C. Devitt, and T. Popic (eds), Health Politics in Europe: A Handbook.

Eikemo, T. A., Avrami, L., Cavounidis, J., Mouriki, A., Gkiouleka, A., McNamara, C. L., and Stathopoulou, T. (2018). 'Health in Crises. Migration, Austerity and Inequalities in Greece and Europe: Introduction to the Supplement', European Journal of Public Health, 28(suppl_5): 1–4.

Elango, S., Szymczak, J. E., Bennett, I. M., Beidas, R. S., and Werner, R. M. (2018). 'Changing Antibiotic Prescribing in a Primary Care Network: The Role of Readiness to Change and Group Dynamics in Success', *American Journal of Medical Quality*, 33(2): 154–61.

Ensor, T. (2004). 'Informal Payments for Health Care in Transition Economies', *Social Science & Medicine*, 58(2): 237–46.

Epihack (n.d.) [website]. *What Is an EpiHack?* Retrieved from https://epihack.org/what-is-epihack (accessed 25 January 2019).

Ericson, K. M. M., and Laibson, D. I. (2019). 'Intertemporal Choice', in B. D. Bernheim, S. Della Vigna, and D. I. Laibson (eds), *Handbook of Behavioral Economics: Foundations and Applications, Volume 2*. Amsterdam: North Holland, 1–67.

Ericson, K. M. M., and Starc, A. (2016). 'How Product Standardization Affects Choice: Evidence From the Massachusetts Health Insurance Exchange', *Journal of Health Economics*, 50: 71–85.

Esping-Andersen, G. (2002). *Why We Need a New Welfare State*. Oxford: Oxford University Press.

Esping-Andersen, G. (1990). *The Three Worlds of Welfare Capitalism*. Princeton: Princeton University Press.

Esping-Andersen, G. (1987). 'Citizenship and Socialism: Decommodification and Solidarity in the Welfare State', in M. Rein, G. Esping-Andersen, and L. Rainwater (eds), *Stagnation and Renewal in Social Policy: The Rise and Fall of Policy Regimes*. Armonk, NY: M.E. Sharpe, 78–101.

Esping-Andersen, G. (1985). *Politics Against Markets: The Social Democratic Road to Power*. Princeton: Princeton University Press.

Estacio, E. V., Whittle, R., and Protheroe, J. (2017). 'The Digital Divide: Examining Socio-demographic Factors Associated With Health Literacy, Access and Use of Internet to Seek Health Information', *Journal of Health Psychology*, doi: 10.1177/1359105317695429.

European Commission (2015). Global Overview of Ebola Research. Brussels: European Commission.

European Social Survey Cumulative File, ESS 1-8 (2018). Data file edition 1.0. NSD - Norwegian Centre for Research Data, Norway - Data Archive and distributor of ESS data for ESS ERIC. DOI:10.21338/NSD-ESS-CUMULATIVE.

Eurostat (2019) [website]. *EU Statistics on Income and Living Conditions [2008–2018]*. Retrieved from https://appsso.eurostat.ec.europa.eu/nui/show.do?dataset=hlth_silc_14&lang=en (accessed 28 May 2019).

Eurostat (2018) [website]. *Database* (indicator code hlth_silc_10). Retrieved from https://appsso.eurostat.ec.europa.eu/nui/show.do?dataset=hlth_silc_10&lang=en.

Executive Board, 138. (2016). *2014 Ebola Virus Disease Outbreak and Issues Raised: Follow-up to the Special Session of the Executive Board on the Ebola Emergency (Resolution EBSS3.R1) and the Sixty-eighth World Health Assembly (Decision WHA68(10)): High-level Design for a New WHO Health Emergencies Programme: Report by the Director-General*. Retrieved from http://www.who.int/iris/handle/10665/250754 (accessed 9 May 2019).

Fahy, N., Hervey, T., Greer, S., Jarman, H., Stuckler, D., Galsworthy, M., and McKee, M. (2019). 'How Will Brexit Affect Health Services in the UK? An Updated Evaluation', *The Lancet*, 393(10174): 949–58.

Falkenbach, M., and Greer, S. L. (2018). 'Political Parties Matter: The Impact of the Populist Radical Right on Health', *European Journal of Public Health*, 28(suppl_3): 15–8.

Fan, V., Jamison, D., and Summers, L. (2016). The Inclusive Cost of Pandemic Influenza Risk. NBER Working Paper. Cambridge, MA: National Bureau of Economic Research.

Farrar, J. J., and Piot, P. (2014). 'The Ebola Emergency—Immediate Action, Ongoing Strategy', *The New England Journal of Medicine*, 371(16): 1545–6.

Ferrera, M. (1996). 'The "Southern Model" of Welfare in Social Europe', *Journal of European Social Policy*, 6(1): 17–37.

Fidler, D. P. (2005). 'From International Sanitary Conventions to Global Health Security: The New International Health Regulations', *Chinese Journal of International Law*, 4(2): 325–92.

FIND (Foundation for Innovative New Diagnostics) (2019) [website]. *CEPI Backs Expansion of FIND's Lassa Fever Response Programme to Support Pandemic Preparedness in Nigeria*. Retrieved from https://www.finddx.org/publication/pr-16jan19/ (accessed 27 March 2019).

FIND (2018). Diagnostics for Epidemic Preparedness: Outbreak Strategy 2018. Geneva: FIND.

Fink, S. (2014) [website]. *Cuts at WHO Hurt Response to Ebola Crisis*. Retrieved from https://www.nytimes.com/2014/09/04/world/africa/cuts-at-who-hurt-response-to-ebola-crisis.html (accessed 10 April 2019).

Fischer, B., Jones, W., and Rehm, J. (2014). 'Trends and Changes in Prescription Opioid Analgesic Dispensing in Canada 2005–2012: An Update With a Focus on Recent Interventions', *BMC Health Services Research*, 14: 90.

Fitchett, J. R., Lichtman, A., Soyode, D. T., Low, A., Villar de Onis, J., Head, M. G., and Atun, R. (2016). 'Ebola Research Funding: A Systematic Analysis, 1997–2015', *Journal of Global Health*, 6(2): 20703.

Fjær, E. L., Stornes, P., Borisova, L. V., McNamara, C. L., and Eikemo, T. A. (2017). 'Subjective Perceptions of Unmet Need for Health Care in Europe Among Social Groups: Findings From the European Social Survey (2014) Special Module on the Social Determinants of Health', *European Journal of Public Health*, 27(suppl_1): 82–9.

Földes, M. É. (forthcoming). 'Hungary', in E. M. Immergut, K. M. Anderson, C. Devitt, and T. Popic (eds), *Health Politics in Europe: A Handbook*.

Forster, T., Kentikelenis, A., and Bambra, C. (2018). Health Inequalities in Europe: Setting the Stage for Progressive Policy Action. Dublin: Think Tank for Action on Social Change.

Fox, N. J., and Ward, K. J. (2008). 'What Governs Governance, and How Does It Evolve? The Sociology of Governance-in-action', *The British Journal of Sociology*, 59(3): 519–38.

Freeman, R., and Rothgang, H. (2010). 'Health', in F. G. Castles, S. Leibfried, J. Lewis, H. Obinger, and C. Pierson (eds), *The Oxford Handbook of the Welfare State*. Oxford: Oxford University Press, 367–77.

Freidson, E. (2001). *Professionalism: The Third Logic*. Cambridge: Polity.

Frenk, J., and Donabedian, A. (1987). 'State Intervention in Medical Care: Types, Trends and Variables', *Health Policy and Planning*, 2(1): 17–31.

Frenk, J., Gómez-Dantés, O., and Moon, S. (2014). 'From Sovereignty to Solidarity: A Renewed Concept of Global Health for an Era of Complex Interdependence', *The Lancet*, 383(9911): 94–7.

de Freytas-Tamura, K. (2018) [website]. *Trek Into Congo Forest Reveals an Ebola Crisis Fueled by Violence*. Retrieved from https://www.nytimes.com/2018/12/26/world/africa/ebola-congo.html (accessed 13 March 2019).

Friel, S. (2018) [website]. *Global Health Disruptors: Doha Declaration*. Retrieved from https://blogs.bmj.com/bmj/2018/11/28/global-health-disruptors-doha-declaration/ (accessed 10 April 2019).

Funke, M., Schularick, M., and Trebesch, C. (2016). 'Going to Extremes: Politics After Financial Crises, 1870–2014', *European Economic Review*, 88: 227–60.

G7 (2018) [website]. *Official Documents: 2018 Charlevoix Summit*. Retrieved from http://www.g8.utoronto.ca/summit/2018charlevoix/index.html (accessed 9 May 2019).

G7 (2017). *G7 Milan Health Ministers' Communiqué: 5–6 November, 2017*. Retrieved from http://www.g7italy.it/en/meeting/health/ (accessed 14 February 2019).

G7 (2016). *G7 Ise-Shima Vision for Global Health*. Retrieved from https://extranet.who.int/sph/g7-ise-shima-vision-global-health (accessed 19 March 2019).

G7 (2015). G7 Presidency 2015: Final Report by the Federal Government on the G7 Presidency 2015. Berlin: Press and Information Office of the Federal Government of Germany.

Galizzi, M. M., and Wiesen, D. (2018). 'Behavioral Experiments in Health Economics', in *Oxford Research Encyclopedia of Economics and Finance*. Retrieved from https://oxfordre.com/economics/view/10.1093/acrefore/9780190625979.001.0001/acrefore-9780190625979-e-244 (accessed 9 June 2019).

Gamble, A. (2009). *The Spectre at the Feast: Capitalist Crisis and the Politics of Recession*. Basingstoke: Palgrave Macmillan.

Garcia del Pozo, J., Carvajal, A., Viloria, J. M., Velasco, A., and Garcia del Pozo, V. (2008). 'Trends in the Consumption of Opioid Analgesics in Spain: Higher Increases as Fentanyl Replaces Morphine', *European Journal of Clinical Pharmacology*, 64(4): 411–5.

García del Pozo, J., Carvajal García-Pando, A., Rueda de Castro, A. M., Cano del Pozo, M. I., and Martín Arias, L. H. (1999). 'Opioid Consumption in Spain: The Significance of a Regulatory Measure', *European Journal of Clinical Pharmacology*, 55(9): 681–3.

Garrett, G. (2001). 'Globalization and Government Spending Around the World', *Studies in Comparative International Development*, 35(4): 3–29.

Garritzmann, J. L., Häusermann, S., Palier, B., and Zollinger, C. (2017). The World Politics of Social Investment. LIEPP Working Paper 64. Paris: Sciences Po - LIEPP.

Garthwaite, K., Collins, P. J., and Bambra, C. (2015). 'Food for Thought: An Ethnographic Study of Negotiating Ill Health and Food Insecurity in a UK Goodbank', *Social Science & Medicine*, 132: 38–44.

Gauld, R. (2014). 'Ahead of Its Time? Reflecting on New Zealand's Pharmac Following Its 20th Anniversary', *PharmacoEconomics*, 32(10): 937–42.

Gauld, R. (2009). *The New Health Policy*. Maidenhead: Open University Press.

Gauld, R. (2007). 'Public Sector Information System Project Failures: Lessons From a New Zealand Hospital Organization', *Government Information Quarterly*, 24(1): 102–14.

Gauld, R., Burgers, J., Dobrow, M., Minhas, R., Wendt, C., Cohen, A. B., and Luxford, K. (2014). 'Healthcare System Performance Improvement: A Comparison of Key Policies in Seven High-income Countries', *Journal of Health Organization and Management*, 28(1): 2–20.

Gauld, R., and Goldfinch, S. (2006). *Dangerous Enthusiasms: E-government, Computer Failure and Information System Development*. Dunedin: Otago University Press.

Gauld, R., and Williams, S. (2009). 'Use of the Internet for Health Information: A Study of Australians and New Zealanders', *Informatics for Health and Social Care*, 34(3): 149–58.

Gelormino, E., Bambra, C., Spadea, T., Bellini, S., and Costa, G. (2011). 'The Effects of Health Care Reforms on Health Inequalities: A Review and Analysis of the European Evidence Base', *International Journal of Health Services: Planning, Administration, Evaluation*, 41(2): 209–30.

Gerber, J. S., Prasad, P. A., Fiks, A. G., Localio, A. R., Bell, L. M., Keren, R., and Zaoutis, T. E. (2014). 'Durability of Benefits of an Outpatient Antimicrobial Stewardship Intervention After Discontinuation of Audit and Feedback', *JAMA*, 312(23): 2569–70.

Gerdtham, U. G., and Jönsson, B. (2000). 'International Comparisons of Health Expenditure', in A. J. Culyer, and J. P. Newhouse (eds), *Handbook of Health Economics*. 1st ed. Amsterdam: Elsevier, 11–53.

GHRF Commission (Commission on a Global Health Risk Framework for the Future) (2016). *The Neglected Dimension of Global Security: A Framework to Counter Infectious Disease Crises*. Washington, DC: National Academies Press.

Giaimo, S., and Manow, P. (1999). 'Adapting the Welfare State: The Case of Health Care Reform in Britain, Germany, and the United States', *Comparative Political Studies*, 32(8): 967–1000.

Gibson, M., Petticrew, M., Bambra, C., Sowden, A. J., Wright, K. E., and Whitehead, M. (2011). 'Housing and Health Inequalities: A Synthesis of Systematic Reviews of Interventions Aimed at Different Pathways Linking Housing and Health', *Health & Place*, 17(1): 175–84.

Gilson, L., and Raphaely, N. (2008). 'The Terrain of Health Policy Analysis in Low and Middle Income Countries: A Review of Published Literature 1994–2007', *Health Policy and Planning*, 23(5): 294–307.

Gingrich, J., and Greer, S. (forthcoming). 'Regional Outlook: The United Kingdom and Ireland', in E. M. Immergut, K. M. Anderson, C. Devitt, and T. Popic (eds), *Health Politics in Europe: A Handbook.*

Giridharadas, A. (2018). *Winners Take All: The Elite Charade of Changing the World*. New York: Alfred A. Knopf.

Glassman, A., Datema, B., and McClelland, A. (2018) [website]. *Financing Outbreak Preparedness: Where Are We and What Next?* Retrieved from https://www.cgdev.org/blog/financing-outbreak-preparedness-where-are-we-and-what-next (accessed 10 April 2019).

Global Burden of Disease Collaborative Network (2018) [website]. *Global Burden of Disease Study 2017 (GBD 2017) Results*. Retrieved from http://ghdx.healthdata.org/gbd-results-tool.

Global Health Crises Task Force (2017). *Global Health Crises Task Force Final Report*. Retrieved from https://www.un.org/en/global-health-crises-task-force/ (accessed 13 February 2019).

Global Virome Project (n.d.) [website]. *About the Global Virome Project*. Retrieved from https://www.globalviromeproject.org/overview/ (accessed 25 January 2019).

Godlee, F. (1997). 'WHO Reform and Global Health', *BMJ Clinical Research Edition*, 314(7091): 1359.

Gomes, T., Tadrous, M., Mamdani, M. M., Paterson, J. M., and Juurlink, D. N. (2018). 'The Burden of Opioid-related Mortality in the United States', *JAMA Network Open*, 1(2): e180217.

Gostin, L. O., Tomori, O., Wibulpolprasert, S., Jha, A. K., Frenk, J., Moon, S., Phumaphi, J., Piot, P., Stocking, B., Dzau, V. J., and Leung, G. M. (2016). 'Toward a Common Secure Future: Four Global Commissions in the Wake of Ebola', *PLoS Medicine*, 13(5): e1002042.

Gould, D. J., Moralejo, D., Drey, N., Chudleigh, J. H., and Taljaard, M. (2017). 'Interventions to Improve Hand Hygiene Compliance in Patient Care', *The Cochrane Database of Systematic Reviews*, 9: CD005186.

Grant, A. M., and Hofmann, D. A. (2011). 'It's Not All About Me: Motivating Hand Hygiene Among Health Care Professionals by Focusing on Patients', *Psychological Science*, 22(12): 1494–9.

Green, A. (2019). 'DR Congo Ebola Virus Treatment Centres Attacked', *The Lancet*, 393(10176): 1088.

Greenberg, A. J., Falisi, A. L., Finney Rutten, L. J., Chou, W.-Y. S., Patel, V., Moser, R. P., and Hesse, B. W. (2017). 'Access to Electronic Personal Health Records Among Patients With Multiple Chronic Conditions: A Secondary Data Analysis', *Journal of Medical Internet Research*, 19(6): e188.

Guha, S. (2016) [website]. *At Landmark BRICS Meet, India Raises Public Health, Pharma Sector Concerns*. Retrieved from https://www.firstpost.com/world/at-landmark-brics-meet-india-raises-public-health-pharma-sector-concerns-2797052.html (accessed 10 April 2019).

Guillen, A. M. (2002). 'The Politics of Universalisation: Establishing National Health Services in Southern Europe', *West European Politics*, 25(4): 49–68.

Habibov, N. (2016). 'Effect of Corruption on Healthcare Satisfaction in Post-Soviet Nations: A Cross-country Instrumental Variable Analysis of Twelve Countries', *Social Science & Medicine*, 152: 119–24.

Hacker, J. S. (2004). 'Dismantling the Health Care State? Political Institutions, Public Policies and the Comparative Politics of Health Reform', *British Journal of Political Science*, 34(4): 693–724.

Hacker, J. S. (1998). 'The Historical Logic of National Health Insurance: Structure and Sequence in the Development of British, Canadian, and US Medical Policy', *Studies in American Political Development*, 12(1): 57–130.

Hadland, S. E., Cerdá, M., Li, Y., Krieger, M. S., and Marshall, B. D. L. (2018). 'Association of Pharmaceutical Industry Marketing of Opioid Products to Physicians With Subsequent Opioid Prescribing', *JAMA Internal Medicine*, 178(6): 861–3.

Hall, C. S., Fottrell, E., Wilkinson, S., and Byass, P. (2014). 'Assessing the Impact of mHealth Interventions in Low- and Middle-income Countries—What Has Been Shown to Work?', *Global Health Action*, 7: 25606.

Hallsworth, M., Berry, D., Sanders, M., Sallis, A., King, D., Vlaev, I., and Darzi, A. (2015). 'Stating Appointment Costs in SMS Reminders Reduces Missed Hospital Appointments: Findings From Two Randomised Controlled Trials', *PloS One*, 10(9): e0137306.

Hallsworth, M., Chadborn, T., Sallis, A., Sanders, M., Berry, D., Greaves, F., Clements, L., and Davies, S. C. (2016). 'Provision of Social Norm Feedback to High Prescribers of Antibiotics in General Practice: A Pragmatic National Randomised Controlled Trial', *The Lancet*, 387(10029): 1743–52.

Hallsworth, M., Snijders, V., Burd, H., Prestt, J., Judah, G., Huf, S., and Halpern, D. (2016). Applying Behavioural Insights: Simple Ways to Improve Health Outcomes. Doha, Qatar: WISH Behavioral Insights Forum.

Hamine, S., Gerth-Guyette, E., Faulx, D., Green, B. B., and Ginsburg, A. S. (2015). 'Impact of mHealth Chronic Disease Management on Treatment Adherence and Patient Outcomes: A Systematic Review', *Journal of Medical Internet Research*, 17(2): e52.

Hamunen, K., Paakkari, P., and Kalso, E. (2009). 'Trends in Opioid Consumption in the Nordic Countries 2002–2006', *European Journal of Pain*, 13(9): 954–62.

Handel, B. R. (2013). 'Adverse Selection and Inertia in Health Insurance Markets: When Nudging Hurts', *The American Economic Review*, 103(7): 2643–82.

Handel, B. R., Kolstad, J. T., and Spinnewijn, J. (2019). 'Information Frictions and Adverse Selection: Policy Interventions in Health Insurance Markets', *The Review of Economics and Statistics*, 101(2): 326–40.

Hankins, C. (2016). Good Participatory Practice Guidelines for Trials of Emerging (and Re-emerging) Pathogens That Are Likely to Cause Severe Outbreaks in the Near Future and for Which Few or No Medical Countermeasures Exist. Outcome Document of the Consultative Process. Geneva: WHO.

Hanlon, P., Nicholl, B. I., Jani, B. D., Lee, D., McQueenie, R., and Mair, F. S. (2018). 'Frailty and Pre-frailty in Middle-aged and Older Adults and Its Association With Multimorbidity and Mortality: A Prospective Analysis of 493 737 UK Biobank Participants', *The Lancet Public Health*, 3(7): e323-e332.

Harper, I., and Parker, M. (2014). 'The Politics and Anti-politics of Infectious Disease Control', *Medical Anthropology*, 33(3): 198–205.

Harris, G., and Huetteman, E. (2016) [website]. *Actions by Congress on Opioids Haven't Included Limiting Them*. Retrieved from https://www.nytimes.com/2016/05/19/us/politics/opioid-dea-addiction.html (accessed 4 January 2019).

Held, D., Kickbusch, I., McNally, K., Piselli, D., and Told, M. (2019). 'Gridlock, Innovation and Resilience in Global Health Governance', *Global Policy*, 13(5): 519.

Hemerijck, A. (2018). 'Social Investment as a Policy Paradigm', *Journal of European Public Policy*, 25(6): 810–27.

Hemerijck, A. (ed) (2017). *The Uses of Social Investment*. Oxford: Oxford University Press.

Hemerijck, A. (2015). 'The Quiet Paradigm Revolution of Social Investment', *Social Politics: International Studies in Gender, State & Society*, 22(2): 242–56.

Henao-Restrepo, A. M., Camacho, A., Longini, I. M., Watson, C. H., Edmunds, W. J., Egger, M., Carroll, M. W., Dean, N. E., Diatta, I., Doumbia, M., Draguez, B., Duraffour, S., Enwere, G., Grais, R., Gunther, S., Gsell, P.-S., Hossmann, S., Watle, S. V., Kondé, M. K., Kéïta, S., Kone, S., Kuisma, E., Levine, M. M., Mandal, S., Mauget, T., Norheim, G., Riveros, X., Soumah, A., Trelle, S., Vicari, A. S., Røttingen, J.-A., and Kieny, M.-P. (2017). 'Efficacy and Effectiveness of an rVSV-vectored Vaccine in Preventing Ebola Virus Disease: Final Results From the Guinea Ring Vaccination, Open-label, Cluster-randomised Trial (Ebola Ça Suffit!)', *The Lancet*, 389(10068): 505–18.

Herten-Crabb, A., Vaidya, R., Spencer, J., Moon, S., and Lillywhite, L. (2017). Infectious Disease Outbreaks, Travel and Tourism: Monitoring for Preparedness. London: Chatham House, The Royal Institute of International Affairs.

Heymann, D. L., Chen, L., Takemi, K., Fidler, D. P., Tappero, J. W., Thomas, M. J., Kenyon, T. A., Frieden, T. R., Yach, D., Nishtar, S., Kalache, A., Olliaro, P. L., Horby, P., Torreele, E., Gostin, L. O., Ndomondo-Sigonda, M., Carpenter, D., Rushton, S., Lillywhite, L., Devkota, B., Koser, K., Yates, R., Dhillon, R. S., and Rannan-Eliya, R. P. (2015). 'Global Health Security: The Wider Lessons From the West African Ebola Virus Disease Epidemic', *The Lancet*, 385(9980): 1884–901.

Hiam, L., and Dorling, D. (2018). 'Rise in Mortality in England and Wales in First Seven Weeks of 2018', *BMJ Clinical Research Edition*, 360: k1090.

Hider-Mlynarz, K., Cavalié, P., and Maison, P. (2018). 'Trends in Analgesic Consumption in France Over the Last 10 Years and Comparison of Patterns Across Europe', *British Journal of Clinical Pharmacology*, 84(6): 1324–34.

Higham, S., and Bernstein, L. (2017) [website]. *The Drug Industry's Triumph Over the DEA*. Retrieved from https://www.washingtonpost.com/graphics/2017/investigations/dea-drug-industry-congress/ (accessed 4 January 2019).

High-Level Panel on the Global Response to Health Crises (2016). Protecting Humanity From Future Health Crises. New York: UN General Assembly.

Hillier-Brown, F., Thomson, K., Mcgowan, V., Cairns, J., Eikemo, T. A., Gil-Gonzále, D., and Bambra, C. (forthcoming). 'The Effects of Social Protection Policies on Health Inequalities: Evidence From Systematic Reviews', *Scandinavian Journal of Public Health*, doi: 10.1177/1403494819848276.

Hoeksema, K., Wee, R., Macdonald, A., Guilford, P., Wall, J., and Cornwall, J. (2017). 'Where to From Here? Posthumous Healthcare Data, Digital e(lectronic)-Mortality and New Zealand's Healthcare Future', *The New Zealand Medical Journal*, 130(1459): 64–70.

Hofman, M. and Au, S. (eds) (2017). *The Politics of Fear: Médecins sans Frontières and the West African Ebola Epidemic*. New York: Oxford University Press.

Holmberg, S., and Rothstein, B. (2011). 'Dying of Corruption', *Health Economics, Policy, and Law*, 6(4): 529–47.

Honigsbaum, M. (2019). 'Disease X and Other Unknowns', *The Lancet*, 393(10180): 1496–7.

Hood, A., and Waters, T. (2017). *Living Standards, Poverty and Inequality in the UK: 2016–17 to 2021–22*. London: Institute for Fiscal Studies.

Hood, C. (1991). 'A Public Management for All Seasons?', *Public Administration*, 69(1): 3–19.

Hopkins, S. (2006). 'Economic Stability and Health Status: Evidence From East Asia Before and After the 1990s Economic Crisis', *Health Policy*, 75(3): 347–57.

Horvath, A., and Powell, W. W. (2016). 'Contributory or Disruptive: Do New Forms of Philanthropy Erode Democracy?', in R. Reich, L. Bernholz, and C. Cordelli (eds), *Philanthropy in Democratic Societies: History, Institutions, Values*. Chicago: The University of Chicago Press, 87–112.

Hu, Y., van Lenthe, F. J., Judge, K., Lahelma, E., Costa, G., Gelder, R. de, and Mackenbach, J. P. (2016). 'Did the English Strategy Reduce Inequalities in Health? A Difference-in-difference Analysis Comparing England With Three Other European Countries', *BMC Public Health*, 16(1): 865.

Huber, E., and Stephens, J. D. (2001a). *Development and Crisis of the Welfare State: Parties and Policies in Global Markets*. Chicago: The University of Chicago Press.

Huber, E., and Stephens, J. D. (2001b). 'Welfare State and Production Regimes in the Era of Retrenchment', in P. Pierson (ed), *The New Politics of the Welfare State*. Oxford: Oxford University Press, 107–45.

Hudec, R., Tisonova, J., Foltan, V., and Kristova, V. (2013). 'Consumption of Three Strong Opioids (Morphine, Oxycodone and Fentanyl) in Seven European Countries During Seven Years (2003-2009)', *Bratislavske lekarske listy*, 114(10): 581–3.

Huijts, T., Gkiouleka, A., Reibling, N., Thomson, K. H., Eikemo, T. A., and Bambra, C. (2017). 'Educational Inequalities in Risky Health Behaviours in 21 European Countries: Findings From the European Social Survey (2014) Special Module on the Social Determinants of Health', *European Journal of Public Health*, 27(suppl_1): 63–72.

Hurrelmann, K. (1989). *Human Development and Health*. New York: Springer.

Hurrelmann, K. and Laaser, U. (eds) (1996). *International Handbook of Public Health*. Westport, CT: Greenwood Press.

Hurrelmann, K., Rathmann, K., and Richter, M. (2011). 'Health Inequalities and Welfare State Regimes A Research Note', *Journal of Public Health*, 19(1): 3–13.

IHME (Institute for Health Metrics and Evaluation) (2019). Financing Global Health 2018: Countries and Programs in Transition. Seattle: IHME.

IMHE (Institute for Health Metrics and Evaluation) (2018) [website]. *GBD Compare Data Visualization*. Retrieved from http://vizhub.healthdata.org/gbd-compare.

IHME (Institute for Health Metrics and Evaluation) (2016). Financing Global Health 2015: Development Assistance Steady on the Path to New Global Goals. Seattle: IHME.

ILO (International Labour Organization) (2014). Addressing the Global Health Crisis: Universal Health Protection Policies. Social Protection Policy Papers 13. Geneva: ILO.

Immergut, E. M. (2011). 'Democratic Theory and Policy Analysis: Four Models of "Policy, Politics and Choice"', *der moderne staat - dms*, 4(1): 69–86.

Immergut, E. M. (1992). *Health Politics: Interests and Institutions in Western Europe*. Cambridge: Cambridge University Press.

Immergut, E. M., Anderson, K. M., Devitt, C. and Popic, T. (eds) (forthcoming). *Health Politics in Europe: A Handbook*.

Immergut, E. M., and Wendt, C. (forthcoming). 'Germany', in E. M. Immergut, K. M. Anderson, C. Devitt, and T. Popic (eds), *Health Politics in Europe: A Handbook*.

Institute of Medicine (2001). *Crossing the Quality Chasm: A New Health System for the 21st Century*. Washington, DC: Institute of Medicine.

Inter-Agency Standing Committee (2016). Level 3 (L3) Activation Procedures for Infectious Disease Events. Geneva: World Health Organization.

IPCC (Intergovernmental Panel on Climate Change) (2018) [website]. Global Warming of 1.5°C. An IPCC Special Report on the Impacts of Global Warming of 1.5°C Above Pre-industrial levels and Related Global Greenhouse Gas Emission Pathways, in the Context of Strengthening the Global Response to the Threat of Climate Change, Sustainable Development, and Efforts to Eradicate Poverty. Retrieved from https://www.ipcc.ch/sr15/ (accessed 10 April 2019).

ISSP (International Social Survey Programme) (2018) [website]. *ISSP 2016 - 'Role of Government V' – ZA No. 6900*. Retrieved from https://www.gesis.org/issp/modules/issp-modules-by-topic/role-of-government/2016/ (accessed 9 December 2018).

Iversen, T., and Stephens, J. D. (2008). 'Partisan Politics, the Welfare State, and Three Worlds of Human Capital Formation', *Comparative Political Studies*, 41(4-5): 600–37.

Iyengar, A., Kundu, A., and Pallis, G. (2018). 'Healthcare Informatics and Privacy', *IEEE Internet Computing*, 22(2): 29–31.

Jain, A., Nundy, S., and Abbasi, K. (2014). 'Corruption: Medicine's Dirty Open Secret', *BMJ Clinical Research Edition*, 348: g4184.

Jansen, L. (2008). 'Collaborative and Interdisciplinary Health Care Teams: Ready or Not?', *Journal of Professional Nursing*, 24(4): 218–27.

Jenkinson, C. E., Dickens, A. P., Jones, K., Thompson-Coon, J., Taylor, R. S., Rogers, M., Bambra, C. L., Lang, I., and Richards, S. H. (2013). 'Is Volunteering a Public Health Intervention? A Systematic Review and Meta-analysis of the Health and Survival of Volunteers', *BMC Public Health*, 13: 773.

Jenson, J. (2009). 'Lost in Translation: The Social Investment Perspective and Gender Equality', *Social Politics: International Studies in Gender, State & Society*, 16(4): 446–83.

Johnson, E. J., and Goldstein, D. (2003). 'Medicine. Do Defaults Save Lives?', *Science*, 302(5649): 1338–9.

Kamau, M., Chasek, P., and O'Connor, D. (2018). *Transforming Multilateral Diplomacy: The Inside Story of the Sustainable Development Goals*. London: Routledge.

Kaminska, M. E., and Wulfgramm, M. (2018). 'Universal or Commodified Healthcare? Linking Out-of-pocket Payments to Income-related Inequalities in Unmet Health Needs in Europe', *Journal of European Social Policy*, 29(3), 345–60.

Kamradt-Scott, A. (2016). 'WHO's to Blame? The World Health Organization and the 2014 Ebola Outbreak in West Africa', *Third World Quarterly*, 37(3): 401–18.

Karanges, E. A., Blanch, B., Buckley, N. A., and Pearson, S.-A. (2016). 'Twenty-five Years of Prescription Opioid Use in Australia: A Whole-of-population Analysis Using Pharmaceutical Claims', *British Journal of Clinical Pharmacology*, 82(1): 255–67.

Karanikolos, M., Mladovsky, P., Cylus, J., Thomson, S., Basu, S., Stuckler, D., Mackenbach, J. P., and McKee, M. (2013). 'Financial Crisis, Austerity, and Health in Europe', *The Lancet*, 381(9874): 1323–31.

Katz, R., and Seifman, R. (2016). 'Opportunities to Finance Pandemic Preparedness', *The Lancet Global Health*, 4(11): e782–3.

Kelly-Cirino, C. D., Nkengasong, J., Kettler, H., Tongio, I., Gay-Andrieu, F., Escadafal, C., Piot, P., Peeling, R. W., Gadde, R., and Boehme, C. (2019). 'Importance of Diagnostics in Epidemic and Pandemic Preparedness', *BMJ Global Health*, 4: e001179.

Kennedy, S. B., Bolay, F., Kieh, M., Grandits, G., Badio, M., Ballou, R., Eckes, R., Feinberg, M., Follmann, D., Grund, B., Gupta, S., Hensley, L., Higgs, E., Janosko, K., Johnson, M., Kateh, F., Logue, J., Marchand, J., Monath, T., Nason, M., Nyenswah, T., Roman, F., Stavale, E., Wolfson, J., Neaton, J. D., and Lane, H. C. (2017). 'Phase 2 Placebo-controlled Trial of Two Vaccines to Prevent Ebola in Liberia', *The New England Journal of Medicine*, 377(15): 1438–47.

Kenyon, C. C., Gruschow, S. M., Quarshie, W. O., Griffis, H., Leach, M. C., Zorc, J. J., Bryant-Stephens, T. C., Miller, V. A., and Feudtner, C. (2019). 'Controller Adherence Following

Hospital Discharge in High Risk Children: A Pilot Randomized Trial of Text Message Reminders', *The Journal of Asthma*, 56(1): 95–103.

Keogh-Brown, M. R., and Smith, R. D. (2008). 'The Economic Impact of SARS: How Does the Reality Match the Predictions?', *Health Policy*, 88(1): 110–20.

Kessler, J. B., Troxel, A. B., Asch, D. A., Mehta, S. J., Marcus, N., Lim, R., Zhu, J., Shrank, W., Brennan, T., and Volpp, K. G. (2018). 'Partners and Alerts in Medication Adherence: A Randomized Clinical Trial', *Journal of General Internal Medicine*, 33(9): 1536–42.

Kesternich, I., Schumacher, H., and Winter, J. (2015). 'Professional Norms and Physician Behavior: Homo Oeconomicus or Homo Hippocraticus ?', *Journal of Public Economics*, 131: 1–11.

Kiang, M. V., Basu, S., Chen, J., and Alexander, M. J. (2019). 'Assessment of Changes in the Geographical Distribution of Opioid-Related Mortality Across the United States by Opioid Type, 1999–2016', *JAMA Network Open*, 2(2): e190040.

Kickbusch, I. (2013). 'A Game Change in Global Health: The Best Is Yet to Come', *Public Health Reviews*, 35(1): 1–20.

Kickbusch, I. (2007). 'Health Governance: The Health Society', in D. V. McQueen, I. Kickbusch, L. Potvin, J. M. Pelikan, L. Balbo, and T. Abel (eds), *Health and Modernity: The Role of Theory in Health Promotion*. New York: Springer, 144–61.

Kickbusch, I., and Cassels, A. (2018) [website]. *Disruptions That Shape Global Health*. Retrieved from https://blogs.bmj.com/bmj/2018/11/26/ilona-kickbusch-and-andrew-cassels-disruptions-that-shape-global-health (accessed 10 April 2019).

Kickbusch, I., and Gleicher, D. (2012). *Governance for Health in the 21st Century*. Copenhagen: WHO Regional Office for Europe.

Kickbusch, I., Orbinski, J., Winkler, T., and Schnabel, A. (2015). 'We Need a Sustainable Development Goal 18 on Global Health Security', *The Lancet*, 385(9973): 1069.

Kim, R. H., Day, S. C., Small, D. S., Snider, C. K., Rareshide, C. A. L., and Patel, M. S. (2018). 'Variations in Influenza Vaccination by Clinic Appointment Time and an Active Choice Intervention in the Electronic Health Record to Increase Influenza Vaccination', *JAMA Network Open*, 1(5): e181770.

Kimmel, S. E., Troxel, A. B., French, B., Loewenstein, G., Doshi, J. A., Hecht, T. E. H., Laskin, M., Brensinger, C. M., Meussner, C., and Volpp, K. (2016). 'A Randomized Trial of Lottery-based Incentives and Reminders to Improve Warfarin Adherence: The Warfarin Incentives (WIN2) Trial', *Pharmacoepidemiology and Drug Safety*, 25(11): 1219–27.

King, D., Vlaev, I., Everett-Thomas, R., Fitzpatrick, M., Darzi, A., and Birnbach, D. J. (2016). '"Priming" Hand Hygiene Compliance in Clinical Environments', *Health Psychology*, 35(1): 96–101.

Kitson, M., Martin, R., and Tyler, P. (2011). 'The Geographies of Austerity', *Cambridge Journal of Regions, Economy and Society*, 4(3): 289–302.

Koivusalo, M., Tynkkynen, L.-K., and Keskimäki, I. (forthcoming). 'Finland', in E. M. Immergut, K. M. Anderson, C. Devitt, and T. Popic (eds), *Health Politics in Europe: A Handbook*.

Kolodny, A., Courtwright, D. T., Hwang, C. S., Kreiner, P., Eadie, J. L., Clark, T. W., and Alexander, G. C. (2015). 'The Prescription Opioid and Heroin Crisis: A Public Health Approach to an Epidemic of Addiction', *Annual Review of Public Health*, 36: 559–74.

Kolstad, J. T. (2013). 'Information and Quality When Motivation Is Intrinsic: Evidence From Surgeon Report Cards', *American Economic Review*, 103(7): 2875–910.

Koplan, J. P., and McPheeters, M. (2004). 'Plagues, Public Health, and Politics', *Emerging Infectious Diseases*, 10(11): 2039–43.

Kozul-Wright, R., and Gallagher, K. P. (2019) [website]. *Toward a Global Green New Deal*. Retrieved from https://www.project-syndicate.org/commentary/global-green-new-deal-by-richard-kozul-wright-and-kevin-p-gallagher-2019-04 (accessed 10 April 2019).

Krech, R., Kickbusch, I., Franz, C., and Wells, N. (2018). 'Banking for Health: The Role of Financial Sector Actors in Investing in Global Health', *BMJ Global Health*, 3: e000597.

Krieger, N. (2011). *Epidemiology and the People's Health: Theory and Context*. New York: Oxford University Press.

Krieger, N., Rehkopf, D. H., Chen, J. T., Waterman, P. D., Marcelli, E., and Kennedy, M. (2008). 'The Fall and Rise of US Inequities in Premature Mortality: 1960-2002', *PLoS Medicine*, 5(2): e46.

Krnic, D., Anic-Matic, A., Dosenovic, S., Draganic, P., Zezelic, S., and Puljak, L. (2015). 'National Consumption of Opioid and Nonopioid Analgesics in Croatia: 2007–2013', *Therapeutics and Clinical Risk Management*, 11: 1305–14.

Kuhlmann, E., Blank, R. H., Bourgeault, I. L., and Wendt, C. (2015a). 'Healthcare Policy and Governance in International Perspective', in E. Kuhlmann, R. H. Blank, I. L. Bourgeault, and C. Wendt (eds), *The Palgrave International Handbook of Healthcare Policy and Governance*. Basingstoke: Palgrave Macmillan, 3–19.

Kuhlmann, E., Blank, R. H., Bourgeault, I. L. and Wendt, C. (eds) (2015b). *The Palgrave International Handbook of Healthcare Policy and Governance*. Basingstoke: Palgrave Macmillan.

Kuhlmann, E., Groenewegen, P. P., Bond, C., Burau, V., and Hunter, D. J. (2018). 'Primary Care Workforce Development in Europe: An Overview of Health System Responses and Stakeholder Views', *Health Policy*, 122(10): 1055–62.

Kyu, H. H., Abate, D., Abate, K. H., et al. (2018). 'Global, Regional, and National Disability-adjusted Life-years (DALYs) for 359 Diseases and Injuries and Healthy Life Expectancy (HALE) for 195 Countries and Territories, 1990–2017: A Systematic Analysis for the Global Burden of Disease Study 2017', *The Lancet*, 392(10159): 1859–922.

Labonté, R., and Ruckert, A. (2019). *Health Equity in a Globalizing Era: Past Challenges, Future Prospects*. Oxford: Oxford University Press.

Lagarde, C. (2019) [website]. *A Delicate Moment for the Global Economy: Three Priority Areas for Action*. Retrieved from https://www.imf.org/en/News/Articles/2019/03/29/sp040219-a-delicate-moment-for-the-global-economy (accessed 10 April 2019).

Lalic, S., Ilomäki, J., Bell, J. S., Korhonen, M. J., and Gisev, N. (2019). 'Prevalence and Incidence of Prescription Opioid Analgesic Use in Australia', *British Journal of Clinical Pharmacology*, 85(1): 202–15.

Langer, A., Meleis, A., Knaul, F. M., Atun, R., Aran, M., Arreola-Ornelas, H., Bhutta, Z. A., Binagwaho, A., Bonita, R., Caglia, J. M., Claeson, M., Davies, J., Donnay, F. A., Gausman, J. M., Glickman, C., Kearns, A. D., Kendall, T., Lozano, R., Seboni, N., Sen, G., Sindhu, S., Temin, M., and Frenk, J. (2015). 'Women and Health: The Key for Sustainable Development', *The Lancet*, 386(9999): 1165–210.

Leape, L., Berwick, D., Clancy, C., Conway, J., Gluck, P., Guest, J., Lawrence, D., Morath, J., O'Leary, D., O'Neill, P., Pinakiewicz, D., and Isaac, T. (2009). 'Transforming Healthcare: A Safety Imperative', *Quality and Safety in Health Care*, 18(6): 424–8.

Lehmann, B. A., Chapman, G. B., Franssen, F. M. E., Kok, G., and Ruiter, R. A. C. (2016). 'Changing the Default to Promote Influenza Vaccination Among Health Care Workers', *Vaccine*, 34(11): 1389–92.

Leibfried, S. (1993). 'Towards a European Welfare State? On Integrating Poverty Regimes Into the European Community', in C. Jones (ed), *New Perspectives on the Welfare State in Europe*. London: Routledge, 133–56.

Leigh, J., Moon, S., Garcia, E., and Fitzgerald, G. (2018). Is Global Capacity to Manage Outbreaks Improving? An Analysis. Geneva: Graduate Institute of International and Development Studies, Global Health Centre.

Leist, A. (forthcoming). 'Luxembourg', in E. M. Immergut, K. M. Anderson, C. Devitt, and T. Popic (eds), *Health Politics in Europe: A Handbook*.

Levy, A. E., Huang, C., Huang, A., and Michael Ho, P. (2018). 'Recent Approaches to Improve Medication Adherence in Patients With Coronary Heart Disease: Progress Towards a Learning Healthcare System', *Current Atherosclerosis Reports*, 20(1): 5.

Levy, D. T., Yuan, Z., Luo, Y., and Mays, D. (2018). 'Seven Years of Progress in Tobacco Control: An Evaluation of the Effect of Nations Meeting the Highest Level MPOWER Measures between 2007 and 2014', *Tobacco Control*, 27: 50–7.

Lidén, J. (2013). The Grand Decade for Global Health: 1998–2008. Centre on Global Health Security Working Group Papers: Working Group on Governance 2. London: Chatham House.

Lin, S., Gao, L., Reyes, M., Cheng, F., Kaufman, J., and El-Sadr, W. M. (2016). 'China's Health Assistance to Africa: Opportunism or Altruism?', *Globalization and Health*, 12(1): 83.

Linder, J. A., Meeker, D., Fox, C. R., Friedberg, M. W., Persell, S. D., Goldstein, N. J., and Doctor, J. N. (2017). 'Effects of Behavioral Interventions on Inappropriate Antibiotic Prescribing in Primary Care 12 Months After Stopping Interventions', *JAMA*, 318(14): 1391–2.

Liu, J., and Torreele, E. (2019) [website]. *Open Letter to CEPI Board Members: Revise CEPI's Access Policy*. Retrieved from https://msfaccess.org/open-letter-cepi-board-members-revise-cepis-access-policy (accessed 13 April 2019).

Love-Koh, J., Peel, A., Rejon-Parrilla, J. C., Ennis, K., Lovett, R., Manca, A., Chalkidou, A., Wood, H., and Taylor, M. (2018). 'The Future of Precision Medicine: Potential Impacts for Health Technology Assessment', *PharmacoEconomics*, 36(12): 1439–51.

Lozano, R., Fullman, N., Abate, D., et al. (2018). 'Measuring Progress From 1990 to 2017 and Projecting Attainment to 2030 of the Health-related Sustainable Development Goals for 195 Countries and Territories: A Systematic Analysis for the Global Burden of Disease Study 2017', *The Lancet*, 392(10159): 2091–138.

Luhby, T. (2019) [website]. *The Top 26 Billionaires Own $1.4 Trillion—As Much as 3.8 Billion Other People*. Retrieved from https://edition.cnn.com/2019/01/20/business/oxfam-billionaires-davos/index.html (accessed 10 April 2019).

Lukes, S. (2008). *Moral Relativism*. London: Profile Books.

Mackenbach, J. P. (2012). 'The Persistence of Health Inequalities in Modern Welfare States: The Explanation of a Paradox', *Social Science & Medicine*, 75(4): 761–9.

Mackenbach, J. P. (2011a). 'Can We Reduce Health Inequalities? An Analysis of the English Strategy (1997–2010)', *Journal of Epidemiology and Community Health*, 65(7): 568–75.

Mackenbach, J. P. (2011b). 'The English Strategy to Reduce Health Inequalities', *The Lancet*, 377(9782): 1986–8.

Mackenbach, J. P. (2010). 'Has the English Strategy to Reduce Health Inequalities Failed?', *Social Science & Medicine*, 71(7): 1249–53.

Mackenbach, J. P. (2009). 'Politics Is Nothing but Medicine at a Larger Scale: Reflections on Public Health's Biggest Idea', *Journal of Epidemiology and Community Health*, 63(3): 181–4.

Mackenbach, J. P., Kulhánová, I., Artnik, B., Bopp, M., Borrell, C., Clemens, T., Costa, G., Dibben, C., Kalediene, R., Lundberg, O., Martikainen, P., Menvielle, G., Östergren, O., Prochorskas, R., Rodríguez-Sanz, M., Strand, B. H., Looman, C. W. N., and de Gelder, R. (2016). 'Changes in Mortality Inequalities Over Two Decades: Register Based Study of European Countries', *BMJ Clinical Research Edition*, 353: i1732.

Mackenbach, J. P., Meerding, W. J., and Kunst, A. E. (2011). 'Economic Costs of Health Inequalities in the European Union', *Journal of Epidemiology and Community Health*, 65(5): 412–9.

Mackert, M., Mabry-Flynn, A., Champlin, S., Donovan, E. E., and Pounders, K. (2016). 'Health Literacy and Health Information Technology Adoption: The Potential for a New Digital Divide', *Journal of Medical Internet Research*, 18(10): e264.

Mackey, T. K., and Novotny, T. A. (2012) [website]. 'Improving United Nations Funding to Strengthen Global Health Governance: Amending the Helms–Biden Agreement', *Global Health Governance Journal*, VI(1). Retrieved from http://blogs.shu.edu/ghg/2012/12/31/improving-united-nations-funding-to-strengthen-global-health-governance-amending-the-helms-biden-agreement/ (accessed 20 March 2019).

Mackintosh, M. (2013). 'Health Care Commercialisation: A Core Development Issue', Third Annual Development Studies Lecture, 16 May. London: Birkbeck, University of London. Retrieved from https://backdoorbroadcasting.net/2013/05/maureen-mackintosh-health-care-commercialisation-a-core-development-issue/ (accessed 6 March 2016).

MacLeavy, J. (2011). 'A "New Politics" of Austerity, Workfare and Gender? The UK Coalition Government's Welfare Reform Proposals', *Cambridge Journal of Regions, Economy and Society*, 4(3): 355–67.

Maier, C. B., Batenburg, R., Birch, S., Zander, B., and Busse, R. (2018). 'Health Workforce Planning: Which Countries Include Nurse Practitioners and Physician Assistants and to What Effect?', *Health Policy*, 122(10): 1085–92.

Manlan, C. (2017) [website]. *A CDC for Africa: But the Body Modeled After the US Agency Needs Funding*. Retrieved from https://www.scientificamerican.com/article/a-cdc-for-africa/ (accessed 14 April 2019).

Mann, J. A., MacDonald, B. A., Kuo, I.-H., Li, X., and Broadbent, E. (2015). 'People Respond Better to Robots Than Computer Tablets Delivering Healthcare Instructions', *Computers in Human Behavior*, 43: 112–7.

Manow, P. (2015). 'Workers, Farmers and Catholicism: A History of Political Class and the South-European Welfare State Regime', *Journal of European Social Policy*, 25(1): 32–49.

Manow, P. (2004). 'The Good, the Bad, and the Ugly'. Esping-Andersen's Regime Typology and the Religious Roots of the Western Welfare State. MPIfG Working Paper 04/3. Cologne: Max Planck Institute for the Study of Societies.

Manow, P., Palier, B., and Schwander, H. (2018a). 'Introduction: Welfare Democracies and Party Politics—Explaining Electoral Dynamics in Times of Changing Welfare Capitalism', in P. Manow, B. Palier, and H. Schwander (eds), *Welfare Democracies and Party Politics: Explaining Electoral Dynamics in Times of Changing Welfare Capitalism*. Oxford: Oxford University Press, 1–26.

Manow, P., Palier, B. and Schwander, H. (eds) (2018b). *Welfare Democracies and Party Politics: Explaining Electoral Dynamics in Times of Changing Welfare Capitalism*. Oxford: Oxford University Press.

Marmor, T. R., and Okma, K.G.H. (1998). 'Cautionary Lessons From the West: What (Not) to Learn From Other Countries' Experiences in the Financing and Delivery of Health Care', in P. Flora, P. R. de Jong, J. Le Grand, and J.-Y. Kim (eds), *The State of Social Welfare, 1997: International Studies on Social Insurance and Retirement, Employment, Family Policy and Health Care*. Aldershot: Ashgate, 327–50.

Marmot, M., Allen, J., Goldblatt, P., Boyce, T., McNeish, D., Grady, M., and Geddes, I. (2010). *Fair Society, Healthy Lives: The Marmot Review*. London: Marmot Review.

Marmot, M., Siegrist, J., and Theorell, T. (2006). 'Health and the Psychosocial Environment at Work', in M. Marmot, and R. G. Wilkinson (eds), *Social Determinants of Health*. 2nd ed. Oxford: Oxford University Press, 97–130.

Marquette, H., and Peiffer, C. (2018). 'Grappling With the "Real Politics" of Systemic Corruption: Theoretical Debates Versus "Real-world" Functions', *Governance*, 31(3): 499–514.

Marshall, T. H. (1950). *Citizenship and Social Class, and Other Essays*. Cambridge: Cambridge University Press.

Marten, R. (2018) [website]. *Global Health Disruptors: Millennium Development Goals*. Retrieved from https://blogs.bmj.com/bmj/2018/11/26/global-health-disruptors-millennium-development-goals/ (accessed 10 April 2019).

Massachusetts Suffolk County Superior Court (2019). Commonwealth of Massachusetts v. Purdue Pharma LP. Boston: Massachusetts Suffolk County Superior Court.

Matfess, H. (2018) [website]. *Layered Insecurity in North Kivu: Violence and the Ebola Response*. Retrieved from https://www.acleddata.com/2018/10/26/layered-insecurity-in-north-kivu-violence-and-the-ebola-response/ (accessed 23 March 2019).

Mattheys, K., Warren, J., and Bambra, C. (2018). '"Treading in Sand": A Qualitative Study of the Impact of Austerity on Inequalities in Mental Health', *Social Policy & Administration*, 52(7): 1275–89.

McCaskill, C. (2018). Fueling an Epidemic: Exposing the Financial Ties Between Opioid Manufacturers and Third Party Advocacy Groups. Washington, DC: US Senate Homeland Security and Governmental Affairs Committee.

McDaid, D., Sassi, F. and Merkur, S. (eds) (2015). *Promoting Health, Preventing Disease: The Economic Case*. Maidenhead: Open University Press.

McGlone, P. (2019) [website]. *As More Museums Say No to Sackler Donations, Family Trust Halts Its Giving*. Retrieved from https://www.washingtonpost.com/entertainment/museums/as-more-museums-say-no-to-sackler-donations-family-trust-halts-its-giving/2019/03/25/83ac5ab4-4f22-11e9-88a1-ed346f0ec94f_story.html (accessed 15 April 2019).

McGreal, C. (2018). *American Overdose: The Opioid Tragedy in Three Acts*. London: Guardian Books.

McNamara, C. L., Balaj, M., Thomson, K. H., Eikemo, T. A., and Bambra, C. (2017a). 'The Contribution of Housing and Neighbourhood Conditions to Educational Inequalities in Non-communicable Diseases in Europe: Findings From the European Social Survey (2014) Special Module on the Social Determinants of Health', *European Journal of Public Health*, 27(suppl_1): 102–6.

McNamara, C. L., Balaj, M., Thomson, K. H., Eikemo, T. A., Solheim, E. F., and Bambra, C. (2017b). 'The Socioeconomic Distribution of Non-communicable Diseases in Europe: Findings From the European Social Survey (2014) Special Module on the Social Determinants of Health', *European Journal of Public Health*, 27(suppl_1): 22–6.

McPhail, S. M. (2016). 'Multimorbidity in Chronic Disease: Impact on Health Care Resources and Costs', *Risk Management and Healthcare Policy*, 9: 143–56.

Meagher, P. (2006). 'Governance in Bulgaria's Pharmaceutical Selection and Procurement Systems', in Transparency International (ed), *Global Corruption Report 2006*. London: Pluto Press, 346–9.

Mehta, S. J., Feingold, J., Vandertuyn, M., Niewood, T., Cox, C., Doubeni, C. A., Volpp, K. G., and Asch, D. A. (2017). 'Active Choice and Financial Incentives to Increase Rates of Screening Colonoscopy: A Randomized Controlled Trial', *Gastroenterology*, 153(5): 1227–9.

Metabiota (n.d.) [website]. *Home: Confronting the Risk You Can't See*. Retrieved from http://metabiota.com/ (accessed 25 January 2019).

Mettler, M. (2016). 'Blockchain Technology in Healthcare: The Revolution Starts Here', in *2016 IEEE 18th International Conference on e-Health Networking, Applications and Services (Healthcom): 14-16 Sept. 2016*. Piscataway, N.J.: IEEE, 1–3.

Michaud, J., Moss, K., and Kates, J. (2017). *The US Government and Global Health Security*. Retrieved from https://www.kff.org/global-health-policy/issue-brief/the-u-s-government-and-global-health-security/ (accessed 18 March 2019).

Midgley, J., Dahl, E., and Conley Wright, A. (2017). *Social Investment and Social Welfare: International and Critical Perspectives*. Cheltenham, UK: Edward Elgar Publishing.

Milkman, K. L., Beshears, J., Choi, J. J., Laibson, D., and Madrian, B. C. (2013). 'Planning Prompts as a Means of Increasing Preventive Screening Rates', *Preventive Medicine*, 56(1): 92–3.

Milkman, K. L., Beshears, J., Choi, J. J., Laibson, D., and Madrian, B. C. (2011). 'Using Implementation Intentions Prompts to Enhance Influenza Vaccination Rates', *Proceedings of the National Academy of Sciences of the United States of America*, 108(26): 10415–20.

Milton, B., Attree, P., French, B., Povall, S., Whitehead, M., and Popay, J. (2012). 'The Impact of Community Engagement on Health and Social Outcomes: A Systematic Review', *Community Development Journal*, 47(3): 316–34.

Moon, S. (2018) [website]. *Global Health Disruptors: SARS and Ebola*. Retrieved from https://blogs.bmj.com/bmj/2018/11/28/global-health-disruptors-sars-and-ebola/ (accessed 10 April 2019).

Moon, S., Leigh, J., Woskie, L., Checchi, F., Dzau, V., Fallah, M., Fitzgerald, G., Garrett, L., Gostin, L., Heymann, D. L., Katz, R., Kickbusch, I., Morrison, J. S., Piot, P., Sands, P., Sridhar, D., and Jha, A. K. (2017). 'Post-Ebola Reforms: Ample Analysis, Inadequate Action', *BMJ Clinical Research Edition*, 356: j280.

Moon, S., and Vaidya, R. (2018). Investing for a Rainy Day: Challenges in Financing National Preparedness for Outbreaks. Global Health Centre Working Paper 18. Geneva: Graduate Institute of International and Development Studies, Global Health Centre.

Moran, M. (2000). 'Understanding the Welfare State: The Case of Health Care', *The British Journal of Politics and International Relations*, 2(2): 135–60.

Morel, N., Palier, B. and Palme, J. (eds) (2012). *Towards a Social Investment Welfare State? Ideas, Policies and Challenges*. Bristol: Policy Press.

Morel, N., and Palme, J. (2017). 'A Normative Foundation for the Social Investment Approach?', in A. Hemerijck (ed), *The Uses of Social Investment*. Oxford: Oxford University Press, 150–9.

Morhard, R. (2019). *Global Health Security*. Retrieved from https://weforum.ent.box.com/v/HealthSecurity-2017 (accessed 16 April 2019).

Morrison, S. (2018) [website]. *Global Health Disruptors: Decay of the Postwar Multilateral Western Order*. Retrieved from https://blogs.bmj.com/bmj/2018/11/29/stephen-morrison-decay-of-the-postwar-multilateral-western-order/ (accessed 10 April 2019).

Moynihan, R., and Henry, D. (2006). 'The Fight Against Disease Mongering: Generating Knowledge for Action', *PLoS Medicine*, 3(4): e191.

Mueller, T., and Östergren, P.-O. (2016). 'The Correlation Between Regulatory Conditions and Antibiotic Consumption Within the WHO European Region', *Health Policy*, 120(8): 882–9.

Müller, A. M., Alley, S., Schoeppe, S., and Vandelanotte, C. (2016). 'The Effectiveness of e- and mHealth Interventions to Promote Physical Activity and Healthy Diets in Developing Countries: A Systematic Review', *The International Journal of Behavioral Nutrition and Physical Activity*, 13(1): 109.

Murauskiene, L. (forthcoming). 'Lithuania', in E. M. Immergut, K. M. Anderson, C. Devitt, and T. Popic (eds), *Health Politics in Europe: A Handbook*.

Murray, C. J. L., Callender, C. S. K. H., Kulikoff, X. R., et al. (2018). 'Population and Fertility by Age and Sex for 195 Countries and Territories, 1950–2017: A Systematic Analysis for the Global Burden of Disease Study 2017', *The Lancet*, 392(10159): 1995–2051.

Murtin, F., Mackenbach, J., Jasilionis, D., and d'Ercolei, M. M. (2017). *Inequalities in Longevity by Education in OECD Countries: Insights From New OECD Estimates*. Paris: OECD.

Mur-Veeman, I., Hardy, B., Steenbergen, M., and Wistow, G. (2003). 'Development of Integrated Care in England and the Netherlands: Managing Across Public–Private Boundaries', *Health Policy*, 65(3): 227–41.

National Academies of Science, Engineering, and Medicine (2017). *Integrating Clinical Research Into Epidemic Response: The Ebola Experience*. Washington, DC: National Academies Press.

National Safety Council (n.d.a) [website]. *Injury Facts: Drug Overdoses*. Retrieved from https://injuryfacts.nsc.org/home-and-community/safety-topics/drugoverdoses/ (accessed 4 January 2019).

National Safety Council (n.d.b) [website]. *Injury Facts: Preventable Deaths*. Retrieved from https://injuryfacts.nsc.org/all-injuries/preventable-death-overview/odds-of-dying/ (accessed 4 January 2019).

Newhouse, J. P. (1992). 'Medical Care Costs: How Much Welfare Loss?', *Journal of Economic Perspectives*, 6(3): 3–21.

Nguyen, V.-K. (2019). 'An Epidemic of Suspicion: Ebola and Violence in the DRC', *The New England Journal of Medicine*, 380(14): 1298–9.

Nicholson, C., Jackson, C., and Marley, J. (2013). 'A Governance Model for Integrated Primary/Secondary Care for the Health-reforming First World: Results of a Systematic Review', *BMC Health Services Research*, 13(1): 11.

Niedzwiedz, C. L., Mitchell, R. J., Shortt, N. K., and Pearce, J. R. (2016). 'Social Protection Spending and Inequalities in Depressive Symptoms Across Europe', *Social Psychiatry and Psychiatric Epidemiology*, 51(7): 1005–14.

Nikogosian, H., and Kickbusch, I. (2018). 'Interface of Health and Trade: A View Point From Health Diplomacy', *BMJ Global Health*, 3: e000491.

Nikoloski, Z., and Mossialos, E. (2013). 'Corruption, Inequality and Population Perception of Healthcare Quality in Europe', *BMC Health Services Research*, 13: 472.

Nolte, E., and McKee, M. (2011). 'Variations in Amenable Mortality—Trends in 16 High-income Nations', *Health Policy*, 103(1): 47–52.

Nordahl, H., Lange, T., Osler, M., Diderichsen, F., Andersen, I., Prescott, E., Tjønneland, A., Frederiksen, B. L., and Rod, N. H. (2014). 'Education and Cause-specific Mortality: The Mediating Role of Differential Exposure and Vulnerability to Behavioral Risk Factors', *Epidemiology*, 25(3): 389–96.

Nordmann, S., Pradel, V., Lapeyre-Mestre, M., Frauger, E., Pauly, V., Thirion, X., Mallaret, M., Jouanjus, E., and Micallef, J. (2013). 'Doctor Shopping Reveals Geographical Variations in Opioid Abuse', *Pain Physician*, 16(1): 89–100.

Nuffield Department of Women's and Reproductive Health (n.d.) [website]. *Zika Online Data-sharing Platform*. Retrieved from https://www.wrh.ox.ac.uk/research/zika-online-data-sharing-platform (accessed 30 April 2019).

Nurse, J., Dorey, S., Yao, L., Sigfrid, L., Yfantopolous, P, McDaid, D., Yfantopolous, J., Moreno, J. M. (2014). The Case for Investing in Public Health. Copenhagen: WHO Regional Office for Europe.

Nussbaum, M. C. (2000). *Women and Human Development: The Capabilities Approach*. Cambridge: Cambridge University Press.

Nuzzo, J. (2017) [website]. *Johns Hopkins Center for Health Security Teams With NTI and the Economist Intelligence Unit to Develop a Global Health Security Index*. Retrieved from http://www.bifurcatedneedle.com/new-blog/2017/3/6/johns-hopkins-center-for-health-security-teams-with-nti-and-the-economist-intelligence-unit-to-develop-a-global-health-security-index (accessed 10 February 2019).

O'Campo, P., Molnar, A., Ng, E., Renahy, E., Mitchell, C., Shankardass, K., St John, A., Bambra, C., and Muntaner, C. (2015). 'Social Welfare Matters: A Realist Review of When, How, and Why Unemployment Insurance Impacts Poverty and Health', *Social Science & Medicine*, 132: 88–94.

OECD (Organisation for Economic Co-operation and Development) (2019). *Social Expenditure Database (SOCX)*. Retrieved from http://www.oecd.org/social/expenditure.htm (accessed 29 January 2019).

OECD (2018a). *Focus on Spending on Health: Latest Trends*. Retrieved from http://www.oecd.org/els/health-systems/health-data.htm (accessed 29 January 2019).

OECD (2018b). *Health Expenditure and Financing: Health Expenditure Indicators*. Retrieved from http://dx.doi.org/10.1787/data-00349-en (accessed 7 May 2019).

OECD (2018c). *States of Fragility 2018*. Paris: OECD Publishing.

OECD (2017a). *Health at a Glance 2017: OECD Indicators*. Paris: OECD Publishing.

OECD (2017b). *How's Life? 2017: Measuring Well-being*. Paris: OECD Publishing.

OECD (2016). *The Economic Consequences of Brexit: A Taxing Decision*. Retrieved from https://www.oecd.org/eco/the-economic-consequences-of-brexit-a-taxing-decision.htm (accessed 15 April 2019).

OECD (2009). *Health at a Glance 2009: OECD Indicators*. Paris: OECD Publishing.

OECD Social Policy Division (2015). *CO2.2 Child Poverty*. Retrieved from http://www.oecd.org/els/family/database.htm (accessed 12 March 2019).

Office of US Congressman Hal Rogers (2017) [website]. *Clark, Rogers to WHO: Don't Let the Opioid Epidemic Go Global*. Retrieved from https://halrogers.house.gov/press-releases?ID=311C2A46-7843-4EDB-9786-6E121EA3545E (accessed 11 June 2019).

Olberg, B., Fuchs, S., Panteli, D., Perleth, M., and Busse, R. (2017). 'Scientific Evidence in Health Technology Assessment Reports: An In-depth Analysis of European Assessments on High-risk Medical Devices', *Value in Health*, 20(10): 1420–6.

Olshan, D., Rareshide, C. A. L., and Patel, M. S. (2019). 'Longer-term Durability of Using Default Options in the Electronic Health Record to Increase Generic Prescribing Rates', *Journal of General Internal Medicine*, 34(3): 349–50.

Omaswa, F. (2018). *Global Health Disruptors: The End of The Cold War*. Retrieved from https://blogs.bmj.com/bmj/2018/11/26/global-health-disruptors-the-end-of-the-cold-war/ (accessed 10 April 2019).

Osborne, D., and Gaebler, T. (1992). *Reinventing Government: How the Entrepreneurial Spirit Is Transforming the Public Sector*. Reading, MA: Addison-Wesley.

Osborne, S. P. (2010). *The New Public Governance? Emerging Perspectives on the Theory and Practice of Public Governance*. London: Routledge.

Osborne, S. P. (2006). 'The New Public Governance?', *Public Management Review*, 8(3): 377–87.

Pablos-Méndez, A., and Raviglione, M. C. (2018). 'A New World Health Era', *Global Health, Science and Practice*, 6(1): 8–16.

PAIN (Prescription Addiction Intervention Now) (n.d.) [website]. *Mission Statement*. Retrieved from https://www.sacklerpain.org/mission-statement (accessed 15 April 2019).

Palladino, R., Tayu Lee, J., Ashworth, M., Triassi, M., and Millett, C. (2016). 'Associations Between Multimorbidity, Healthcare Utilisation and Health Status: Evidence From 16 European Countries', *Age and Ageing*, 45(3): 431–5.

Palmer, M. J., Barnard, S., Perel, P., and Free, C. (2018). 'Mobile Phone-based Interventions for Improving Adherence to Medication Prescribed for the Primary Prevention of Cardiovascular Disease in Adults', *The Cochrane Database of Systematic Reviews*, 6: CD012675.

Papacharissi, Z. (2018). *A Networked Self and Human Augmentics, Artificial Intelligence, Sentience*. London: Routledge.

Patel, A., Cass, A., Peiris, D., Usherwood, T., Brown, A., Jan, S., Neal, B., Hillis, G. S., Rafter, N., Tonkin, A., Webster, R., Billot, L., Bompoint, S., Burch, C., Burke, H., Hayman, N., Molanus, B., Reid, C. M., Shiel, L., Togni, S., and Rodgers, A. (2015). 'A Pragmatic Randomized Trial of a Polypill-based Strategy to Improve Use of Indicated Preventive

Treatments in People at High Cardiovascular Disease Risk', *European Journal of Preventive Cardiology*, 22(7): 920–30.

Patel, M. S., Day, S. C., Halpern, S. D., Hanson, C. W., Martinez, J. R., Honeywell, S., and Volpp, K. G. (2016). 'Generic Medication Prescription Rates After Health System-wide Redesign of Default Options Within the Electronic Health Record', *JAMA Internal Medicine*, 176(6): 847–8.

Patel, M. S., Volpp, K. G., Small, D. S., Wynn, C., Zhu, J., Yang, L., Honeywell, S., and Day, S. C. (2016). 'Using Active Choice Within the Electronic Health Record to Increase Physician Ordering and Patient Completion of High-value Cancer Screening Tests', *Healthcare*, 4(4): 340–5.

Patel, M. S., Volpp, K. G., Small, D. S., Wynne, C., Zhu, J., Yang, L., Honeywell, S., and Day, S. C. (2017). 'Using Active Choice Within the Electronic Health Record to Increase Influenza Vaccination Rates', *Journal of General Internal Medicine*, 32(7): 790–5.

Patrick, S. W., Schumacher, R. E., Benneyworth, B. D., Krans, E. E., McAllister, J. M., and Davis, M. M. (2012). 'Neonatal Abstinence Syndrome and Associated Health Care Expenditures: United States, 2000–2009', *JAMA*, 307(18): 1934–40.

Pavot, V. (2016). 'Ebola Virus Vaccines: Where Do We Stand?', *Clinical Immunology*, 173: 44–9.

Payne, S. (2019). *Boris Johnson Calls for UK's Aid Department to be Closed*. Retrieved from https://www.ft.com/content/03bb726a-157d-11e9-a581-4ff78404524e (accessed 10 April 2019).

Pearce, J. (2013). 'Commentary: Financial Crisis, Austerity Politics, and Geographical Inequalities in Health', *Environment and Planning A: Economy and Space*, 45(9): 2030–45.

Pearce, J., and Dorling, D. (2006). 'Increasing Geographical Inequalities in Health in New Zealand, 1980–2001', *International Journal of Epidemiology*, 35(3): 597–603.

Pearce, J., Dorling, D., Wheeler, B., Barnett, R., and Rigby, J. (2006). 'Geographical Inequalities in Health in New Zealand, 1980–2001: The Gap Widens', *Australian and New Zealand Journal of Public Health*, 30(5): 461–6.

Pedersen, L., and Andersen, S. K. (2014). A Time of Reforms. Regulation of Labour Market and Welfare Since 1990. Danish Country Report. Oslo: Fafo.

Penno, E., and Gauld, R. (2017). 'Change, Connectivity, and Challenge: Exploring the Role of Health Technology in Shaping Health Care for Aging Populations in Asia Pacific', *Health Systems & Reform*, 3(3): 224–35.

Persson, A., Rothstein, B., and Teorell, J. (2019). 'Getting the Basic Nature of Systemic Corruption Right: A Reply to Marquette and Peiffer', *Governance*, 43(3): 57.

Phelan, J. C., Link, B. G., Diez-Roux, A., Kawachi, I., and Levin, B. (2004). '"Fundamental Causes" of Social Inequalities in Mortality: A Test of the Theory', *Journal of Health and Social Behavior*, 45(3): 265–85.

Pierson, P. (2001). 'Coping With Permanent Austerity: Welfare State Restructuring in Affluent Democracies', in P. Pierson (ed), *The New Politics of the Welfare State*. Oxford: Oxford University Press, 410–56.

Pierson, P. (2000). 'Increasing Returns, Path Dependence, and the Study of Politics', *American Political Science Review*, 94(2): 251–67.

Pierson, P. (1996). 'The New Politics of the Welfare State', *World Politics*, 48(2): 143–79.

Piot, P., Russell, S., and Larson, H. (2007). 'Good Politics, Bad Politics: The Experience of AIDS', *American Journal of Public Health*, 97(11): 1934–6.

Polanyi, K. (1944). *The Great Transformation*. Boston: Beacon Press.

Pollitt, C. (1994). 'The Citizen's Charter: A Preliminary Analysis', *Public Money & Management*, 14(2): 9–14.

Pollitt, C., and Bouckaert, G. (2011). *Public Management Reform: A Comparative Analysis - New Public Management, Governance, and the Neo-Weberian State*. 3rd ed. Oxford, New York: Oxford University Press.

References

Ponizovsky, A. M., Marom, E., Weizman, A., and Schwartzberg, E. (2018). 'Changes in Consumption of Opioid Analgesics in Israel 2009 to 2016: An Update Focusing on Oxycodone and Fentanyl Formulations', *Pharmacoepidemiology and Drug Safety*, 27(5): 535–40.

Ponizovsky, A. M., Marom, E., Zeldin, A., and Cherny, N. I. (2011). 'Trends in Opioid Analgesics Consumption, Israel, 2000–2008', *European Journal of Clinical Pharmacology*, 67(2): 165–8.

Ponizovsky, A. M., Pchelintsev, M. V., Marom, E., and Zvartau, E. E. (2012). 'Differences in the Consumption Rates and Regulatory Barriers to the Accessibility of Strong Opioid Analgesics in Israel and St. Petersburg', *European Journal of Clinical Pharmacology*, 68(1): 89–95.

Popic, T. (forthcoming a). 'Czech Republic', in E. M. Immergut, K. M. Anderson, C. Devitt, and T. Popic (eds), *Health Politics in Europe: A Handbook*.

Popic, T. (forthcoming b). 'Slovenia', in E. M. Immergut, K. M. Anderson, C. Devitt, and T. Popic (eds), *Health Politics in Europe: A Handbook*.

Priebe, S., Bremner, S. A., Lauber, C., Henderson, C., and Burns, T. (2016). 'Financial Incentives to Improve Adherence to Antipsychotic Maintenance Medication in Non-adherent Patients: A Cluster Randomised Controlled Trial', *Health Technology Assessment*, 20(70): 1–122.

Raphael, D. (2015). 'Beyond Policy Analysis: The Raw Politics Behind Opposition to Healthy Public Policy', *Health Promotion International*, 30(2): 380–96.

Ravelo, J. L. (2018). *18 Months in, How Is WHO's Health Emergencies Program Working?* Retrieved from https://www.devex.com/news/18-months-in-how-is-who-s-health-emergencies-program-working-91956 (accessed 13 February 2019).

Ravelo, J. L. (2017). *WHO's Budget and the Tasks for the Next Director-General.* Retrieved from https://www.devex.com/news/who-s-budget-and-the-tasks-for-the-next-director-general-90385 (accessed 13 February 2019).

Ravelo, J. L. (2016). *Margaret Chan Attempts One Last WHO Funding Boost.* Retrieved from https://www.devex.com/news/margaret-chan-attempts-one-last-who-funding-boost-89064 (accessed 15 April 2019).

Rawls, J. (1971). *A Theory of Justice.* Cambridge, MA: Belknap Press of Harvard University Press.

Ray, W. A., Chung, C. P., Murray, K. T., Hall, K., and Stein, C. M. (2016). 'Prescription of Long-acting Opioids and Mortality in Patients With Chronic Noncancer Pain', *JAMA*, 315(22): 2415–23.

Raymond, L., Paré, G., Ortiz de Guinea, A., Poba-Nzaou, P., Trudel, M.-C., Marsan, J., and Micheneau, T. (2015). 'Improving Performance in Medical Practices Through the Extended Use of Electronic Medical Record Systems: A Survey of Canadian Family Physicians', *BMC Medical Informatics and Decision Making*, 15: 27.

Reddy, A., Huseman, T. L., Canamucio, A., Marcus, S. C., Asch, D. A., Volpp, K., and Long, J. A. (2017). 'Patient and Partner Feedback Reports to Improve Statin Medication Adherence: A Randomized Control Trial', *Journal of General Internal Medicine*, 32(3): 256–61.

Reese, P. P., Bloom, R. D., Trofe-Clark, J., Mussell, A., Leidy, D., Levsky, S., Zhu, J., Yang, L., Wang, W., Troxel, A., Feldman, H. I., and Volpp, K. (2017). 'Automated Reminders and Physician Notification to Promote Immunosuppression Adherence Among Kidney Transplant Recipients: A Randomized Trial', *American Journal of Kidney Diseases*, 69(3): 400–9.

Reeves, A., Basu, S., McKee, M., Marmot, M., and Stuckler, D. (2013). 'Austere or Not? UK Coalition Government Budgets and Health Inequalities', *Journal of the Royal Society of Medicine*, 106(11): 432–6.

Reeves, A., Karanikolos, M., Mackenbach, J., McKee, M., and Stuckler, D. (2014). 'Do Employment Protection Policies Reduce the Relative Disadvantage in the Labour

Market Experienced by Unhealthy People? A Natural Experiment Created by the Great Recession in Europe', *Social Science & Medicine*, 121: 98–108.

Reibling, N. (2010). 'Healthcare Systems in Europe: Towards an Incorporation of Patient Access', *Journal of European Social Policy*, 20(1): 5–18.

Reibling, N., and Wendt, C. (2012). 'Gatekeeping and Provider Choice in OECD Healthcare Systems', *Current Sociology*, 60(4): 489–505.

Reid, P., Kukutai, T., and Cormack, D. (2018). 'Indigenous Data and Health: Critical Research Approaches and Indigenous Data Governance', *European Journal of Public Health*, 28(suppl_1): 28–49.

Review on Antimicrobial Resistance (2014). Antimicrobial Resistance: Tackling a Crisis for the Health and Wealth of Nations. London: Wellcome Trust, HM Government.

Robinson, H., MacDonald, B., and Broadbent, E. (2014). 'The Role of Healthcare Robots for Older People at Home: A Review', *International Journal of Social Robotics*, 6(4): 575–91.

Robinson, T., Brown, H., Norman, P. D., Fraser, L. K., Barr, B., and Bambra, C. (2019). 'The Impact of New Labour's English Health Inequalities Strategy on Geographical Inequalities in Infant Mortality: A Time-trend Analysis', *Journal of Epidemiology and Community Health*, 73(6): 564–8.

Rönnerstrand, B., and Lapuente, V. (2017). 'Corruption and Use of Antibiotics in Regions of Europe', *Health Policy*, 121(3): 250–6.

Rosenbaum, S. (2019). 'Reproductive Health: Assessing the Damage', *The Milbank Quarterly*, doi: 10.1111/1468-0009.12382.

Rosling, H., Rosling, O., and Rosling Rönnlund, A. (2018). *Factfulness: Ten Reasons We're Wrong About the World—and Why Things Are Better Than You Think*. London: Spectre.

Ross, N. A., Wolfson, M. C., Dunn, J. R., Berthelot, J. M., Kaplan, G. A., and Lynch, J. W. (2000). 'Relation Between Income Inequality and Mortality in Canada and in the United States: Cross Sectional Assessment Using Census Data and Vital Statistics', *BMJ Clinical Research Edition*, 320(7239): 898–902.

Roth, G. A., Abate, D., Abate, K. H., et al. (2018). 'Global, Regional, and National Age-sex-specific Mortality for 282 Causes of Death in 195 Countries and Territories, 1980–2017: A Systematic Analysis for the Global Burden of Disease Study 2017', *The Lancet*, 392(10159): 1736–88.

Rothgang, H., Cacace, M., Frisina, L., Grimmeisen, S., Schmid, A., and Wendt, C. (2010). *The State and Healthcare: Comparing OECD Countries*. Basingstoke: Palgrave Macmillan.

Rothgang, H., Cacace, M., Grimmeisen, S., and Wendt, C. (2005). 'The Changing Role of the State in Healthcare Systems', *European Review*, 13(S1): 187–212.

Rüefli, C. (forthcoming). 'Switzerland', in E. M. Immergut, K. M. Anderson, C. Devitt, and T. Popic (eds), *Health Politics in Europe: A Handbook*.

Ruscitto, A., Smith, B. H., and Guthrie, B. (2015). 'Changes in Opioid and Other Analgesic Use 1995–2010: Repeated Cross-sectional Analysis of Dispensed Prescribing for a Large Geographical Population in Scotland', *European Journal of Pain*, 19(1): 59–66.

Ryan, M. J., Giles-Vernick, T., and Graham, J. E. (2019). 'Technologies of Trust in Epidemic Response: Openness, Reflexivity and Accountability During the 2014–2016 Ebola Outbreak in West Africa', *BMJ Global Health*, 4(1): e001272.

Sachs, J. D., Schmidt-Traub, G., and Fajans-Turner, V. (2019). *Fully Filling the Global Fund*. Retrieved from https://www.project-syndicate.org/commentary/global-fund-aids-tb-malaria-replenishment-round-by-jeffrey-d-sachs-et-al-2019-01 (accessed 10 April 2019).

Samet, J. H., and Kertesz, S. G. (2018). 'Suggested Paths to Fixing the Opioid Crisis: Directions and Misdirections', *JAMA Network Open*, 1(2): e180218.

Savedoff, W. D. (2011). Governance in the Health Sector: A Strategy for Measuring Determinants and Performance. Policy Research Working Paper 5655. Washington, DC: World Bank.

Savedoff, W. D., and Hussmann, K. (2006). 'Why Are Health Systems Prone to Corruption?', in Transparency International (ed), *Global Corruption Report 2006*. London: Pluto Press, 4–13.

Schedlbauer, A., Davies, P., and Fahey, T. (2010). 'Interventions to Improve Adherence to Lipid Lowering Medication', *The Cochrane Database of Systematic Reviews*, (3): CD004371.

Schneider, S., Rathmann, K., and Roots, A. (forthcoming). 'Health Outcomes and Health Inequalities', in E. M. Immergut, K. M. Anderson, C. Devitt, and T. Popic (eds), *Health Politics in Europe: A Handbook*.

Schneider, S. M., and Popic, T. (2018). 'Cognitive Determinants of Healthcare Evaluations - A Comparison of Eastern and Western European Countries', *Health Policy*, 122(3): 269–78.

Schokkaert, E., Steel, J., and van de Voorde, C. (2017). 'Out-of-pocket Payments and Subjective Unmet Need of Healthcare', *Applied Health Economics and Health Policy*, 15(5): 545–55.

Schrecker, T., and Bambra, C. (2015). *How Politics Makes Us Sick: Neoliberal Epidemics*. Basingstoke: Palgrave Macmillan.

Scott, J. (2001). *Power*. Oxford: Polity.

Scott-Samuel, A., Bambra, C., Collins, C., Hunter, D. J., McCartney, G., and Smith, K. (2014). 'The Impact of Thatcherism on Health and Well-being in Britain', *International Journal of Health Services: Planning, Administration, Evaluation*, 44(1): 53–71.

Seifmann, R., and Pannenborg, O. (2018). *The Need for a Geopolitical Shift in Global Health*. Retrieved from https://www.thelancet.com/journals/langlo/blog (accessed 10 April 2019).

Sen, A. (2009). *The Idea of Justice*. London: Allen Lane.

Sen, A. (1992). *Inequality Reexamined*. New York: Russell Sage Foundation.

Shaikh, M., and Gandjour, A. (2019). 'Pharmaceutical Expenditure and Gross Domestic Product: Evidence of Simultaneous Effects Using a Two-step Instrumental Variables Strategy', *Health Economics*, 28(1): 101–22.

Shaw, C., Blakely, T., Atkinson, J., and Crampton, P. (2005). 'Do Social and Economic Reforms Change Socioeconomic Inequalities in Child Mortality? A Case Study: New Zealand 1981–1999', *Journal of Epidemiology and Community Health*, 59(8): 638–44.

Sheikh, K., Bennett, S. C., El Jardali, F., and Gotsadze, G. (2017). 'Privilege and Inclusivity in Shaping Global Health Agendas', *Health Policy and Planning*, 32(3): 303–4.

Shiovitz-Ezra, S., and Ayalon, L. (2010). 'Situational Versus Chronic Loneliness as Risk Factors for All-cause Mortality', *International Psychogeriatrics*, 22(3): 455–62.

Simou, E., and Koutsogeorgou, E. (2014). 'Effects of the Economic Crisis on Health and Healthcare in Greece in the Literature From 2009 to 2013: A Systematic Review', *Health Policy*, 115(2-3): 111–9.

Singleton, N., and Rubin, J. (2014). 'What Is Good Governance in the Context of Drug Policy?', *The International Journal on Drug Policy*, 25(5): 935–41.

Sligo, J., Gauld, R., Roberts, V., and Villa, L. (2017). 'A Literature Review for Large-scale Health Information System Project Planning, Implementation and Evaluation', *International Journal of Medical Informatics*, 97: 86–97.

Smith, R. D. (1995). 'The WHO: Change or Die', *BMJ Clinical Research Edition*, 310(6979): 543–4.

Song, J. (2018). *Boosted by Belt and Road Initiative, Spread of TCM Speeds Up*. Retrieved from http://global.chinadaily.com.cn/a/201806/04/WS5b14ab0fa31001b82571dfaf.html (accessed 10 April 2019).

Special Advisory Committee on the Epidemic of Opioid Overdoses (2019). *National Report: Apparent Opioid-related Deaths in Canada (January 2016 to September 2018)*. Retrieved from https://infobase.phac-aspc.gc.ca/datalab/national-surveillance-opioid-mortality.html (accessed 15 April 2019).

Sridhar, D., and Woods, N. (2013). 'Trojan Multilateralism: Global Cooperation in Health', *Global Policy*, 4(4): 325–35.

Staats, B. R., Dai, H., Hofmann, D., and Milkman, K. L. (2017). 'Motivating Process Compliance Through Individual Electronic Monitoring: An Empirical Examination of Hand Hygiene in Healthcare', *Management Science*, 63(5): 1563–85.

Stafford, M., and McCarthy, M. (2006). 'Neighbourhoods, Housing and Health', in M. Marmot, and R. G. Wilkinson (eds), *Social Determinants of Health*. 2nd ed. Oxford: Oxford University Press, 78–96.

Stanaway, J. D., Afshin, A., Gakidou, E., et al. (2018). 'Global, Regional, and National Comparative Risk Assessment of 84 Behavioural, Environmental and Occupational, and Metabolic Risks or Clusters of Risks for 195 Countries and Territories, 1990–2017: A Systematic Analysis for the Global Burden of Disease Study 2017', *The Lancet*, 392(10159): 1923–94.

Stein, F., and Sridhar, D. (2017). 'Health as a "Global Public Good": Creating a Market for Pandemic Risk', *BMJ Clinical Research Edition*, 358: j3397.

Stolarova-Demuth, G. (forthcoming). 'Bulgaria', in E. M. Immergut, K. M. Anderson, C. Devitt, and T. Popic (eds), *Health Politics in Europe: A Handbook*.

Strunk, B. C., Ginsburg, P. B., and Banker, M. I. (2006). 'The Effect of Population Aging on Future Hospital Demand', *Health Affairs*, 25(3): w141–9.

Stuckler, D., and Basu, S. (2013). *The Body Economic: Why Austerity Kills*. New York: Basic Books.

Stuckler, D., Basu, S., Suhrcke, M., Coutts, A., and McKee, M. (2009). 'The Public Health Effect of Economic Crises and Alternative Policy Responses in Europe: An Empirical Analysis', *The Lancet*, 374(9686): 315–23.

Stuenkel, O. (2016). *Post-western World: How Emerging Powers Are Remaking Global Order*. Cambridge: Polity Press.

Suhrcke, M., Mazzuco, S., McKee, M., Urban, D., and Steinherr, A. (2007). *Economic Consequences of Noncommunicable Diseases and Injuries in the Russian Federation*. Copenhagen: WHO Regional Office for Europe.

Susumpow, P., Pansuwan, P., Sajda, N., and Crawley, A. W. (2014). 'Participatory Disease Detection Through Digital Volunteerism: How the DoctorMe Application Aims to Capture Data for Faster Disease Detection in Thailand', in C.-W. Chung (ed), *WWW '14 Companion: Proceedings of the 23rd International Conference on World Wide Web April 7–11, 2014, Seoul, Korea*. New York: ACM Press, 663–6.

't Hoen, E. (2002). 'TRIPS, Pharmaceutical Patents, and Access to Essential Medicines: A Long Way From Seattle to Doha', *Chicago Journal of International Law*, 3(1): 27–46.

Tan, X., Liu, X., and Shao, H. (2017). 'Healthy China 2030: A Vision for Health Care', *Value in Health Regional Issues*, 12: 112–4.

Tang, H., and Ng, J. H. K. (2006). 'Googling for a Diagnosis—Use of Google as a Diagnostic Aid: Internet Based Study', *BMJ Clinical Research Edition*, 333(7579): 1143–5.

Tannenbaum, D., Fox, C. R., and Rogers, T. (2017). 'On the Misplaced Politics of Behavioural Policy Interventions', *Nature Human Behaviour*, 1(7): 663.

Taylor-Robinson, D., Lai, E., Wickham, S., Rose, T., Bambra, C., Whitehead, M., and Barr, B. (forthcoming). 'Child Poverty and Inequalities in Infant Mortality in England 2000–17: Time-trend Analysis'.

Thaler, R. H., and Sunstein, C. R. (2008). *Nudge: Improving Decisions About Health, Wealth, and Happiness*. New Haven: Yale University Press.

The BMJ (2018). *Global Health Disruptors*. Retrieved from https://www.bmj.com/global-health-disruptors (accessed 10 April 2019).

The Global Fund to Fight AIDS, Tuberculosis and Malaria (2018). *India Supports Global Fund Efforts to Mobilize Funds*. Retrieved from https://www.theglobalfund.org/en/news/2018-09-05-india-supports-global-fund-efforts-to-mobilize-funds (accessed 10 April 19).

Thomson, K., Hillier-Brown, F., Todd, A., McNamara, C., Huijts, T., and Bambra, C. (2018). 'The Effects of Public Health Policies on Health Inequalities in High-income Countries: An Umbrella Review', *BMC Public Health*, 18(1): 869.

Touati, N., Roberge, D., Denis, J.-L., Pineault, R., Cazale, L., and Tremblay, D. (2007). 'Governance, Health Policy Implementation and the Added Value of Regionalization', *Healthcare Policy/Politiques de Santé*, 2(3): 97–114.

Townsend, J. (2015). 'Curbing Tobacco Smoking', in D. McDaid, F. Sassi, and S. Merkur (eds), *Promoting Health, Preventing Disease: The Economic Case*. Maidenhead: Open University Press, 53–80.

Transparency International (2016). *Global Corruption Barometer 2016: Results for Europe and Central Asia*. Retrieved from https://www.transparency.org/news/feature/governments_are_doing_a_poor_job_at_fighting_corruption_across_europe (accessed May 2019).

Trenfield, S. J., Awad, A., Goyanes, A., Gaisford, S., and Basit, A. W. (2018). '3D Printing Pharmaceuticals: Drug Development to Frontline Care', *Trends in Pharmacological Sciences*, 39(5): 440–51.

Tulic, S. (2019). *The Human Condition, the Museum, and OxyContin*. Retrieved from https://artwriting.sva.edu/journal/post/human-condition-museum-oxycontin (accessed 15 April 2019).

UC Davis Veterinary Medicine (n.d.) [website]. *PREDICT Project*. Retrieved from https://ohi.vetmed.ucdavis.edu/programs-projects/predict-project (accessed 30 April 2019).

UN OCHA (United Nations Office for the Coordination of Humanitarian Affairs) (2017). *The Communication and Community Engagement Initiative: Towards a Collective Service for More Effective Humanitarian Responses*. Retrieved from https://reliefweb.int/report/world/communication-community-engagement-initiative-towards-collective-service-more-effective (accessed 15 January 2019).

UNAIDS (Joint United Nations Programme on HIV and AIDS) (2018). UNAIDS Data 2018. Geneva: UNAIDS.

UNDESA (United Nations Department of Economic and Social Affairs) (2017). The Sustainable Development Goals Report 2017. New York: UNDESA.

UNDESA (2015a). The Millennium Development Goals Report 2015. New York: United Nations.

UNDESA (2015b). World Population Ageing 2015. Retrieved from https://www.un.org/en/development/desa/population/publications/ageing/WPA2015_Infochart.asp (accessed 20 February 2019).

United Nations (2017). Transforming Our World: The 2030 Agenda for Sustainable Development. New York: United Nations.

United Nations (2015). *Launch of New Sustainable Development Agenda to Guide Development Actions for the Next 15 Years*. Retrieved from https://www.un.org/sustainabledevelopment/blog/2015/12/launch-of-new-sustainable-development-agenda-to-guide-development-actions-for-the-next-15-years (accessed 10 April 2019).

US General Accounting Office (2003). OxyContin Abuse and Diversion and Efforts to Address the Problem GAO-04-110. Washington, DC: US General Accounting Office.

van Kersbergen, K., and Manow, P. (2017). 'The Welfare State', in D. Caramani (ed), *Comparative Politics*. 4th ed. Oxford: Oxford University Press, 363–80.

van Oorschot, W. (2006). 'Making the Difference in Social Europe: Deservingness Perceptions Among Citizens of European Welfare States', *Journal of European Social
Policy*, 16(1): 23–42.

van Oorschot, W., and Roosma, F. (2015). The Social Legitimacy of Differently Targeted
Benefits. ImProvE Working Paper No. 15/11. Antwerp: Herman Deleeck Centre for
Social Policy – University of Antwerp.

van Rensburg, A. J., Petersen, I., Wouters, E., Engelbrecht, M., Kigozi, G., Fourie, P., van
Rensburg, D., and Bracke, P. (2018). 'State and Non-state Mental Health Service Col-
laboration in a South African District: A Mixed Methods Study', *Health Policy and
Planning*, 33(4): 516–27.

van Rensburg, A. J., Rau, A., Fourie, P., and Bracke, P. (2016). 'Power and Integrated Health
Care: Shifting From Governance to Governmentality', *International Journal of Integrated Care*, 16(3): 17.

van Zee, A. (2009). 'The Promotion and Marketing of Oxycontin: Commercial Triumph,
Public Health Tragedy', *American Journal of Public Health*, 99(2): 221–7.

Vandenbroucke, F., Hemerijck, A., and Palier, B. (2011). The EU Needs a Social Investment
Pact. OSE Paper Series Opinion Paper No. 5. Brussels: Observatoire Social Européen.

Vayena, E., Blasimme, A., and Cohen, I. G. (2018). 'Machine Learning in Medicine:
Addressing Ethical Challenges', *PLoS Medicine*, 15(11): e1002689.

Vian, T. (2008). 'Review of Corruption in the Health Sector: Theory, Methods and Interventions', *Health Policy and Planning*, 23(2): 83–94.

Volpp, K. G., Troxel, A. B., Mehta, S. J., Norton, L., Zhu, J., Lim, R., Wang, W., Marcus, N.,
Terwiesch, C., Caldarella, K., Levin, T., Relish, M., Negin, N., Smith-McLallen, A., Sny-
der, R., Spettell, C. M., Drachman, B., Kolansky, D., and Asch, D. A. (2017). 'Effect of
Electronic Reminders, Financial Incentives, and Social Support on Outcomes After
Myocardial Infarction: The HeartStrong Randomized Clinical Trial', *JAMA Internal
Medicine*, 177(8): 1093–101.

Vrangbæk, K. (forthcoming). 'Denmark', in E. M. Immergut, K. M. Anderson, C. Devitt,
and T. Popic (eds), *Health Politics in Europe: A Handbook*.

Vranken, M. J. M., Mantel-Teeuwisse, A. K., Schutjens, M.-H. D. B., Scholten, W. K., Jünger,
S., and Leufkens, H. G. M. (2018). 'Access to Strong Opioid Analgesics in the Context of Legal and Regulatory Barriers in Eleven Central and Eastern European Countries', *Journal of Palliative Medicine*, 21(7): 963–9.

Walt, G. (1993). 'WHO Under Stress: Implications for Health Policy', *Health Policy*, 24(2):
125–44.

Watson, S. (2008). 'The Left Divided: Parties, Unions, and the Resolution of Southern
Spain's Agrarian Social Question', *Politics & Society*, 36(4): 451–77.

Wegrich, K., and Ziaja, S. (2018). 'Governance Capacities After the Global Financial and
Economic Crisis: Depleted, Refilled, or Steady State?', in Hertie School of Governance (ed), *The Governance Report 2018*. Oxford: Oxford University Press, 47–63.

Wendt, C. (2019). 'Social Health Insurance in Europe: Basic Concepts and New Principles', *Journal of Health Politics, Policy and Law*, 44(4).

Wendt, C. (2015). 'Healthcare Policy and Finance', in E. Kuhlmann, R. H. Blank, I. L.
Bourgeault, and C. Wendt (eds), *The Palgrave International Handbook of Healthcare
Policy and Governance*. Basingstoke: Palgrave Macmillan, 54–68.

Wendt, C. (2014). 'Changing Healthcare System Types', *Social Policy & Administration*,
48(7): 864–82.

Wendt, C. (2009). 'Mapping European Healthcare Systems: A Comparative Analysis of
Financing, Service Provision and Access to Healthcare', *Journal of European Social
Policy*, 19(5): 432–45.

Wendt, C., Frisina, L., and Rothgang, H. (2009). 'Healthcare System Types: A Conceptual
Framework for Comparison', *Social Policy & Administration*, 43(1): 70–90.

West, D. M. (2005). *Digital Government: Technology and Public Sector Performance*. Princeton, NJ: Princeton University Press.

Westbrook, J. I., Reckmann, M., Li, L., Runciman, W. B., Burke, R., Lo, C., Baysari, M. T., Braithwaite, J., and Day, R. O. (2012). 'Effects of Two Commercial Electronic Prescribing Systems on Prescribing Error Rates in Hospital In-patients: A Before and After Study', *PLoS Medicine*, 9(1): e1001164.

Whitehead, M. (1992). 'The Concepts and Principles of Equity and Health', *International Journal of Health Services: Planning, Administration, Evaluation*, 22(3): 429–45.

Whitehead, M., and Popay, J. (2010). 'Swimming Upstream? Taking Action on the Social Determinants of Health Inequalities', *Social Science & Medicine*, 71(7): 1234–6.

WHO (World Health Organization) (2019a). A Heavy Burden: The Productivity Cost of Illness in Africa. Brazzaville: WHO Regional Office for Africa.

WHO (2019b). *Ten Threats to Global Health in 2019*. Retrieved from https://www.who. int/emergencies/ten-threats-to-global-health-in-2019 (accessed 10 April 2019).

WHO (2018a). *9 out of 10 People Worldwide Breathe Polluted Air, but More Countries Are Taking Action*. Retrieved from https://www.who.int/news-room/detail/02-05-2018-9-out-of-10-people-worldwide-breathe-polluted-air-but-more-countries-are-taking-action (accessed 10 April 2019).

WHO (2018b). *Definition of Regional Groupings*. Retrieved from https://www.who.int/ healthinfo/global_burden_disease/definition_regions/en/ (accessed 21 February 2019).

WHO (2018c). Draft Thirteenth General Programme of Work 2019–2023: Promote Health, Keep the World Safe, Serve the Vulnerable. Geneva: WHO.

WHO (2018d). Financing of the Programme Budget 2018–2019: Report by the Director-General. Geneva: WHO.

WHO (2018e). *Global Health Observatory Data Repository*. Retrieved from http://apps. who.int/gho/data/node.home (accessed 20 January 2019).

WHO (2018f). Global Tuberculosis Report 2018. Geneva: WHO.

WHO (2018g). *Neglected Tropical Diseases*. Retrieved from https://www.who.int/ neglected_diseases/diseases/en/ (accessed 20 February 2019).

WHO (2018h). *WHO and World Bank Group Join Forces to Strengthen Global Health Security*. Retrieved from https://www.worldbank.org/en/news/press-release/2018/ 05/24/who-and-world-bank-group-join-forces-to-strengthen-global-health-secu rity (accessed 23 March 2019).

WHO (2018i). World Health Statistics 2018: Monitoring Health for the SDGs. Geneva: WHO.

WHO (2018j). World Malaria Report 2018. Geneva: WHO.

WHO (2017a). *An R&D Blueprint for Action to Prevent Epidemics: Accelerating R&D and Saving Lives*. Retrieved from http://apps.who.int/blueprint-brochure/ (accessed 10 April 2019).

WHO (2017b). Emergency Response Framework. 2nd ed. Geneva: WHO.

WHO (2017c). Promoting Health in the SDGs: Report on the 9th Global Conference for Health Promotion: All for Health, Health for All, 21–24 November 2016. Geneva: WHO.

WHO (2016a). Joint External Evaluation Tool: International Health Regulations (2005). Geneva: WHO.

WHO (2016b). WHO's Financing Dialogue 2016. A Proposal for Increasing the Assessed Contribution: Ensuring Sustainable Financing for WHO. Geneva: WHO.

WHO (2015a). Anticipating Emerging Infectious Disease Epidemics, Meeting Report: WHO Informal Consultation. Geneva: WHO.

WHO (2015b). Global Action Plan on Antimicrobial Resistance. Geneva: WHO.

WHO (2015c). Health in 2015: From MDGs to SDGs. Geneva: WHO.

WHO (2015d). Report of the Ebola Interim Assessment Panel - July 2015. Geneva: WHO.

WHO (2015e). State of Inequality: Reproductive, Maternal, Newborn and Child Health. Geneva: WHO.

WHO (2014a). Health Systems Governance for Universal Health Coverage. Action Plan. Geneva: WHO.

WHO (2014b). Report of the Sage Working Group on Vaccine Hesitancy. Geneva: WHO.

WHO (2012). *Q&A: Why Are Some Tropical Diseases Called 'Neglected'?* Retrieved from https://www.who.int/features/qa/58/en/ (accessed 20 February 2019).

WHO (2009). WHO Guidelines on Hand Hygiene in Health Care. Geneva: WHO.

WHO (2008). The World Health Report 2008: Primary Health Care (Now More Than Ever). Geneva: WHO.

WHO (2005). International Health Regulations. 3rd ed. Geneva: WHO.

WHO (1999). The World Health Report 1999: Making a Difference. Geneva: WHO.

WHO (1946). Constitution of the World Health Organization. Geneva: WHO.

WHO (n.d.a) [website]. *FluID: Global Influenza Epidemiological Data Collection Tool.* Retrieved from https://www.who.int/influenza/surveillance_monitoring/fluid/en/ (accessed 25 January 2019).

WHO (n.d.b) [website]. *JEE Dashboard, Strategic Partnership for International Health Regulations (2005) and Health Security (SPH).* Retrieved from https://extranet.who.int/sph/jee-dashboard (accessed 5 April 2019).

WHO and World Bank (2015). Tracking Universal Health Coverage: First Global Monitoring Report. Geneva: WHO.

WHO Global Observatory for eHealth (2016). *Global Diffusion of eHealth: Making Universal Health Coverage Achievable, Report of the Third Global Survey on eHealth.* Geneva: World Health Organization.

Whyte, L. E., Mulvihill, G., and Wieder, B. (2016) [website]. *Politics of Pain: Drugmakers Fought State Opioid Limits Amid Crisis.* Retrieved from https://publicintegrity.org/state-politics/politics-of-pain-drugmakers-fought-state-opioid-limits-amid-crisis/ (accessed 4 January 2019).

Wickström Östervall, L. (2017). 'Nudging to Prudence? The Effect of Reminders on Antibiotics Prescriptions', *Journal of Economic Behavior and Organization*, 135: 39–52.

Widmer, R. J., Collins, N. M., Collins, C. S., West, C. P., Lerman, L. O., and Lerman, A. (2015). 'Digital Health Interventions for the Prevention of Cardiovascular Disease: A Systematic Review and Meta-analysis', *Mayo Clinic Proceedings*, 90(4): 469–80.

Wiklund, H. (2005). 'A Habermasian Analysis of the Deliberative Democratic Potential of ICT-enabled Services in Swedish Municipalities', *New Media & Society*, 7(2): 247–70.

Wilensky, H. L. (1975). *The Welfare State and Equality: Structural and Ideological Roots of Public Expenditures.* Berkeley: University of California Press.

Wilkinson, R. G., and Pickett, K. (2009). *The Spirit Level: Why More Equal Societies Almost Always Do Better.* London: Allen Lane.

Willem, A., and Gemmel, P. (2013). 'Do Governance Choices Matter in Health Care Networks? An Exploratory Configuration Study of Health Care Networks', *BMC Health Services Research*, 13: 229.

Wolf, M. (2015). *The Shifts and the Shocks: What We've Learned—and Have Still to Learn—From the Financial Crisis.* London: Penguin Press.

Wolinsky, H. (2005). 'Disease Mongering and Drug Marketing: Does the Pharmaceutical Industry Manufacture Diseases as well as Drugs?', *EMBO Reports*, 6(7): 612–4.

World Bank (2018a). Money and Microbes: Strengthening Research Capacity to Prevent Epidemics. Washington, DC: World Bank Group.

World Bank (2018b). *World Bank Group's Pandemic Emergency Financing Facility (PEF) Makes First $12 Million Commitment to Bridge Financing Gap for Ebola Response in DRC*. Retrieved from https://www.worldbank.org/en/news/press-release/2018/05/22/world-bank-groups-pandemic-emergency-financing-facility-pef-makes-first-12-million-commitment-to-bridge-financing-gap-for-ebola-response-in-drc (accessed 24 March 2019).

World Bank (2017a). Drug Resistant Infections: A Threat to Our Economic Future. Washington, DC: World Bank.

World Bank (2017b). From Panic and Neglect to Investing in Health Security: Financing Preparedness at a National Level. Washington, DC: World Bank Group.

World Bank (2017c). Pandemic Emergency Financing Facility (PEF) Framework. Washington, DC: World Bank.

World Bank (2017d). *Pandemic Emergency Financing Facility: Frequently Asked Questions*. Retrieved from http://www.worldbank.org/en/topic/pandemics/brief/pandemic-emergency-facility-frequently-asked-questions (accessed 24 March 2019).

World Bank (2017e). World Development Report 2017: Governance and the Law. Washington, DC: World Bank.

World Travel and Tourism Council (2018). Impact of the Ebola Epidemic on Travel and Tourism. London: World Travel and Tourism Council.

Xu, K., Soucat, A., Kutzin, J., Brindley, C., Vande Maele, N., Toure, H., Garcia, M. A., Li, D., Barroy, H., Flores, G., Roubal, T., Indikadahena, C., Cherilova, V., and Siroka, A. (2018). Public Spending on Health: A Closer Look at Global Trends. WHO/HIS/HGF/HF Working Paper 18.3. Geneva: World Health Organization.

Zaugg, V., Korb-Savoldelli, V., Durieux, P., and Sabatier, B. (2018). 'Providing Physicians With Feedback on Medication Adherence for People With Chronic Diseases Taking Long-term Medication', *The Cochrane Database of Systematic Reviews*, 1: CD012042.

Zhang, S., Liao, R., Alpert, J., Kong, J., Spetzger, U., Milia, P., Thiriet, M., and Wortley, D. (2018). 'Digital Medicine: Emergence, Definition, Scope, and Future', *Digital Medicine*, 4(1): 1.

Zin, C. S., Chen, L. C., and Knaggs, R. D. (2014). 'Changes in Trends and Pattern of Strong Opioid Prescribing in Primary Care', *European Journal of Pain*, 18(9): 1343–51.

Zuboff, S. (2019). *The Age of Surveillance Capitalism: The Fight for a Human Future at the New Frontier of Power*. New York: PublicAffairs.

About the Contributors

Clare Bambra is Professor of Public Health at the Faculty of Medical Sciences, Newcastle University, UK. She is an interdisciplinary social scientist with expertise across health politics and policy, health geography, and social epidemiology. Her mixed methods research examines the social, political, and economic determinants of health inequalities. She has published widely on these topics, including several books. She is a Senior Investigator in the Centre for Global Health Inequalities Research (CHAIN); Fuse: Centre for Translational Research in Public Health; and the NIHR School for Public Health Research. She works regularly with policy and practice organisations including Public Health England, Eurohealthnet, and WHO Europe.

Elodie Besnier is a PhD candidate at the Department of Sociology and Political Science at the Norwegian University of Science and Technology (NTNU) in Trondheim, Norway. Her research at the Centre for Global Health Inequalities Research (CHAIN) focuses primarily on public health interventions and health inequalities in children in low- and middle-income countries. Before joining NTNU, Elodie worked in the policy and advocacy sector for public health and health non-profit organisations across Europe.

Anna Bezruki is a Master of International Affairs candidate at the Graduate Institute of International and Development Studies in Geneva. Previously, she worked on ensuring quality of care for people living with HIV/AIDS in New York at the New York State Department of Health and assisted with global health research as an intern at the Council on Foreign Relations. She completed her undergraduate degree at Bryn Mawr College.

Piet Bracke is Professor at the Department of Sociology at Ghent University (Belgium). In his research and teaching, he strongly focuses on mental health and mental health services and on comparative health sociology. Current research topics are the development of institutional theories about educational health inequalities, participation in cancer screening programmes and fundamental cause theory, mental health stigma, and mental health professional care-seeking.

Terje Andreas Eikemo is Professor of Sociology at the Department of Sociology and Political Science at the Norwegian University of Science and Technology (NTNU) in Trondheim, Norway. He is the leader of the Centre for Global Health Inequalities Research (CHAIN), which aims to monitor, explain, and reduce socioeconomic inequalities in health in all world regions. He is also the Editor-in-Chief of the *Scandinavian Journal of Public Health.*

Robin Gauld is Pro-Vice-Chancellor (Commerce) and, since December 2016, Dean, Otago Business School (New Zealand). Previously, he was Head of the Department of Preventive and Social Medicine at the Otago Medical School, where he was based for twenty years following a PhD in public administration from the University of Hong Kong. Robin is Co-Director, Centre for Health Systems and Technology, which spans the Business School and Health Sciences Division at the University of Otago. He has authored more than 150 peer-reviewed journal articles, many book chapters, and several books including *The New Health Policy* (Open University Press, 2009), awarded First Prize in category at the 2010 British Medical Association Medical Book Awards. His most recent co-edited book is *Health Systems in Developing Counties in Asia* (Routledge, 2017).

Klaus Hurrelmann is Professor of Public Health and Education at the Hertie School (Berlin, Germany). He was the founding dean of the first German School of Public Health at the University of Bielefeld, where he spent twelve years as Director of the Research Center on Prevention and Intervention in Childhood and Adolescence. From 1992 to 2006, he led the German contribution to the international comparative study Health Behaviour in School Children for the World Health Organization and is currently in the directorial team of several national surveys covering the development of family, children, youth, and young adults. Klaus was educated as a social scientist at the University of Münster and the University of California, Berkeley, ultimately earning his doctorate in education systems and society.

Ellen M. Immergut is Professor of Political Science at the European University Institute in Florence (Italy) and Humboldt University Berlin (Germany). She led the NORFACE Welfare States Futures (WSF) HEALTHDOX project, which investigated health policy reforms in Europe from 1989 to the present. She is also Scientific Programme Coordinator for the entire WSF Programme.

Ilona Kickbusch is Director of the Global Health Centre at the Graduate Institute of Geneva. She is a member of the Global Preparedness Monitoring Board and the WHO High-Level Independent Commission on Non-communicable Diseases and is co-chair of UHC2030. She chairs the Council of the World Health Summit in Berlin and the international advisory board for the development of the German global health strategy.

Austin Liu is a policy analyst on global health. He was previously a research assistant to Ilona Kickbusch at the Global Health Centre at the Graduate Institute of Geneva, where he obtained his master's degree in development studies.

Suerie Moon is Director of Research at the Global Health Centre and Visiting Lecturer at the Graduate Institute of International and Development Studies (Geneva). Her research and teaching focus on global governance, the political economy of global health (in particular, innovation and access to medicines; outbreak preparedness and response; trade, investment, and intellectual property rules; and development assistance for health), and the evolution of international regimes. Prior to joining the Graduate Institute, she was Study Director of the Harvard-LSHTM Independent Panel on the Global Response to Ebola. She received her PhD from the Harvard Kennedy School of Government.

Andra Roescu is Max Weber Fellow at the European University Institute (Italy) and was previously Research Fellow at the University of Southampton (UK). She holds a PhD in political science. Her research interests are political attitudes and behaviour as well as welfare and healthcare policies.

Björn Rönnerstrand is a researcher at the SOM Institute at the University of Gothenburg (Sweden). He holds a PhD from the Department of Political Science at the same university and was a postdoctoral researcher in the NORFACE-funded research project HEALTHDOX. He has published on social capital, corruption, public opinion, and health policy.

Hanna Schwander is Professor of Public Policy at the Hertie School (Berlin, Germany). Located at the intersection between comparative politics, political sociology, and political economy, her research examines how post-industrial transformations of welfare states, labour markets, and societies affect various aspects of political life. Prior to joining the Hertie School, she was Senior Researcher with an Ambizione project on women's political alignment at the Department of Political Science of the University of Zürich and worked at the Research Center on Inequality and Social Policy (SOCIUM) in Bremen, the University of Oxford, and the European University Institute.

Mujaheed Shaikh is Professor of Health Governance at the Hertie School (Berlin, Germany) and lead for the Hertie School's involvement in the Robert Bosch Stiftung's initiative 'Restart! A Health Care Reform Workshop' ('Neustart!'). His research concentrates on health economics and management with a focus on health expenditures, hospital efficiency and competition, and health insurance. He also has a keen interest in policy issues related to international donor funding for diseases and health in developing countries. Previously, Mujaheed was employed at the Health Economics and Policy Division of Vienna University of Economics and Business. He holds a doctorate in economics from the Frankfurt School of Finance and Management.

Christian Traxler is Professor of Economics at the Hertie School (Berlin, Germany). Using experimental policy evaluation approaches, he pursues questions in public and behavioural economics. Christian studied economics at the University of Vienna, Carlos III de Madrid, and the Ludwig-Maximilians-Universität Munich, where he received his PhD in 2006. Between 2006 and 2011, he was Senior Researcher at the Max Planck Institute for Research on Collective Goods (Bonn) and held visiting positions at the Universities of Amsterdam and Michigan (Ann Arbor). Before joining the Hertie School in 2013, he held a Chair for Public Economics at the University of Marburg.

André J. van Rensburg is a senior researcher at the Centre for Rural Health, University of KwaZulu-Natal (Durban, South Africa). He is a member of Health Systems Global, Emerging Voices for Global Health, and the National Institute for Health Research (NIHR) Global Health Academy. The bulk of his work relates to the political economy of mental healthcare in post-apartheid South Africa and the development of integrated platforms of care in low-resource settings. Currently he is involved in the Southern African Consortium for Mental Health Integration (S-MhINT) as well as in the NIHR Global Health Research Unit on Health Systems Strengthening in Sub-Saharan Africa (ASSET).

Claus Wendt is Professor of Sociology of Health and Healthcare Systems at the University of Siegen (Germany). His research interests include international comparisons of welfare states and healthcare systems, health policy and demographic change, and the sociology of health. Claus has been a 2008-09 Harkness/Bosch Fellow of Health Policy and Practice at Harvard School of Public Health and J. F. Kennedy Fellow at Harvard's Center for European Studies. Prior to joining the University of Siegen, he was Senior Researcher at the Mannheim Center for European Studies, the University of Bremen, and the University of Heidelberg, where he received his PhD in 2003.

Also in the OUP Governance Report series:

The Governance Report 2018
Economic Crisis | Financial Stress | Responses | Global Coordination | Governing Capacity | Trust
(Hertie School of Governance, Ed.)

The Governance Report 2017
Democracy | Innovations | Participation | Legitimacy | Indicators
(Hertie School of Governance, Ed.)

Governance Indicators: Approaches, Progress, Promise
(Helmut K. Anheier, Matthias Haber, and Mark A. Kayser, Eds.)

The Governance Report 2016
Infrastructure | Trade-offs | Productivity | Delivery | Innovations | Indicators
(Hertie School of Governance, Ed.)

The Governance of Infrastructure
(Kai Wegrich, Genia Kostka, and Gerhard Hammerschmid, Eds.)

The Governance Report 2015
Eurozone Crisis | Economic Governance | Institutional Dilemmas | Constitutionalism | Indicators
(Hertie School of Governance, Ed.)

Beyond the Crisis: The Governance of Europe's Economic, Political, and Legal Transformation
(Mark Dawson, Henrik Enderlein, and Christian Joerges, Eds.)

The Governance Report 2014
Public Administration | Performance | Capacity | Problem-solving | Innovation | Indicators
(Hertie School of Governance, Ed.)

The Problem-solving Capacity of the Modern State: Governance Challenges and Administrative Capacities
(Martin Lodge and Kai Wegrich, Eds.)

The Governance Report 2013
Sovereignty | Fiscal Policy | Innovations | Trade-offs | Indicators
(Hertie School of Governance, Ed.)

Governance Challenges and Innovations: Financial and Fiscal Governance
(Helmut K. Anheier, Ed.)

Notes

Notes